Beauties

ALSO BY JAMES DUTHIE

The Guy on the Left:
Sports Stories from the Best Seat in the House

The Day I (Almost) Killed Two Gretzkys:
And Other Off-the-Wall Stories about Sports . . . and Life

They Call Me Killer: Tales from Junior Hockey's Legendary
Hall-of-Fame Coach (co-author with Brian Kilrea)

James Duthie

with a foreword by Roberto Luongo

BEAUTIES

HOCKEY'S GREATEST
UNTOLD STORIES

HarperCollins*Publishers*Ltd

Published by HarperCollins Publishers Ltd

First edition

HarperCollins books may be purchased for educational, business,
or sales promotional use through our Special Markets Department.

HarperCollins Publishers Ltd
Bay Adelaide Centre, East Tower
22 Adelaide Street West, 41st Floor
Toronto, Ontario, Canada
M5H 4E3

www.harpercollins.ca

Library and Archives Canada Cataloguing in Publication

Title: Beauties : hockey's greatest untold stories / James Duthie.
Names: Duthie, James, 1966- author.
Identifiers: Canadiana (print) 20200299778 | Canadiana (ebook) 20200299786 |
ISBN 9781443460750 (hardcover) | ISBN 9781443460767 (ebook)
Subjects: LCSH: Hockey—Anecdotes. | LCSH: Hockey players—Anecdotes. |
LCSH: National Hockey League—Anecdotes.
Classification: LCC GV848.5.A1 D89 2020 | DDC 796.962092/2—dc23

Printed and bound in the United States of America
LSC/H 10 9 8 7 6 5 4 3 2 1

For my mom

Contents

Beauties

Foreword

by Roberto Luongo

I'm about to get this book off to a crappy start.

No, no, no, I mean that literally! The book is great! (Especially my chapter.) But yeah, this foreword is full of . . . you know.

It's May 3, 2007, Game 5 of our second-round series against the Anaheim Ducks. My Vancouver Canucks are down, three games to one. We're hanging on for dear life. I've had a good night, not gonna lie: 46 saves on 47 shots. Blind squirrel, 46 nuts!

But with about seven minutes left in the third period of a 1–1 tie, I get a stomach ache. I'm thinking, "This is weird." I never get stomach aches during a game. *Before* the game is a different story. I go to the bathroom five times a day on game day. I'm talking number two here. I may have been a number one goalie most of my career, but I'm all about number two on game days.

I go once in the morning when I get up, once at the morning skate, once after I wake up from my nap, once after the pre-game meeting, and once after warm-up, just in case. I don't want any accidents during the game. It's a skill.

The guys on my team all know about it. They see my big-ass toes sticking out from under the stall door and say, "Lui's goin' again."

I finish the third, and we're going to overtime. So I get back to my stall in the dressing room, and the tummy is rumbly, and I'm wondering, "Do I have to go? Or is this one of those times when I don't really have to go and once I get back into the game, it'll just go away?" After contemplating for a couple of minutes, I figure, "Just relax, it'll go away."

With about six minutes left on the intermission clock, I put all my gear back on and go out into the tunnel to get ready to go back on the ice. That's my routine. But about two minutes before we go out, my stomach says, "Lui, we're not gonna make it." I call Red, our trainer, over and say, "Red, I gotta go to the bathroom. What are we gonna do?!"

Red says, "Hold on, I'm gonna go talk to the referee." So Red runs over to the ref's room to talk to Bill McCreary. He comes running back 30 seconds later and says, "You're fine. Bill says they'll wait for you."

So I run to the bathroom, peel off my gear, and I go. And go. And go. I'm trying to hurry, but figuring I'm okay because Red said they wouldn't start without me. Then, after about four minutes, I hear the play start! I'm like, "Wait, *what*?! What happened to waiting for me?"

You can find footage from the CBC broadcast of the game on YouTube. I'll give you Jim Hughson's exact commentary right before the overtime starts, and add my own analysis for you.

HUGHSON: *This has been one of the most unusual, most curious playoff games I have ever seen, and it gets curiouser and curiouser. Dany Sabourin has led the Vancouver Canucks out and will be playing goal to start overtime. Roberto Luongo is not on the bench and is nowhere to be seen.*

Yeah, I'm taking a dump, Jim. Also, is *curiouser* a word?

HUGHSON: *[Luongo] finished the third period, he's had a spectacular night, he's stopped 46 of 47 shots . . .*

Told you guys I was awesome.

HUGHSON: *Markus Naslund did come out early and was speaking with the referee as though he might be trying to buy some time . . .*

That's a good captain right there, stalling while his goalie's butt explodes.

HARRY NEALE: *Dehydrated, maybe?*

I will be shortly, Harry, seeing that it's been a back-end waterfall in here for the last five minutes.

HUGHSON: *And overtime is under way . . .*

WTF?!
I'm sitting on the toilet with my pants on the floor, and overtime has started in an elimination game in the Stanley Cup playoffs! So, now I'm in a full panic. Don't want to gross you out (I know . . . too late for that), but I'm not sure I even wipe. I just throw my gear back on and rush to the bench.

And of course, there are no whistles. The play goes on for two or three minutes. I'm dying. The Ducks get a bunch of Grade A chances. Sabourin is making unbelievable saves. All I keep thinking is, "If they score, I will never get over this. It will be the worst thing in my life. For-*ever*." (Or at least until Boston in 2011. Freakin' Bruins.)

A whistle! Finally! I get back in. And yeah, I know what you're asking in your head. It had stopped. Mostly. I think I've gotten so anxious and panicked that everything . . . er . . . has tightened up . . . if you know what I mean.

No one scores in the first OT, and back in the dressing room, there is no chance I am going again.

Lui's five-hole—and six-hole—is not open.

Funny thing is, I make 56 saves. It's probably one of the best games of my career. Until the end.

Four and a half minutes into double overtime, Jannik Hansen gets levelled by Rob Niedermayer out near our blue line. It distracts me, just for a millisecond. I put my arm up, looking to the refs for a penalty. Just as I do that, Rob's brother Scott just throws the puck at the net and I'm caught off guard. It's in. Game over. Series over. Season over.

And now I'm feeling sick all over again. And this stomach ache lasts all summer.

===

I still don't know what went wrong that night with my stomach. There was no bad shrimp. Maybe Ducks defenceman Chris Pronger poisoned my water bottle. He's always looked like a Bond villain. It had never happened before, and it never happened again. Thanks, hockey gods, or stomach gods, or whatever gods control this crap. Maybe it could have been a pre-season game in Edmonton instead of an elimination game in the playoffs?!

Sorry, still sour.

A few nights later, we are having our season-ending party at a place on Kits Beach in Vancouver. It's right on the corner of a street. And I am sitting at the corner table with a bunch of the guys, having a few beers. A fire truck drives by, and one of the firefighters yells, "Hey, Luongo!" and throws a roll of toilet paper onto my table.

I guess that was the 2007 Canucks' version of a ticker-tape parade. Chucking toilet paper at Mr. Poopy Pants.

It was painful at the time (the loss *and* the diarrhea). But I can laugh now. Years go by, and these are the stories we tell endlessly over beers.

And that's what this book is. I've known James a long time. He loves to hear, and loves to tell, a great hockey story. This book is full of them. Most will make you laugh. A few might make you cry. Hopefully, none will send you running for the toilet.

Hockey is full of characters. You know how we always say, "That guy's a beauty"? This book is full of beauties.

And there is no way I'm letting James restrict me to a foreword about the time I couldn't stop pooping and we lost. Strombone needs a happy ending. So, you'll hear the 2010 Olympic story later. You should probably just flip to that chapter. It's poetry.

Oh, and by the way, I usually only tweet. This was a lot of words I had to write. Duthie should have paid me more.

My contract sucks. Again.

Introduction

———

Here's how the book's first interview goes.

One morning, I'm lying on my couch in my underwear (too much already?), eating a bowl of oatmeal, watching *SportsCentre*, when my phone rings.

"Hey, James. Bobby Orr. You have a few minutes now?"

"Uhhh . . . of course, Bobby . . . Mr. Orr . . . just give me one second."

I'd emailed Bobby about doing a story for the book the night before, expecting it might take a few weeks or months for the greatest defenceman ever to get back to me. It's taken 10 hours— three, if you don't count sleep. I sprint towards the kitchen, where my wife—wonderful . . . loving . . . beautiful . . . zero sense of urgency—is on the phone with some trendy clothing store, trying to buy a gift for our daughter.

I need her phone, like *now*. I'm an idiot when it comes to technology, so the only way I've figured out how to record phone interviews for the book is to talk to the subject with my speaker on, and record to the voice memo folder on my wife's phone. (I know. There are better ways. I've found them since. But Orr's call comes early in the process. This is all I've got.)

I come sliding across the hardwood, full Joel-in-*Risky Business*, half-whispering, half-gesturing to indicate my desperation. "Babe, it's Bobby Orr!" (Miming a shot with a pretend hockey stick.) "For my book!" (Drawing a square with fingers.) "I need your phone!" (Pointing at the phone with one hand, putting the other hand to my ear to indicate . . . "phone.")

She gives me a casual "get lost" wave.

Desperate, I resort to my outside voice, my hand covering my phone. *"It's Bobby freakin' Orr!!!* I need your phone NOW!"

She rolls her eyes and talks on. Now I'm throwing everything at her. Gesticulating wildly at my phone, and then hers. Making loud wounded-animal noises. Mandated-round-the-clock-supervision-type behaviour.

Finally, she gives. "I'll have to call you back," she says with a sigh. "My husband is having a seizure."

I grab her phone and bolt back to my office.

"Bobby, you still there?" He is, thankfully. "So, so sorry about that . . . okay . . . just give me one more sec . . . annnddd . . . we're recording. So. Tell me a great hockey story."

Thankfully, the rest of the interviews for the book are less sitcom-ish. But they all start with that same basic request: "Tell me a great hockey story."

There are no other rules. Long. Short. Funny. Serious. Inspirational. It could be the greatest game of your career. It could be the worst. It might be the funniest moment you've ever seen on the ice. Or in the bar after.

Some shared one story. Some shared a few. You will hear from current NHL superstars, Hall of Famers, journeymen, minor leaguers, coaches, refs, broadcasters, agents, trainers, hockey moms and dads, fans—everyone in the game.

Don't try to make sense of the list of storytellers. I prefer randomness. In real life, you run into someone at the rink, the airport . . . the bar. And they say, "You gotta hear this one."

I started with my friends at TSN—the former players and Insiders I work with daily. My favourite part of nearly two decades on the hockey panel is getting to sit beside characters who spin endless tales. Broadcasters are generally great storytellers. (It's kind of our job.)

Then I called people I've gotten to know in the game—Roberto Luongo, Jordan Eberle, Steven Stamkos—good guys with good tales. Your story tree grows from there. Stamkos says, "You should talk to Teddy Purcell." Kelly Chase says, "Call Jim McKenzie and Garth Butcher—they are gold." Jon Cooper says, "You need Eric Neilson in this book!"

And of course, you talk to the greats. Orr, Gretz, Sid, McDavid . . . they are all here.

An apology to all my journalism profs who demanded multiple sources for every story. I will break that rule, intentionally, many times in this book. Stories are personal. I want you to feel like you are sharing a beer or a coffee with the storyteller. When a chapter needs more voices, you will hear them.

I always hear how hockey players are boring. And maybe in those "keep workin' hard, get pucks in deep" intermission interviews, they mostly are. (By the way, they really do want to get pucks in deep. Their coach just yelled it in their ears for the last 20 minutes. It's ingrained.)

But turn the cameras off and get them away from that sweaty, out-of-breath, towel-around-the-neck, cliché-filled environment, and hockey players usually have a ton of stories. The game is full of characters.

Enjoy their stories. They were a pleasure to write.

Darryl

Sidney Crosby and His Wild Junior Hockey Roommate, Eric Neilson

―――――

"Holy shit!" Eric Neilson says from his seat in the stands. "This kid is insane!"

It's September 2003. The Rimouski Océanic of the Quebec Major Junior Hockey League (the Q) are playing their first pre-season game at home against Baie-Comeau. Neilson and some other Océanic vets have the night off, and they sit together in the stands, watching 16-year-old Sidney Crosby make magic in his first junior appearance. By the third period, the phenom from Cole Harbour, Nova Scotia, has four goals and four assists.

"It's a man against boys," Neilson says about the boy, who is playing against several men. "At that time, his nicknames are Sid the Kid, the Swayner, the Next One . . . really stupid nicknames. So, as a group of veterans—me, Mark Tobin, Érick Tremblay, Danny Stewart—we figure we have to come up with a new nickname for this guy.

"With about five minutes left in the game, Mark says to me, 'Neily, who is that Toronto Maple Leafs captain who got 10 points in a game?' And I go, 'That's Darryl Sittler.' So Mark says, 'Let's call him Darryl!'

"After the game, we go into the room and we're all saying, 'Hey, Darryl! Great game, Darryl! Way to go, Darryl!' And he's like,

'Why are you guys calling me Darryl?' We won't tell him. 'You're a rookie. You don't get to know where your nickname comes from!'"

"I'm pretty happy with that nickname," Crosby (Darryl) laughs. "For a 16-year-old rookie in junior, I'm sure they could have come up with much worse."

The next day, the vets take white tape and a black marker and write DARRYL over CROSBY on everything that bears his name—his locker nameplate, his sticks, his flip-flops . . . everywhere: 87 DARRYL.

A couple of media outlets eventually get wind of the story, and it gets back to the original Darryl, Sittler. When Crosby returns from the World Juniors in January, there is a package waiting from Ontario. It is a framed photo of Sittler and his 10-point-game scoresheet, signed by Darryl: *To Darryl.*

Neilson almost never got to be Darryl's teammate. The season before Crosby's arrival, 2002–03, Rimouski is the worst junior team in Canada. And Neilson spirals.

"I just go off track," he says. "The partying, the girls, the missed curfews. I'm an assistant captain, and the team gives me multiple chances. Finally, they call me into the office just before Christmas, and they have a one-way bus ticket back to Freddy [Fredericton, Neilson's hometown]. They say, 'You're off the team. You are not the player we thought you were when we brought you here.'

"It's like an instant epiphany for me. I have this flashback of being back home, working for my dad—Neilson's Heating and Ventilation—doing heat pumps and ductwork. Then I have another flashback to being a young hockey player, going to the gym and being the first one there, sacrificing everything to make it to the Quebec League. And it's like an instant 180. I rip the bus ticket up, throw it on the ground, and say, 'Boys, give me one more chance!' Everybody says no, except assistant coach Donald Dufresne. He says, 'All right, but this is it. You have one more chance, and then you're done.'"

For the rest of the season, Neilson works harder than he ever has, stays out of trouble and earns back the trust of the Océanic brass. The team finishes dead last, winning just 11 games, but he's saved his career. He gets called back into the team office.

"They say, 'We're going to draft this kid from Nova Scotia. You've shown us the kind of player and person you can be, and we want you to be his roommate and mentor him. Is that something you'd want to do?'

"I go, 'Yeah, sure, who is it?' They say, 'Sidney Crosby.' And I go, 'Who is that?' I'd never heard of Sidney Crosby."

Their first night as teammates/housemates doesn't go well.

Crosby and their billets pick up Neilson at the bus station. "He walks off the bus, best mushroom cut I've ever seen, full of energy, and I could just tell right away he's a great guy to be around," Crosby says. "Then, that night, he says, 'Make sure you open my window tonight.' We have bedrooms next to each other in our billet's basement. He tells me he is going to wait to make sure there isn't a curfew call, and then sneak out. He needs his window open to get back in. Of course, I fall asleep and forget. I wake up at 3 a.m. to this banging and crashing. But I don't know what it is, so I fall back asleep.

"In the morning, I open his bedroom door and it's just freezing. His window is demolished! I wake him up, he rolls over, and he's so mad at me. So we don't get off to the best start."

Luckily, it's easy to forgive a guy who is about to turn your franchise around. Eric and Crosby quickly become best buds. A local Mazda dealership gives them a sponsor car. Crosby doesn't have his licence yet, so the dealership puts his name and number on the passenger-side door: 87 CROSBY. And on the driver's side, NEILSON 29.

"It's *Driving Miss Daisy!*" Neilson laughs. "I'm his personal chauffeur. Everywhere Darryl needs to go, I take him. I try to teach him how to drive in the local parking lots. He's a horrible driver. Can't handle a stick." Irony! "Still a way better hockey player than he is a driver."

These are golden days for the boys. With Crosby, the Océanic go from the basement to instant contender. And Neilson has a driver's-side view of the future of hockey. But one night he almost blows that last chance the Océanic have given him.

"We're out late after a game," he says. "I'm the driver. I'm taking a couple of drunk teammates home and there are two girls in the back. I'm showing off. Coming around a corner, I try to do this e-brake *Tokyo Drift* thing, and I lose control. Now I'm doing donuts on the streets of Rimouski at 2 a.m. I hit the curb, bounce over it, hit three street signs and land in the other lane, facing the wrong way.

"My heart is in my throat because I know I've messed up. The police officer shows up, and one of the girls in my car is talking to him. Finally, he comes up and says, 'I know it was a mistake. I'll make sure you don't get in any trouble. I just need one favour: I want two autographed Crosby cards.'"

"Done," Neilson says before the officer finishes the sentence. A tow truck takes away the Mazda, and the police officer drives Neilson back to his billet's house.

"I run into Darryl's room, grab the cards and a marker from his desk, and shake him awake," Neilson says. "Now, Darryl is a real heavy sleeper, he's hard to wake up, and he doesn't remember much when you do wake him up from his beauty sleep. I manage to semi-revive him and I'm like, 'Darryl, you gotta sign these cards!' He scribbles his name, half-asleep. I go give them to the cop, and it's done.

"The next morning, Darryl comes down for breakfast and he's got marker ink all over his face and his chest . . . everywhere! He kept the marker in his hand as he went back to sleep. And I'm like, 'Darryl, you better go look in the mirror!' He thinks we pranked him."

"I just figure they wrote all over me while I was sleeping," Crosby says. "Then he tells me the whole story. Interesting way to wake up. Car is totalled and I'm covered in marker."

"He's pretty mad when I tell him the real story," Neilson says. "I don't think he usually gives autographs to cops to keep idiot teammates out of trouble."

So, it is true what they say: Sidney Crosby can make brilliant plays in his sleep.

For the next two years, Darryl rides shotgun in Neilson's (repaired) Mazda, and Neilson and the Océanic ride shotgun to Darryl's brilliance on the ice. He puts up 350 points in 143 games and leads Rimouski to the 2005 Quebec League championship.

The next fall, Crosby is off to Pittsburgh, to Stanley Cups and Harts and Golden Goals and one of the greatest careers in hockey history. And Neilson, his old roomie and driver, is off on a 12-year odyssey through the desert and jungle of the minors.

"Mike Angelidis, my old captain in Norfolk and Syracuse, used to say, 'East Coast Hockey League: Easy Come, Hard to Leave'— that's the desert. Then you get the call and you make it to the second three-letter league, the American Hockey League—that's the jungle. 'Cause you never know what's going to happen in the jungle! Then, just maybe you might get called up to the first three-letter league: the NHL. We call that paradise! You go from eating chicken fingers and pizza on a Greyhound bus for eight hours to flying around in a super turbojet, having the filet mignon or sea bass with red or white wine."

Neilson never makes it to paradise. He becomes a journeyman enforcer, mostly in the jungle. But he takes great joy, and a mentor's pride, in watching Crosby become a superstar. The two remain close friends.

Crosby writes DARRYL on his gloves his entire first season in Pittsburgh. At season's end, he gives Neilson, and each of the three other Rimouski vets who nicknamed him, a set of the gloves.

To this day, Neilson refuses to say the names Sidney or Crosby. Sid is Darryl. Darryl only. Darryl forever.

And there is one more night, playing with the Norfolk

Admirals in the jungle, that Neilson could have really used his old roomie.

It's 2011. The Admirals' team Halloween party at a local bar.

"I call Halloween a holiday. It's my favourite night of the year," Neilson says. "I always put a ton of effort into my costume. So that year, I have really long hair and I'd recently watched the movie *Blow* with Johnny Depp. It's about the drug dealer George Jung, back in the '70s. So I figure I can pull that off. I wear the white turtleneck, white suit, white shoes, sunglasses. I go see a professional hairdresser. She does my hair and makeup just perfect. I am George Jung! But I have to have props, right? So I have a rolled-up hundred-dollar bill, a bag of icing sugar for the cocaine, a bag of green tea for the pot, a makeup mirror to do fake snorting, and two fake rolled-up joints with green tea on the inside. I'm buzzing around all night, jokingly asking people if they want a bump. I'm totally in character. Just a great night.

"There's a scene in the movie where Johnny Depp gets arrested outside his parents' house. So I've had a few drinks, and at the end of the night, as I'm leaving, I joke to the manager of the bar, 'You want a bump before I go?' He grabs me and my bag of icing sugar and pulls me outside the bar. This is Halloween night on Granby Street in Norfolk, so there are cops patrolling up and down the street. The manager pulls me over to a cop and says, 'This guy is doing coke in my bar!' And the cop grabs the bag of sugar and says, 'What is this?'

"In the state I'm in, I think everyone is just playing along with my character. The manager and cop must know some of my buddies on the team, and now we're just recreating the arrest scene from the movie! They're all part of the skit! So I yell at the cop in my best Johnny-Depp-as-George-Jung voice, 'What da *fawk* you think it is, man? It's cocaine!' And he starts putting me in the cop car. I see all the other players standing around, watching, so I stay in character, yelling, 'YOU CAN'T TOUCH ME! I'M THE BEST FAWKING DRUG DEALER THERE IS!'

"Now I'm in the back of the car, and the cop gets in. I go, 'That was awesome, man. Thanks for playing along!' And he says, 'What are you talking about? You're under arrest for cocaine possession! You're going to jail.' That's when I realize, 'Oh, shit.'

"He takes my New Brunswick ID, and he's saying, 'This is a fake ID! Where did you get all this cocaine?' I'm desperately trying to explain that I'm a Norfolk Admirals player and this is a Halloween costume. But he isn't buying it. I sit for 45 minutes in the back of the car before the drug unit guys come down and test my bag of cocaine positive for icing sugar. Finally, they let me go. Just another night in the jungle."

Should have called Darryl. And asked for more autographed cards.

The Great One-Liner

The Joke That Leads to
Wayne Gretzky's Greatest Cup Final

———

The most underappreciated part of Wayne Gretzky's game was his ability to finish.

A joke, I mean.

One afternoon, Darren Pang, former NHL goalie turned broadcaster, is out golfing with his long-time pal at Sherwood Country Club in California, where Gretzky lives at the time.

"We're on the tee box of this really long par five, unreachable," says Pang. "And Gretz says, 'I bet you I can get home in two.' I take the bet, because Gretz is a good golfer, but he has zero chance of getting on that green in two shots. So, he hits a nice drive in the fairway. But he's still got a mile to the green. No chance. So, Gretz walks up to his ball, takes a long look at the green—and pulls a wedge out! I'm thinking, 'What is he doing?' And he casually turns to his left and hits the ball into his backyard. 'Home in two!' he says with this big grin.

"Another day, another round. The Great One drains a 60-foot putt for birdie. Without missing a beat, he says casually, 'You gotta earn your nickname.'

"We all just crack up," Pang says. "He's not being cocky. He just does it to give the guys a laugh."

Timing is everything in comedy. And considering the timing,

the stakes and what would happen next, Gretzky's greatest one-liner comes in the 1985 Stanley Cup final.

The series does not start well for the favoured Oilers. The defending Cup champs lose Game 1 to the Philadelphia Flyers, 4–1. Gretzky goes pointless and is a minus-2.

"Glen Sather really gives it to me in the dressing room after," Gretzky says. "Myself and Paul Coffey are the ones who get singled out for not being ready to play. And he just rips us. Everyone thought the Oilers were going to win in four or five, and that first game really could have been 8–1 if not for Grant Fuhr. I just didn't show up for the game. And when you play that way, you deserve it. But the next day, Sather's really positive, building us back up. So by the time Game 2 starts, we are ready to play."

Early in Game 2, the Oilers are killing a penalty when Gretzky tries to freeze a puck in the Flyers zone. Forward Rick Tocchet is all over him. We'll let them handle the play-by-play:

GRETZKY: *In those days, it takes a long time to get a whistle freezing the puck. You have to hold it a while. We end up with seven or eight guys in the same corner while I'm trying to freeze it. Now, that's the year Clarkie [Flyers GM Bob Clarke] makes the Flyers all wear these giant shoulder pads. They were already a big team, but those made them look huge. So they're all around me, and Tocchet is just hacking and whacking me. Everything you can imagine that is semi-legal to do.*

TOCCHET: *Mike Keenan says to me before the series, "You have to go after Gretzky. Do whatever you can to get under his skin." I think he used a little harsher language than that. So I'm cross-checking him, face-washing, you name it.*

GRETZKY: *Finally, thankfully, the whistle goes. I turn to Tocchet and say, "Hey, relax. Lighten up!" And he looks me in the eye and says . . .*

TOCCHET: *"Get used to it! You are getting this every shift! Every period! All seven games long!"*

GRETZKY: *So I look at him and say, "I don't know what series you're playing in, because I'm only playing four more games."*

Boom! A verbal sucker punch.

TOCCHET: *Everyone just stops for a second or two after he says it. And then they all start laughing. Even the guys on my team! I'm not sure what to do. I have no response. I think I just kind of smirk. I have to admit it's pretty funny.*

GRETZKY: *Everyone leaves the corner laughing. We get back to the bench and all the guys are saying, "What was so funny down there?" They thought someone let one go in the corner.*

Can a great chirp actually turn a series? Well, from that moment on, the Great One goes off. Minutes after the Oilers kill the penalty, Coffey feeds Gretzky to open the scoring. The Oilers go on to win, 3–1, to even the series.

In Game 3, Gretzky scores 1:10 in. Fifteen seconds later, he scores again. Ten minutes into the game, he completes the hat trick. He finishes with four points in a 4–3 win.

All three of his goals are scored with each team having a player in the penalty box, which infuriates Keenan, Clarke and the Flyers. It leads to the "Gretzky Rule."

"That game, those three goals, end four-on-four hockey in the NHL," Gretzky says. "Every time we get a four-on-four in that series, we seem to score. Keenan says afterwards that we were purposely taking penalties to play four on four, which is crazy. But because of that playoff, the league dropped it—for seven years! Coincidental minors were now five-on-five, which was just stupid."

Four-on-four, five-on-five . . . it doesn't matter by this point in the series. Philly can't stop 99. Game 4, their last real hope, is tied 3–3 midway through the second when Gretzky scores two straight to win it, 5–3.

Now he's turned Tocchet's words back against him. He is killing the Flyers every shift . . . every period.

In the clincher, Gretzky goes full legend: a goal and three assists in an 8–3 win. Game. Series. Cup.

In the three and three-quarters games since he punchlined Tocchet in the corner, Gretzky has scored seven times and added four assists, and he wins the Conn Smythe Trophy running away.

"That first loss woke us up . . . woke me up," he says.

"Sure, that joke in Game 2 was funny," Tocchet says. "But the problem is, damn, he was right!"

The Flyers and Oilers develop a fierce rivalry over the next few years, meeting again in the Cup final in 1987, with Edmonton winning in seven games. Three months later, Keenan is chosen to coach the Canada Cup team. He assigns Tocchet to room with Gretzky.

"I'm really nervous," Tocchet says. "I remember calling my parents right away to tell them, 'I'm rooming with Wayne freakin' Gretzky!' But right away, he just accepts me and we start hanging out. He's dating Janet Jones secretly at the time. She comes into the room, and he tells me, 'Don't say anything about this.' I think it's pretty cool that he trusts me with the secret."

A couple of days later, Gretzky tells his roomie he's going to get a haircut.

"He doesn't ask me if I want to come, but he just kind of stands there, waiting," Tocchet says. "I realize he's asking me to come without asking me. So I go, and after five minutes, there's about 100 people outside the salon. I quickly learn that's his life, every day, everywhere he goes. I finally figure out that he just doesn't want to go out alone."

The two become close friends. They still are. When I call Tocchet for this story, he's having dinner with Gretzky that night.

And as for the chirp that, just maybe, changed a series?

"I still bring it up to him once in a while," Gretzky says. "We always laugh about it. But I laugh a little harder. He still doesn't find it quite as funny as I do."

Fixing Razor

Ray Emery and the Trainer Who Helped Pull Off One of Hockey's Greatest Comebacks

———

Google Ray Emery's name, and every story that pops up is about the way he died.

"What happened to Ray Emery on the night he tragically drowned?"

"Sadly fitting that Ray Emery's tragic death at 35 comes under a shroud of mystery."

"Police believe Ray Emery's death was a 'case of misadventure.'"

This story is not about the end of Ray's life. This is the other Ray Emery tale—of one of the greatest comebacks in hockey history. And of the man who pushed him every excruciating step of the way.

———

The goalie and the trainer are both hurting when they find each other.

Matt Nichol's hurt comes from being called into a meeting with Brian Burke and Dave Nonis in the spring of 2009 and being told he is no longer the Toronto Maple Leafs' strength coach.

"It had never been my goal to do that job," Matt says. "I had never played hockey, so it wasn't even on my radar. But once I got it, I poured my heart and soul into it. So that was the hard part, getting fired from something I had given myself completely to for seven years. Suddenly, for the first time in a long time, I have no plan. When the season starts, my clients are gone. I literally have zero clients, and no idea what to do with my life."

For Ray Emery, the hurt is mostly physical. It comes from a hip injury that, in all likelihood, will end his hockey career. He'd been a rising star in goal with the Ottawa Senators, helping them reach the Stanley Cup final in 2007, just his second full season in the NHL. But then his career went sideways. Then backwards. Then stopped. He admitted to some bad decisions off the ice, but also believed he didn't deserve the bad-boy reputation that shadowed him. And then all of that became secondary.

Ray develops a condition called avascular necrosis—the head of his femur is disintegrating within his hip socket. For you and me, the fix is a hip replacement. But you can't play goal in the NHL on an artificial hip. So Ray is done.

Wait. Maybe, just maybe, there is one Hail Mary left. An experimental new surgery has been developed at Duke University Medical Center in North Carolina. They will take a chunk of Ray's fibula and use it as a drill bit to get blood back into the hip. It's risky. Ray is told there is a chance he will never walk again. And even if the surgery is a success, something could still go horribly wrong in his rehab, or when—*if*—he plays again.

"He says some crazy things to me during that time," says Eli Wilson, Ray's long-time goalie coach and friend. "He tells me, dead serious, that he doesn't mind spending the rest of his life in a wheelchair, as long as he makes it back to the NHL first. It's the only thing he wants in his life."

Ray has the surgery. Anything for a chance, even if the odds look Powerball Lottery bad. He spends a month in agony in hospital, his only movement pushing the button on the side of his bed to get upright to eat.

And so the goalie and the trainer sit—Ray in his hospital bed, Matt alone in his gym. Two wounded souls, trying to figure out, "What now?"

Ray's agent, J.P. Barry, is also former Leafs captain Mats Sundin's agent. Barry asks Sundin who might be able to help Ray, and he recommends Matt.

"J.P. calls and explains the situation," Matt says. "I know of Ray from the Leafs' battles with the Senators. But I don't know him personally at all. It's a pretty big leap of faith on my part. The odds of him making it back are very remote. It's uncharted waters. There is no one I can call to ask about similar cases: 'What did you do? What exercises? What types of therapy? What's the timeline?' No one has ever done it. I call around to people I know in the league and am told that even if somehow he miraculously gets back, teams may not want to touch him because of his past transgressions."

Still, Matt agrees to meet with Ray. They sit down on a bench in his gym at the back of St. Michael's College School Arena in downtown Toronto. And the trainer lays it all on the table.

"I say, 'Okay, here's the deal. These are the odds of you making it back. Even if we're able to hit a grand slam on this, maybe it means being able to walk, or go for a jog, or ride a bike. Or even go for a skate—that would be a fantastic outcome. But to be able to play NHL hockey as a goaltender, which is so demanding on the hips . . . it's a long shot. And I'm gonna be completely winging it. You may put in all this time and effort and you still might not get back. So what's a successful outcome to you? If we are able to get you good enough to play East Coast League hockey, is that success for you?'"

There is also a deadline looming a few months away when Ray can be declared medically unfit to play. If this happens, he will receive a large insurance payout—at the cost of never being able to play hockey again. If that deadline passes and he doesn't make it back, he gets nothing. Matt reminds him of this, too.

"I don't care about the money," Ray tells Matt. "You fix my hip. I'll worry about playing in the NHL."

The trainer says, "Okay." And starts trying to figure out how to fix Ray.

Neither the rehab nor the relationship comes easy. They spend endless hours in the gym and pool, and Ray says nothing. No small talk, no questions, no conversation at all.

"At one point, I have to call his agent and say, 'Can you ask him how it's going?'" Matt says. "I think I'm about to get fired. We would be in the gym for two hours, twice a day, without a single word. But J.P. says, 'No, he likes you. That's just Ray.'"

Matt isn't the only one to get the silent treatment. He brings in chiropractor Mike Prebeg to help. Prebeg specializes in soft-tissue treatment and neurofunctional acupuncture. His first meeting with Ray doesn't go well.

"I don't know the guy at all," Prebeg says. "I'd heard that he punched out his last therapist in Russia. When he comes in, he's skinnier than a runway model. He's been in bed for a month. There's nothing left of him. I tell him playing in the NHL again is not a realistic goal. His goal should be to walk properly. Ray says, 'Just treat me.' And he doesn't talk to me again for weeks. I work on him in silence."

Those first few weeks of rehab have nothing to do with hockey. Matt is trying to teach Ray's brain and muscles how to sit, stand and walk again. The bone they harvested from the fibula has cost him all his stability and balance. They work endlessly on tiny movements. Matt, as promised, is making it up as he goes.

"We would go to the National Ballet. We'd do Pilates, various forms of yoga, vision training. We just keep throwing a bunch of shit at the wall to see what would stick."

There is one other person who might be able to help. Bo Jackson hears about Ray's injury through the pro sports grapevine and calls him.

"Bo had a similar injury, though not the same surgery," Matt says. "He came back to play baseball, but was never able to play football again. But he is incredibly helpful to Ray."

Matt keeps pushing Ray. To the edge . . . and over it.

"There are so many things we do that are so far outside his comfort zone, and he just takes it all," Matt says. "I knew he was tough—hockey tough. The toughness to throw a punch, to take a punch. But this is a different toughness. It's crazy what he goes through. I can't even imagine the pain. I can see it in his eyes, but he never says a word. He is the toughest person and hardest worker I've ever seen."

"Ray processes pain differently from any human I've met," Prebeg adds. "He likes it. There are things we do to him in treatment that would make most people, even elite athletes, scream in agony. He just takes it. Just watch some of his fights on YouTube. He's getting punched in the face, and he's just smiling. He's a warrior. I truly think pain is what made him feel alive."

As the days and weeks of endless, punishing workouts pass, Ray starts to open up to Matt. They talk. He chirps Matt's bad jokes. He starts to let him in. Matt starts calling him Razor, the nickname Ray's friends use.

"When you get into his inner circle, Razor is one of the kindest, most considerate people I've ever met in my life," Matt says. "He's one of the more misunderstood players of his generation."

Prebeg is also starting to take down Ray's walls, brick by brick.

"One day we have a couple of breakthroughs in treatment," Prebeg says. "I go, 'Hey, try a squat for me.' And he does it! This huge smile comes over his face. I say to myself, 'Holy shit, he might do this.' I learn to love the guy. Once he trusts you, he's incredible. He's the most generous athlete I've ever worked with."

They chip away, day after day, for months. Sitting . . . standing . . . walking . . . squatting . . . getting in and out of the butterfly, moving from side to side. Eli Wilson comes by regularly to show Matt the body positions he needs his goalie to get into, the hip rotations Ray needs to be able to do. Matt creates the exercises to make those movements happen. And slowly, remarkably, Ray does them all.

It's November now. Ray is back in full gear, crouched between two posts. Already doing more than the doctors believed possible.

"I bring some kids who play Junior B to shoot on Ray," Matt says. "He wants to be tested—high glove, high blocker—but they are scared to take real shots. Shooting high on a goalie is risky. You can hit them in the face. Most goalies will yell at you. These guys worry Ray might kill them!

"So I ask Eric Lindros to come out. When I see a player like that taking shots and Ray making some saves, it's the first time I think, 'Maybe.'"

The next day, Lindros and the junior players are testing Ray with breakaways when one of them tucks in a rebound after the goalie has already turned back towards the next skater. The kid does a little celly, and a switch flips in the goalie.

"Ray has been calm and cautious the whole time, but he tells this kid off in some colourful language and slams his stick into both posts," Matt says. "It's like he's saying, 'All right, let's fucking go.' All of a sudden, we have skipped 15 steps in the rehab process. He is moving all over the net. Eric is firing it as hard as he can. Ray is making save after save. I don't think anyone scores on him for the rest of that practice. That is the moment I say, 'This is happening.'"

Word gets around. A few weeks later, Matt gets calls from two NHL general managers, grilling him about how Ray is doing, about his attitude. Eli Wilson gets the same calls. The next day, Ray walks into Matt's gym in street clothes.

"I tell him, 'All right, get changed, let's get this workout going,'" Matt says. "And Ray goes, 'Not working out today. I'm going to Anaheim, bro. I signed with the Ducks.' I'm like, 'Oh my God, Razor, this is incredible!'"

In the movies, this would be the scene with a long embrace,

tears and cheesy "We did it!" lines. But this isn't *Rocky* or *Rudy*. It's Ray.

"He gives me a quick hug and says, 'Thanks, bro, I'll be in touch,' and he walks out of the gym," Matt laughs. "Five months of training twice a day, every day, doing the impossible—going from not being able to walk to making it all the way back to the NHL. And it's 'Thanks, bro,' and he's gone."

Matt shakes his head and laughs at the memory. That's just Ray's way. Besides, the comeback isn't really complete until he shows the world he can still play.

He does. And soon it becomes clear: Ray hasn't just made it back. He's . . . better.

"The amazing thing is, he's a much different goalie after the comeback," Wilson says. "The challenge was never getting down; it was getting back up. Goaltenders get up with their back leg. So, if they are moving to their left, they get up with the right leg. He could never rotate the repaired hip quite as well as the other. He could never get back in position as smoothly. So he figured out how to rework the way he moved. And he became a much better technical goaltender."

There are setbacks along the way. Ray calls Matt after a Ducks playoff game that first spring to tell him he's strained his hip flexor.

"I'm like, 'Oh, please no,'" Matt says. "But Ray is laughing. He says, 'We pulled the goalie and as I'm skating to the bench, I realize I haven't done this!' When we started this whole thing, I told Ray we didn't have time to make him a well-rounded athlete. The training was ultra-specific to make him move in this small space in the net. We never did a sprint, never jogged a single lap of the track. And so he starts racing off the ice and strains his hip flexor. But he's fine. He thinks it's hilarious."

That summer, Ray limps into Matt's gym one day, panicking his trainer again.

"I go, 'What happened? Is it your hip?' And he goes, 'No, it's my ankle. I was playing one on one with Spezz [close friend Jason

Spezza].' Ray shows me his ankle and it's swollen like a beach ball. I try to lecture him, saying, 'You can't do this after everything you did to get back. Did you even warm up or stretch?' And Ray says, 'I'm an athlete, bro. I can play basketball when I want to. There's no way I'm letting Spezz beat me one on one.'"

Ray signs with Chicago in 2011. A season later, he teams up with Corey Crawford to win the Jennings Trophy for best team goaltending. Ray finishes 17–1, with a 1.94 goals-against average. It is one of the greatest seasons a backup goalie has ever had. The Blackhawks win the Stanley Cup. Ray gets his first and only ring.

You wish the story would end here. A miracle comeback, complete. A clean exit. But Ray's life was never that simple. He slides off track again when he retires from hockey three years later. More bad choices.

Maybe that's why Ray fought so hard to get back after the surgery. He needed the game. Life without it was a struggle. "I'm an athlete, bro."

In the years since he retired, Matt hadn't heard much from Ray. A text here, a pic there. "Riding a hoverboard in Dubai or something random like that."

On July 15, 2018, Matt gets a text from another NHL player he trains.

"Have you heard about Ray?"

Emery had drowned while hanging out with friends after a charity hockey game in Hamilton. They say he was trying to swim under water to a dock 100 feet away in the early morning darkness. He never surfaced. He was 35.

"Ray saved me as much as I did him," Matt says. "He gave me a purpose and a reason to get out of bed and be excited about the day ahead at a time when I didn't feel great about myself or my situation. We ended up in each other's lives when we really needed each other. I miss him."

Remember when Ray signed with Anaheim and walked out of Matt's gym with just a simple "Thanks, bro"? A couple of weeks later, a handwritten letter arrived in Matt's mailbox, followed by an autographed jersey. Matt keeps the contents of the letter to himself. To this day, Ray's jersey remains the only one that hangs in his office. The inscription on the jersey reads:

Matty,

You motivated me to do something that nobody thought we could do. You are the best trainer out there. I owe my career to you.

Your bro,
Razor

Noodles, the Puffin and the Report Card

Goalie Jamie McLennan Takes Heat from Coaches Billy Smith and Darryl Sutter

———

In 1991, the New York Islanders draft a skinny, mulleted goalie from Alberta named Jamie McLennan. Or, as most know him, Noodles. He earns the nickname in junior, for constantly cooking pasta on a tiny portable stove on the team bus.

During his rookie year, Noodles joins the Islanders' American Hockey League team in Newfoundland for two games against the St. John's Maple Leafs, Toronto's farm team. The Isles' goaltending coach is Billy Smith, a hockey legend renowned both for his ability to stop the puck—he backstopped all four Islanders Stanley Cup wins—and his temper. When Billy played, you took your life in your hands if you went near his crease.

"Billy is flying in to watch the games in St. John's, and I want to make a good impression on him," Noodles says. "He has the reputation of being a hard-ass, a guy who doesn't take any shit. So I'm excited, but nervous, when I skate onto the ice for the first period. St. John's has a mascot—it's this weird-looking bird. I find out years later his name is Buddy the Puffin.

"As I take the ice for the start of the game, this bird is flopping around the ice, putting on a show. He's standing in my crease, kind of giving me a hex as I skate towards him. I want to scrape my crease and do my stretching, but he's in my space. So I skate up and gently push him out of the way. He gives me a little push back. The crowd kind of chuckles, but I don't think much of it because I'm locked in, ready for my first start."

Noodles has a solid period and is feeling good as he skates out for the start of the second. But there is Buddy the Puffin, back in his crease.

"I have to skate the whole length of the ice to start the period, a 200-foot skate, and as I approach my net, there's that bird, flapping his wings and standing in my crease. As I get to him, he kind of gives me a shot, and I give him a little shot. It's playful, but I want to get him the hell out of my way because I need to get focused. Finally, he leaves, and again, I don't think much more of it the rest of the game."

Noodles plays well and walks into the dressing room proudly after the game, feeling he's made a good impression on his legendary goalie coach.

"I go into the room and Billy Smith is sitting in my stall," Noodles says. "So I'm thinking he's going to congratulate me and praise me for my performance."

But Billy's face does not read praise. He looks at Noodles sternly and says, 'I need to speak to you outside."

"I'm thinking, 'What the hell is going on here?'" Noodles says. "'Where's my high-five?' Instead, he takes me out in the hallway and says, 'Don't you ever let that fucking bird stand in your crease again! He embarrassed you! If he's there again on Thursday, you run that fucking bird over!' Now I'm rattled. I thought I'd played a good game, and my goalie coach is yelling at me over a giant bird mascot!"

Noodles barely sleeps that night, and quietly prays he doesn't get the start in the Thursday night game. But during the off-day practice, coach Butch Goring skates by and says, "You're going tomorrow."

"I'm like, 'Shit! I have to face the puffin again!'" Noodles says. "I can't sleep again. Buddy is in my head! When I go out to start the game, I get a break. Buddy is there, but this time he isn't really in my crease, so I just leave him alone. But I'm a mess in the first. I'm thinking, 'Just pull me so I don't have to deal with this bird again at the start of the second.'"

But Goring leaves the rookie in. And as Noodles takes to the ice for the second, Buddy is back in his net . . . waiting . . . taunting.

"So I say, 'To hell with it. I'm taking him out.' I pick up speed. By the blue line, I'm really moving. And I just bury that fucking bird! I hit him as hard as I can, and he goes flying into the corner.

"I guess the scary part is I have no idea who is inside that costume. Could have been a 14-year-old girl, or a senior citizen! Anyway, the bird is down and they have to help it off the ice. The crowd is screaming at me. It's one of the worst nights ever. We lose, and I've killed the puffin."

Noodles slumps back to the dressing room, defeated and embarrassed. And there is Billy Smith, waiting in his stall again.

"I think to myself, 'Here comes the riot act.' Instead, he stands up and has this big grin on his face and says, 'That's how you become a man in this league! That's how you get respect!' I'm in shock. I say, 'Billy, I sucked and we lost!' He says, 'Who gives a shit? They'll never forget the way you stood up for yourself tonight.'

"I swear Billy Smith told Butch Goring to keep playing me just to see how I would deal with this bird. That was my first interaction with a coach in pro hockey. I play well, I get shit. I'm the worst player on the ice the next game, but I run a bird over, so I'm a hero."

Noodles is scarred a little by Buddy the Puffin. But he survives. He goes on to play 15 pro seasons and 254 NHL games for six different teams. And he never has another interaction with a coach quite like the one on that road trip to the Rock with Billy Smith.

Okay, maybe one more.

"I am playing in Calgary for Darryl Sutter, and Roman Turek is our starter," Noodles says. "We're playing Washington one night [March 20, 2003], and Roman gives up a bit of a soft one in the second to make it 3-1 Caps. Darryl gives me the look and says, 'Get the fuck in there!'

"So, I skate in and I'm pretty cold. You want to make a few saves early just to get going. I make this unreal save off Peter Bondra, and I'm feeling really good about myself. And then, right off a draw, I allow this awful five-hole goal from down near the goal line. All of a sudden, I look up and I see Roman coming back in the net. As I skate off, Darryl is just lasering me with his eyes. But when he comes in the room after the second, it's Roman he yells at. 'I don't give a fuck if you allow a hundred goals, you're staying in!' I think he was mad at Roman for not skating that morning."

The Flames lose, 4-1, and when Noodles gets to the rink the next morning, assistant coach Jim Playfair tells him "Big D" wants to talk to him.

"As I walk in, I'm thinking, 'Oh God, this can't be good.' So I get into Darryl's office and he's got this whiteboard there. I say, 'Hey, Darryl, what's up?' and he says, 'Sit down, I want to ask you a few questions.'"

DARRYL: *How do you think you are in the room?*

NOODLES: *I think I'm pretty good. I'm a pretty good leader and I like to get the energy going for the boys.*

DARRYL: *I agree.*

On the whiteboard beside him, Darryl writes an *A* next to *In the room*. Noodles smiles, instantly feeling better about himself.

DARRYL: *How do you think your conditioning is?*

NOODLES: *I'm all right, I think.*

DARRYL: *Yup, could be better, but I think you're a solid B.*

Darryl writes a large *B* beside *Conditioning* on his whiteboard. He then adds the word *Preparation* to his report card.

DARRYL: *When you start games for me, how do you rate your preparation?*

NOODLES: *I'm good. I always feel prepared.*

DARRYL: *I agree! Let's give you a B+.*

Noodles is almost feeling cocky now. He has a better report card going than he did in any of his years at Paul Kane High School in St. Albert, Alberta.

DARRYL: *How are you coming off the bench cold?*

Sutter writes the question down on the whiteboard, and just as Noodles is opening his mouth to answer, the coach answers it himself, hastily writing a giant letter *F* on the board as he does.

DARRYL: *EFFF! Fucking EFFFFFF!!*

NOODLES: *But coach—*

DARRYL: *EFFFFFF!!! You have nothing to say! Get the fuck out of this room! It's an EFFFFFF!!!!*

"I don't even need to open the door to walk out—I'm an inch tall. I can walk under it," Noodles says. "Jimmy Playfair is in the next room, and I'm almost in tears as I walk by him. I go out for

30

practice and I work really hard. Jimmy pulls me aside after practice and says, 'Listen, Darryl was a little wound up. He lets things fester for a while, and he has bullets for everyone, and you happened to take the bullets today.' So Jimmy was the good cop to Darryl's bad cop."

The next time Noodles comes into a game cold, Darryl simply says, "Play well." His goalie does, and their relationship smooths over instantly.

"Darryl is my all-time favourite. I absolutely loved him as a coach," Noodles says. "But I'll never forget the *F* that I got on my Big D report card."

Professor Sutter clearly goes by the grading system where they drop the lowest and highest marks, because he later hires Noodles to be his goalie coach in Calgary.

Noodles always gives his Flames goalies three valuable instructions: stay in control, always keep your eye on the puck, and don't ever, *ever*, let a mascot take your crease.

The Fastest-Skating Girl

Kendall Coyne Schofield Changes Women's Hockey in One Lap

―――――

On a tiny shovelled slice of the frozen Ottawa River, four-year-old Demie Anas takes her mark.

"Ready . . . set . . . *pow!*" her dad, Jimmy, says.

And off she goes. Demie is still learning to skate, so it takes a while to circle the two nets on the rink Dad has cleared. But she gets there. And grins as Dad high-fives her with one hand, capturing the moment on his phone with the other.

Demie had never cared much for hockey. "Change it to P*eppa Pig*!" she'd say when her older brother TJ was watching games. Which was . . . well, always.

But then she sees the girl. "The Fastest-Skating Girl," she calls her.

"I want to be like the Fastest-Skating Girl!" Demie repeats over and over for weeks, running laps around the living room. And skating them on that little rink on the river.

"She genuinely wants to be her," says Demie's mom, Catherine.

Catherine posts the video of Demie skating on Twitter and tags her daughter's inspiration.

@KendallCoyne ever since your awesome showing at the @nhl skills competition, my 4yo daughter Demie wants to be just like you!

Here's her attempt to break your record. Thanks for inspiring little girls everywhere. #skatelikeagirl #hockey #girlscandoanything

Kendall Coyne Schofield beams when she sees it. Just like she does for the thousands of other messages she gets from other little Demies around the world.

All because of 14 seconds. A moment that launches a movement.

=====

First, it's just a thought. Not even an idea yet. A random observation from some guy on a couch.

But he's the right guy, it turns out.

It's February 2014. Patrick Burke is at home, watching women's hockey at the Sochi Olympics. "Damn, Kendall is fast!" he says to himself. "Her first three steps are ridiculous."

Burke works for the NHL in its player safety department. But a year after Sochi, he takes on an additional role, helping to run the NHL All-Star Skills Competition.

Along with Susan Cohig, who leads women's initiatives with the league, Burke pushes hard to bring in some of the top women's players for All-Star Weekend.

So, on January 27, 2018, Hilary Knight, Amanda Kessel and Meghan Duggan are in Tampa, Florida, demonstrating some of the skills the NHL stars will compete in. They crush it. Knight nails all five targets in 11.64 seconds in the shooting accuracy event. It would have placed her third among the NHL All-Stars.

But these are just demos. They're done during commercial breaks and aren't shown on TV, though the networks would run highlights of Knight's performance.

One year later, the NHL invites Kendall, her American teammate Brianna Decker, and Canadians Rebecca Johnston and Renata Fast to do the same thing in San Jose.

Kendall and Renata will demonstrate shooting accuracy. The

league wants to play up the Canada–USA rivalry for fans in the building. They won't bother having anyone demonstrate fastest skater. A lap around the rink doesn't need much of an explanation.

But then fate (or flying frozen rubber) intervenes. In the last game before the All-Star break, Colorado Avalanche star Nathan MacKinnon takes a puck in the foot and ends up in a walking boot. MacKinnon happens to be one of the eight players in the fastest skater event.

Burke has never forgotten Kendall's speed in Sochi. He's been watching her ever since. He starts scheming. He believes she's the perfect replacement for MacKinnon.

"I've been telling anyone who would listen for years that Kendall could do fastest skater," Burke says. "I know she can be competitive with these guys."

First, he needs to prove it. So, when Kendall's plane lands in San Jose the day before the event, there's a text from Burke, asking her to come straight to the rink.

"I fly in from Chicago, with a layover in Burbank," Kendall says. "It's already been a really long travel day, and the second I walk in, Patrick says, 'If you get out there right now, you can try fastest skater. But we only have a couple minutes.' I'm frazzled, scrambling to get my stuff on.

"Dave Fischer from USA Hockey is there. He gives Brianna her jersey and socks and I say, 'Fish, do you have mine?' He looks through his stuff and says, 'I only have one sock! They only sent me three!' I'm panicking. Fish runs to try to find me one and comes back with what looks like Joe Thornton's son's sock. It's a little kid's sock! So Renata pulls her Toronto Fury socks out and says, 'You can wear these!' I make it out there just in time, don't warm up at all, and skate my lap."

Kendall is timed in 14.226 seconds. It would have placed her sixth in the previous year's event.

"That's sixth out of our *All-Stars*!" Burke says. "The best players in the world! I'm sitting on the bench with guys like Shane

Doan, Ray Whitney, and they're going, 'Wow, she could beat some of the guys!' And I'm like, 'Yeah, I've been trying to tell you all that!'"

Burke sells NHL chief content officer Steve Mayer on the idea, and the two approach Commissioner Gary Bettman in the lobby of the Fairmont San Jose hotel that evening.

As PR moves go, it may seem like a no-brainer to include Kendall. But there are those inside the league, and out, who believe the NHL All-Star Weekend should be solely for . . . NHL All-Stars. The league didn't bring in Jack Hughes or Connor McDavid when they were prospects. They don't bring in other NHLers who might be crazy fast or have a cannon of a shot. The All-Stars have worked their entire life to get here, and they deserve to own the weekend.

All valid points. But Burke believes this is a chance for a moment bigger than the game.

"Can she do it?" Bettman asks.

"Absolutely," Burke responds, showing the commissioner her time.

"Great," Bettman says. "You need to get it approved by the NHLPA, because there is prize money. We need to make sure they will be okay with a non-PA player getting the money if she wins. But if you get their approval, let's do it."

The NHL Players' Association loves the idea, too. Kendall is in. But she knows nothing of it when she goes to bed Friday night.

The NHL and NHLPA iron out the details Saturday morning, and Burke calls Kendall to break the news.

He gets no answer. Twice.

"It comes up as an unknown number, and I never answer those," Kendall says, laughing. Burke finally tries sending a text: *It's me, Burkie. You really need to pick up your phone.*

"I call him right back and he says, 'You are going to be the first woman to compete in the NHL All-Star Skills Competition,'" Kendall says. "And I go, 'Huh?' I'm overwhelmed."

With a California city hosting the weekend, it means an after-noon start for the skills competition, so Kendall doesn't have much time. She hangs up and makes three quick calls. The first is to her husband, Michael Schofield, an NFL offensive lineman.

"Oh my gosh! This is unbelievable! You are going to kill it!" he says.

He tries to get a flight from Chicago, but quickly realizes he won't get there on time. The event starts in hours. Kendall then calls her parents, Ahlise and John, and her best friend, Amanda. No time for small talk.

"I'm going to be in the skills tonight! The real thing!" she says. "Try to watch. Love you. Gotta go!"

When she gets to the rink, she needs her skates sharpened but is too shy to ask.

"I don't want to be high-maintenance," Kendall says.

"That shows the humility of women's players," Burke says. "She could have just walked in and asked the trainers, and they would have done it in a second."

There's one detail the NHL hasn't considered: the warm-up. Kendall is the first skater in the first event of the night. But no one has told her whether she is allowed to take part in the warm-up with the All-Stars, so she waits in her dressing room.

"I'm on the bench and someone yells in my earpiece, 'Is Kendall Coyne allowed out for warm-ups?'" Burke says. "I say, 'Of course she is! She's opening the show!'"

She steps on the ice, amongst the greatest players in the world, with dull skates and bright eyes.

"Henrik Lundqvist is in net," Kendall says. "I'm thinking, 'This is the coolest thing ever! I'm going to get to shoot on Henrik Lundqvist! Please don't hit him in the head—all of New York will hate you!' So I just whip one at his pads. I want so bad to pick up the puck and keep it as a souvenir."

She spends a few minutes in one of the All-Star dressing rooms after the warm-up, still starstruck.

Marc-André Fleury comes over and introduces himself.

"I'm like, 'I know who you are!'" Kendall says. "It's so great how many players come up to me. I run into Seth Jones and Cam Atkinson. Cam is one of my competitors, and Seth is giving him grief because he's so nervous. They treat me as an equal competitor. And that means a ton."

It's time. Kendall steps back on the ice and to the start line almost immediately. Chants of "USA! USA!" fill the building.

"The ref is behind me and he's counting me down—30 seconds . . . 20 seconds—but I can't hear anything because the crowd is just erupting," Kendall says. "My heart starts racing. My mouth gets super-dry."

But it's just a lap. A simple loop of the rink in a skills event that really means nothing. Or in this case, maybe it means everything.

"I'm really nervous," Burke says. "My biggest concerns are for Kendall and women's hockey. If it doesn't go well, no one will ever say, 'Kendall Coyne is a bad skater.' They'll say, 'Women can't skate.' It's the double standard that gets thrown on all women athletes. Miro Heiskanen skates right after Kendall and falls, wiping out into the boards. No one will ever say, 'Finnish players can't skate.' But if Kendall Coyne falls or puts up a bad time, it will be, 'Women don't belong here.'"

"If I fall, it takes the game back 10, 15 years," Kendall says. "It changes the narrative to 'I told you so—women don't belong. She can't even skate in a circle!' So I keep thinking, 'Just have a clean run. Just skate like you have since you were three years old.' I always tell kids, 'Believe in yourself.' So I'm like, 'Kendall, take your own advice. Believe in yourself. Just move your legs as fast as you can.'"

The ref blows his whistle.

Burke watches anxiously from the Western Conference bench.

"She takes her first few steps, and I hear this sound, almost an involuntary reaction from all the players, like, 'Oh! Oh! Oh shit!

She's really fast!' They all stand to watch. I've done this event enough to know the fastest skaters are the ones who keep skating around the turns. There's only a few guys who can execute the turns at that speed. And her legs never stop. That's when I know she's really moving."

Kendall hits the line. Her time is 14.346 seconds.

"When I first look up, I'm so disappointed that it's a bit slower than last night's," she says.

There's the competitor. The fire. But no one else in the building knows, or cares, about a tenth of a second. They've just watched a woman fly. To the naked eye, she's every bit as fast as the All-Stars who follow her.

She finishes seventh, beating Clayton Keller of the Arizona Coyotes. (She should place sixth, but Heiskanen got up and skated again, breaking the rules.) Ultimately, Kendall comes in less than a second behind the winner—the fastest and best player on the planet, Connor McDavid.

"It's the most clutch performance I've ever seen from an athlete," Burke says. "To be the first woman to do this? To have that amount of pressure on you? Knowing if you make one little mistake, catch one edge, you're out? And she knocks it out of the park."

Burke's phone blows up instantly. "Great idea!" "What a moment!" "That was amazing!"

Kendall high-fives the players on the bench as she skates by. During a break, she comes over and hugs Burke.

"Did I do okay?" she asks.

"You got a standing ovation from the fans and players," Burke responds. "You put up a great time. You showed everyone watching that women can skate with men. I'd say you did okay."

Kendall goes viral in roughly the same time it takes to skate her lap.

"All these girls see her and say, 'I can do that, too!'" Burke says.

"It changes the narrative of the way people view women in hockey," Kendall says. "I think it opens the eyes of people who have never seen girls or women play before. Now they see us as hockey players. We're not girls. We're not women. We're hockey players. We showcase the same skills. We score highlight-reel goals. We just don't have the platform that our male counterparts do."

One year later, in St. Louis, the NHL holds a three-on-three women's tournament between Team Canada and Team USA. It is the highlight of All-Star Weekend.

"That never happens without Kendall's skate," Burke says.

Kendall Coyne Schofield is 28 now, the captain of Team USA, winner of five world championships and an Olympic gold medal. She continues to lead the push for a new professional women's hockey league.

And she's eternally thankful for those 14 seconds.

"So many things had to happen to get me on that ice," Kendall says. "What if Nathan MacKinnon doesn't get hit with that puck? What if I'm two minutes later and don't get out there to be timed the day before? What if Patrick doesn't advocate so hard to get me in? But most of all, that moment never happens without all the players who have worked so hard to improve the skill and talent in women's hockey over the last 20 years," she says. "I am a firm believer that everything happens for a reason. I was just at the right place at the right time."

Kendall bought one souvenir that weekend in San Jose: a Nathan MacKinnon T-shirt. To honour fate.

———

Demie Anas, the little girl on the Ottawa River, is five now.

She watched the three-on-three women's tournament at the 2020 NHL All-Star Game. Got to see her Fastest-Skating Girl play.

"When Kendall came on, Demie said, 'I'm cheering for Kendall Coyne!'" Her mom laughs. "I said, 'You have to cheer for Canada.' And she goes, 'Okay, Mom, I'll cheer for Canada. But I want Kendall to win.' That moment from the year before, watching Kendall skate, really stuck with her."

When she first saw the video of Demie on Twitter, Kendall sent her an autographed hockey card and a handwritten note:

Demie, I saw the awesome video of you skating. You were moving very fast and you didn't fall down! Always remember, if you fall down, it is OK. Just get right back up. Keep working hard and I know you can beat my score one day!

Follow Your Dream!
—Kendall

Demie started playing hockey this fall.

Biznasty's Last Dance

The Wounds and Wars of
Paul Bissonnette's Final Pro Season

═══════

Paul "Biznasty" Bissonnette's hockey career could have ended multiple times, in multiple ways.

Like, say, when Biz almost gets his Phoenix Coyotes kicked out of a Winnipeg hotel. On a game day.

"We are staying at the Fairmont in Winnipeg, and I'm in a bit of a grumpy mood, probably because we'd just landed in Winnipeg in the dead of winter and it's freezing!" Biz says. "I get to my room, and on the nightstand there is this little bottle of Fiji water, and the tag on it says eight dollars. I'm thinking to myself, 'Eight fucking dollars for a tiny bottle of Fiji water?!' I'd just gotten on Instagram at the time and didn't have much of a following. So I take a picture, post it on my Instagram, and write, 'Fuck off, Fairmont.' And then I go to sleep.

"At the morning skate, Tip [Coyotes coach Dave Tippett] gives me the usual 'Biz, you aren't playing tonight. Keep the morale light in the room. Do your thing.' And I do *my* usual: 'Of course, Tip. No problem. Hopefully, we'll get a big *W* tonight!' And then I get on with my usual bag skate with the assistant coach, Jim Playfair. But halfway through, Tip comes back out and waves Playfair over to him for a little chat. When he's done, the mood has changed. Playfair is usually joking around, but now he's very serious. I get skated *really* hard. Then he taps me on the shin pads at the end and says, 'Tip wants to see you in his office.'

"Now my heart is starting to race. What have I done? I go through my usual checklist: Have I said anything stupid on the radio lately? Nope. Have I tweeted anything stupid? Nope. Have I gotten traded? Nope—no one wants me. But when I get to Tip's office, the Coyotes' travel person is also there, pacing back and forth anxiously. He points at his computer screen and says, 'What is this?' And it's my 'Fuck you, Fairmont' post.

"He says to me, 'They are threatening to kick us out of the hotel on game day because of your stunt!' I have to race back to the Fairmont and kiss ass to the manager, pleading for him to let us stay.

"So a guy who plays two minutes a week almost gets his team kicked out of the hotel, on a game day, in the *National Hockey League*! By the way, I should say, for the record, I love the Fairmont."

Biz learns fast.

Or, his career could have ended after he went on a date with a porn star (arranged by a Phoenix radio station) and she called the radio station the next morning to give them every—er . . . detail.

"It's the morning of a game day in the middle of a playoff race," Biz says. "It's the year we end up going to the conference final. Not great timing. So I get to the rink that morning, and everyone knows about it, and the coaches are, like, 'Heard your "friend" on the radio this morning.' I figure I'm in trouble. But, hey, somehow they keep me around!"

In fact, Biz finds a way to stick around for a dozen years in pro hockey, because of his fists and the fact that teammates and coaches love him.

In the end, it's not a tweet, an Instagram post or an attention-craving porn star who finishes him. It's an injury. Make that two. Or, more accurately, one injury in two places. (It'll make sense soon, I promise.) And it leads to one Biz-arre career finale.

Biz spends his last three pro seasons with the Los Angeles Kings' farm team in the American Hockey League. He wins a Calder Cup with the Manchester Monarchs in 2015, and scores his first career professional playoff goal ("Not a big deee-alll," as Biz likes to say) with the Ontario Reign in 2016. (The Kings had moved their AHL team from Manchester, New Hampshire, to Ontario, California, after that Calder Cup–winning season.)

The next fall, the Reign are playing an early-season game against the Charlotte Checkers, when Biz does what Biz has been doing for a dozen years.

"Me and this guy Kyle Hagel, their fighter, have a rift going the entire game," he says. "Sure as shit, we end up scrapping. As I go to throw a punch and cock back on my right leg, I feel something snap. So I go to the box, and when the period ends, I tell our trainer, Michael Muir, 'My knee feels weird. I think I might have tweaked it.' I finish the rest of the game, and then the doctor looks at it and he says, 'I think you may have torn your ACL.' I go, 'No fucking way I tore my ACL cocking back to throw a punch!' I go get the MRI the next day. Yup. I tore my ACL cocking back to throw a punch."

Biz was already pondering retirement at the end of the season. This clinches it. He's done.

Almost.

"My trainer says, 'Why don't you prehab it, try to play the rest of the season and have the surgery after?' He tells me a lot of soccer players have done that. As long as you build up the muscles around it, so they're firing at all times, you can still play. So, that's what I do."

Biz spends the next two months healing, and strengthening his leg, before returning to the Reign lineup. And on his first shift back, the knee pops again. Back to the gym for another month of careful prehab. His next return comes against the San Jose Barracuda, just a few weeks before the playoffs.

"There are about 200 people in the stands," Biz says. "First period, I get hit and I feel the pop again. But this time . . . on the other knee! There's a TV time out, and I skate by the bench and look at Muirsy and say, 'I think I just tore my other ACL.' And he goes, 'Get the fuck out of here.' But I know this one is torn, because it feels even worse. The crazy part is, I go out and finish the period! I'm Bambi out there. I can't stay up more than about five seconds. I'm just inflicting more and more damage on myself. After the period, Muirsy looks at it, moves it around, and goes, 'Dude, you're right. You tore this one, too.'"

Mike Stothers is the head coach of the Reign. He coached Biz back in junior with the Owen Sound Attack, and he is the guy who brought him back to Manchester after the NHL no longer wanted him.

"Mike gets wind of the injury and comes into the room, and we really have a moment," Biz says. "I break down. He starts crying. It's really tough. We both know this is the end."

Wait. This is where we need to define *end*. Yes, this will be Biz's final game of pro hockey. Of course it will—he has two torn ACLs! But Biz being Biz, his final game isn't over yet.

"I put my shin pads back on and go sit on the bench, just to soak it up," Biz says. "Then I say to Mike, 'Hey, you think you can play me a couple more shifts?'"

Shoeless Joe Jackson, meet Kneeless Paul Bissonnette. He's somehow back on the ice, with ligaments dangling like spaghettini in both legs.

"And my first shift, I fight Zack Stortini!" he says. "I hang in there pretty well, for Bambi. I end up playing four or five more shifts, which is more than I usually do. Legs just flopping everywhere, barely standing on my feet."

There's one last thing this story needs: the Hollywood ending. Where wounded Roy Hobbs, blood leaking through his jersey, goes yard and turns the stadium lights into fireworks.

Here it comes. Third period, Reign down 2–1, looking for a hero. Paul "Biznasty" Bissonnette, wobbling around on two torn

ACLs, fires a laser pass to a teammate, who is wide open for a back-door tap-in! And . . .

"Fuckin' goalie stones him, and we end up losing, 4–1."

Oh. Well, we tried.

"Hey, it's still a pretty cool story to go out on!" Biz laughs. "I got to win a Calder Cup. I got to play in the National League. One time, Nick Lidstrom said to me in warm-up, 'Hey, I love you on Twitter!' And I got to fight Zack Stortini with no ACLs. What more can a kid from Welland, Ontario, ask for?"

Apparently, lots more.

After he retires, Biz gets a job as a radio analyst with the Coyotes, joins a little show called *Spittin' Chiclets*, helps turn it into one of the most popular podcasts on the planet, and basically becomes the king of hockey media.

Not a big deee-alll.

The Accidental Taunter

Mike Johnson Celebrates Goals and Makes Enemies

Mike Johnson is a nice guy. It's hard not to like him. In his 12 years in the NHL, he accumulates a grand total of two fights (Luke Richardson, when MJ is with the Leafs, and Wade Redden, when he is with the Coyotes).

But somehow, MJ manages to antagonize two other opponents into wanting to kill him. Not just for one shift, or one game, for *years*. Both the result (as in every good '70s sitcom plot) of a misunderstanding.

MJ is the Accidental Taunter.

Accident One: The Bonus Celly

"My second year in the league with Toronto (1998–99), Pat Quinn sets a team policy of no individual bonuses," MJ says. "These are the days before all the strict rules of the salary cap. So, the bonus plan is pretty loosely operated and they are all cash bonuses. Our team is doing well that year, so every five-game segment, we have about eight or 10 different categories: goals against, power play, penalty kill . . . whatever. If you meet the team goal in that category, you get 500 bucks or a thousand bucks or whatever it is."

How was this legal?!?

"I'm hoping the statute of limitations on the taxes has expired, because every couple weeks, guys are getting multiple thousands of dollars in their lockers. Sadly, because I am still on my entry-level contract, I am one of two players on the team who doesn't get them. So, every two weeks, the guys are waving these envelopes full of cash in my face. We would all go to the bar, and everyone is throwing around their money. I'm like, 'Oh man, this hurts.'"

The only known cure for the painful medical condition known as bonus envy is to get your own bonus. MJ happens to have one bonus clause in his contract that says he will earn an extra $100,000 if he scores 20 goals that season.

"I am chipping away, taking long shifts at the end of games, trying to get an empty-netter . . . anything I can do to get closer to 20. Finally, I get to 19 with about 15 games left. I know I'm going to get 20. Having said that, I would finish with exactly 20. So, I guess it wasn't a lock," MJ chuckles.

"Anyway, we're playing Tampa and they are terrible. We're crushing them, 5–0. It's the second period and I get a drop pass and sneak a greasy wrister under the arm of their backup goalie, Corey Schwab. It's in the net and I have my 20th!

"Now it's 6–0 in the second period of a game between a second-place team and a last-place team. But I celebrate like I'm in the World Juniors and I just scored in overtime to win the gold medal! I'm pumping my fists and freaking out and jumping into the glass. I swear, if I was Tiger Williams, I would have rode my stick out to centre ice. All I can think about is, 'I got my freaking bonus!' I get back to the bench, and multiple teammates look at me like, 'Okay, kid, that's a little excessive.' But I explain the bonus to them and eventually they kind of understand."

But one of MJ's opponents that night doesn't understand. At all. Lightning captain Chris Gratton has no idea the baby-faced kid on the Leafs has just earned a hundred grand. In Gratton's mind, he's a cocky a-hole breaking an unwritten rule of the NHL:

don't embarrass the other team by over-celebrating a meaningless goal in the second period of a blowout.

"So, for the next year, Gratton chases me around the ice every time we play—slashing me, hacking me, cross-checking me, 'motherfucker'-ing me, and I don't really understand why. I keep saying, 'Grats, what are you doing?' And finally he says, 'Don't you ever embarrass our team by celebrating in a 6–0 game like that!' I say, 'But it was my bonus!' I don't think he cared."

The next year, Johnson gets traded. To Tampa. The hockey gods are clever pranksters.

"One of the first things I think about when I hear it's Tampa is Grats," MJ continues. "So the first time I go out for a meal with the team, I sit down with him to try to explain myself. I flesh out the whole story about the other players getting bonuses all season and apologize for looking like a jerk. Finally, he says, 'That kind of makes sense.' And we end up being really close friends.

"But I learn a valuable lesson: kids, don't *ever* over-celebrate goals that get you a bonus but are meaningless to everyone else in the game and embarrass the other team!"

Accident 2: The Unintentional Celly

Earlier in MJ's 20-goal bonus-celly season, the Maple Leafs are playing a game in Chicago. Much like the Lightning that year, the Blackhawks are awful. And the Leafs are destroying them. It's 9–3 late in the third, and the Hawks are angry. They start running around, taking dumb penalties. Bob Probert gets called for cross-checking. Doug Zmolek goes off for roughing. Toronto has a five-on-three with less than two minutes left.

"It's a blowout, so Pat Quinn is just rolling the lines and they put us out there: Derek King, Alyn McCauley and I," MJ remembers. "The puck gets turned over and hits the ref, and we have a four-on-one. I get a pass and shovel it towards the net. It bounces off a stick and in, and it's 10–3.

"Now, just as I'm scoring, Chicago defenceman Eric Weinrich

tries to lift my stick and misses, and his stick gets up near my face. So, as a reactionary, self-defence move, I lift my hands towards my face to protect myself. But I guess to some Blackhawks, it looks like I have put my stick in the air to celebrate. I swear this isn't like Tampa. I'm innocent on this one! I'm not even excited to score. Even *I* am smart enough to know you don't celebrate a 10–3 goal [if there are no bonuses involved]. I'm just protecting myself, but I guess it doesn't look that way. At least it doesn't to one guy."

For the next seven years, no matter what team he's on, Doug Gilmour is out to kill MJ.

"Every single game, he slashes and whacks me and looks like he wants to end me. And I just don't get it," MJ says. "I'm not a real physical player, not an agitator. Why does Doug Gilmour hate me? I would do charity events with him, see him at golf tournaments in the off-season. I just can't understand why he wants to kill me."

It isn't until Gilmour retires and MJ ends up living in his old house in Montreal that the two finally have a conversation. It goes something like this:

GILMOUR: *You know, you aren't such a bad guy.*

MJ is confused and isn't sure whether to be pleased or offended.

JOHNSON: *Why . . . is . . . that . . . news? Why wouldn't you have thought that before?*

GILMOUR: *Because when I was with Chicago, you scored a five-on-three goal in a blowout and celebrated it.*

JOHNSON: *In 1998?! Killer, it's 2007!*

GILMOUR: *Yeah, it was a fucking joke. Embarrassing.*

Killer had carried the grudge around in his mental hockey bag for almost a decade.

So, as he did with Gratton, MJ tries to explain what really happened with Weinrich and the self-defence move.

"He doesn't buy it as much as Grats did," MJ laughs. "He says, 'I don't think so, bud. Your arms were in the air.' And I keep saying, 'No, Doug, I'm innocent. If I could find the tape, you'd see it! I didn't even smile, I swear!'"

(MJ still hasn't shown Gilmour the tape. Killer moves on . . . eventually.)

"There you go," MJ says. "Two incidents where veteran players were angry at me for years for celebrating inappropriately. In Tampa, I was 100 percent guilty. But Chicago? I want to be exonerated!"

Note: If anyone has possession of, or can locate, conclusive video evidence that Mike Johnson's arms were raised by Eric Weinrich on a 10–3 goal in 1998, you can blow this case wide open and give an innocent man his freedom.

There will be no reward. MJ does not give away his bonuses.

Dino and O-Dog

Road Roomies
Kevin Dineen and Jeff O'Neill

In a Washington hotel hallway, two Hartford Whalers veterans are engaged in an intense conversation. Paul Ranheim and Nelson Emerson are trying to figure out how a trade the night before should affect who rooms with whom on the road. These are critical decisions on a hockey team.

It's December 29, 1995. Kevin Dineen, a Whalers legend, has just been reacquired from the Philadelphia Flyers.

Into this high-level meeting walks 19-year-old Whalers rookie Jeff O'Neill. He doesn't have a say. Ranheim and Emerson have decided they don't want to break up any of the regular road roomies.

"You're going with the new guy," they tell O'Neill.

Dineen has already joined the team in Washington and is in his hotel room when O'Neill walks in.

"He's reading a book and doesn't even say hi to me," O'Neill says. "He just rolls over and keeps reading. And I'm like, 'This is going to be a tough one.'"

Dineen laughs hard when he hears this 25 years later.

"Not sure I engage him in an actual conversation, but I'm pretty sure I at least acknowledge him," he says. "I'm not that ignorant. But there is definitely a feeling-out process in our relationship. I'm 32. I've been around a bit, and he is this young punk."

You know those buddy cop movies where two opposite personalities get stuck together, and tension, hijinks and endless comedy ensue? Well, that awkward hotel hello is scene 1 of an all-time classic NHL buddy flick: *Dino and O-Dog*.

Scene 2
[Still in a hotel room]

O-DOG: *He would piss me off so much. He has about 10 brothers [four, actually] in hockey, and he would always call them up to talk about different players in the league. And I would be lying in the hotel bed across from him, and he's talking to one of them, and it's obvious he's talking about me. He says, "Yeah, the kid's got a lot of talent but is really inconsistent and hasn't figured out how to work yet. Who knows, he'll probably be headed for the minors, and if he doesn't figure it out, he'll be done." He knows I know he's talking about me, but he does it every time! I would lie in my bed, shaking my head, saying, "This guy is such a dick."*

DINO *[laughing]: One hundred percent true. That's how I get the message across. Let's just say he needs a little tap early on. That's my way of giving it to him.*

Scene 3
[Dineen family home in Connecticut, 1996]

Despite the steady and less-than-subtle criticism, Dino has slowly warmed to his young roomie. And when his wife and young daughter move to Hartford, he invites O-Dog over for dinner.

O-DOG: *I walk into the house, and his wife says, "Hi, Jeff, I'm Annie. Kevin's not coming for dinner." I'm thinking, "What?!" She says, "He's out hunting with Kelly Chase." This can't be real! Who invites a guy over for dinner and doesn't show up? Turns out, he shot a deer and wounded it. And he's running around the woods in Hartford, trying to track it down. And I'm left to have this awkward dinner with Annie, who I've never met!*

DINO: *If it makes O feel any better, Annie gets mad at me for that one, too. I feel a little sheepish, but hey, it's my first deer! We have to go back and pick up the deer the next morning. And we have a game that night. I may be one of the only players in history to bring a deer to a game-day skate in the back of my truck. We won that night, too! And for what it's worth, Annie tells me after the dinner that she loves O-Dog, thinks he's a great kid. So the dinner's a success without me!*

Scene 4
[A Pittsburgh sports bar, 1996]

DINO: *We're in to play the Penguins, and we're both injured. We have a game the next night, and neither one of us is playing. So, I say, "Let's go watch hockey at this bar downtown." We're having a beer at a table by the window, and a cab pulls up. Who gets out? Jimmy Rutherford, the Whalers' GM, and the entire coaching staff. And O is like, "Oh my God. Oh my God. What are we going to do?" Because he still isn't legal drinking age. So he gets up and says, "Let's run!"*

O-DOG: *You know when you're a kid, and you wrap yourself in the drapes playing hide-and-seek? I actually try to wrap myself in the bar drapes. It's like we're a couple of nine-year-olds.*

DINO: *At first, I jump up with him, panicked. Then I'm like, "What are we doing? I'm a 32-year-old man! I'm not running out of a bar because we're having a beer. Sit down." It's one of those moments when you remember he's just a kid. We send Jimmy and the guys a beer, and never hear anything about it.*

Scene 5
[Super Bowl week, 1997]

O-DOG: *I get sent to the minors and I'm devastated. I've spent a year and a half with the big club. But we're playing like dogshit. So I get sent down. I only play one game, and then there is a two-day break. And during that break is the Super Bowl. So I call Kevin, who is the captain and, supposedly, my best friend. I say, "Kevin, this is kind of awkward, but which Super Bowl party do you think I should go to?" I'm obviously thinking he's going to say, "Buddy, don't even think twice about it. You have to come to the Whalers party. You are one of us!"*

And he goes, "Jeff, you gotta go to the Springfield Falcons party." I'm like, "What?! I don't even know any guys on that team!" And he just says, "It's for the best. That's your team now." My best friend, my roommate, and he's like, "See ya later."

DINO: *I figure, you've just been sent down. Parties are the single best way to bond with teammates. But there's another layer to this story. There's always another layer with O! He gets called right back up. He's down for one game and gets called right back up. We're taking the team bus to Boston, and he gets a stretch limo to take him to Boston to meet us! Down in the minors for a day, and he takes a stretch limo back to the NHL! So, I'm not sure how much it humbled him.*

Scene 6
[Philadelphia, Christmas 1997]

The education of O continues after he asks Dino to pay back an NHL superstar who has done a favour for him.

O-DOG: *We are playing in Philly, the game before the Christmas break. Eric Lindros is flying back to Toronto after the game on a private jet. Dino has a great relationship with Eric, so he asks if I can come along. It's really cool. Chris Gratton and Steven Rice are on the jet as well. I make it to my Christmas party in King City, north of Toronto, by 11:30 that night! I'm really grateful. The Big E is one of my idols, and it's an unbelievable gesture by him.*

So, the next time we're in Philadelphia, I want to pony up some cash for my share of the flight. That shit's not cheap. I give Dino a thousand dollars to give to Eric.

Later, I ask Dino, "Did you give the Big E the money?" He goes, "No, he wouldn't accept it." So I say, "Well, where's my thousand bucks?" He says, "I gave it to the Flyers' equipment guy. He's a great guy. His name's Rock." What?! I go, "Why did you give my money to someone I have never met in my life? I never played for Philadelphia. I have no idea who Rock is." And Dino goes, "He's just a great guy. He deserved it."

I'm like, "He could be the greatest person on Earth, but why does he just randomly get a thousand of my dollars?" For a week, I am so mad at him. It's my second year in the league. A thousand bucks is still a lot of money to me.

DINO: *I just figure that money would be better spent with Rock.*

O-DOG: *How is that mentoring me? How would that help me in my life? You just wasted my money!*

DINO: *O doesn't take care of his cash, anyway. One day he leaves the hotel room before me and leaves his ATM card on the table. So, I take it and I go to an ATM for kicks. If you are going to go to an ATM with O's card, what number are you going to punch in? 9292. His jersey number! That's the first thing I try. Bingo! It works. I could have taken the max and he would have never noticed. But I just take 20 bucks, give him back his card and say, "Kid, you have to change your code."*

Scene 7
[Airport, Raleigh, North Carolina, 1998]

O-DOG: *One of the first things I buy when I get established in the league is a Porsche 911 convertible. And in Carolina after the Whalers move there, we are allowed to pull our cars right inside the fence, beside the runway. The gate would open and we'd pull up right next to the hangar and just walk right onto the bird.*

So, one day there's a delay. Our plane hasn't shown up yet. I always just leave my keys in my car. Dino disappears, and suddenly he's in my car, burning rubber, driving 100 miles an hour up and down the runway! Coach Paul Maurice is there. Jimmy Rutherford is there. And we're all watching this guy, flying up and down the runway in my 911. Ever since that day, no Carolina Hurricanes player or personnel is allowed to park inside of the fence. All because of Dino!

DINO: *We used to drive together all the time, and it's an absolutely gorgeous car, but it's a mess. He's got candy bar wrappers and cans of chew and spit bottles. It's like a garbage truck—just shit all over it. He doesn't take care of it. So, I just decide it deserves to go for a spin with someone who* *appreciates it. Got it up to 120 miles an hour, I think! But yeah, the Carolina players, past and present, are still mad at me for that one.*

Scene 8
[Present day—the part at the end of every buddy movie when they get mushy]

O-DOG: *He became my best friend. And he showed me how to be a pro. Once, he slapped me in the head because I got out of an elevator before these ladies did. He taught me manners. Like how he always tipped everyone. It drove me crazy at first. If he asked the concierge where a good restaurant was, he'd give him five bucks. Every single time he left the hotel room, he'd always grab all his change and leave it on the pillow for the maid. And now I do exactly the same thing. I really could not have had a better guy for my first four years in the NHL. He's still one of my best friends.*

DINO: *O has this tough exterior to break through. But once you break through it, he has one of the biggest hearts you have ever seen. And he made me laugh—hard—pretty much every day we were teammates.*

Scene 9
[Dino's cottage, summer 2019]

O-DOG: *I bring my girls up to Dino's cottage. And as we're leaving, I look above the fireplace and there's this mounted deer head. I say, "Wait, is that the deer?"*

DINO: *Yup, that's him! My first deer. What a great night that was!*

O-DOG: *You're such an idiot.*

[Roll credits.]

Really hoping Lindros agrees to do the cameo.

"What Is That?"

Bobby Orr Meets Connor McDavid

On Good Friday in 1961, a carload of Boston Bruins scouts drives up to Gananoque, Ontario, to see two young prospects who play for the local team: Doug Higgins and Rick Eaton. Gananoque happens to be playing a team from Parry Sound, featuring an unknown 13-year-old kid with a blond brush cut. His name is Bobby Orr.

"We split up in the rink and decided we would meet up at one end when the game was over," the late Milt Schmidt would tell the *Boston Globe* decades later. "Well, to make a long story short, we all came out of that game with the same knowledge: forget Eaton and Higgins, we'll take that Orr kid!"

The Bruins are so smitten that one of the scouts, Wren Blair, stays in Parry Sound for long stretches, just to be close to Bobby and his family, until the Bruins get his name on a contract. They eventually do. You know the rest.

A half century later, in the summer of 2010, the greatest defenceman in hockey history—now an agent—walks into a rink in Aurora, Ontario, to watch a group of prospects skate. Most are 15 or older. But as Orr sits down in the stands, the smallest player on the ice instantly catches his eye.

"I show up a little late, and the kids are out there, doing all sorts of puck-handling drills," Orr says. "I'm watching them and see this little wee guy, and he is the best one on the ice! Just doing ridiculous things with the puck. And I say, 'What is *that*?'"

That is Connor McDavid.

=====

Before you hear the rest of When Bobby Met Connor, you should know how Bobby met Joe. Because the two tales will weave together two decades later.

In 1989, Joe Quinn is a 27-year-old former junior hockey player, now playing beer-league hockey in the Ottawa Valley. One night his good pal Jimmy Conboy gets cross-checked from behind into the boards. He is left a quadriplegic.

Joe and Jimmy both idolize Bobby Orr. When Joe hears Bobby is coming to the nearby town of Smiths Falls for a golf tournament, he drives Jimmy down to meet him.

"Bobby sees Jimmy in the wheelchair and comes right over to take a photo with us, and asks if he can sign an autograph for Jimmy," Quinn says. "We are just in awe. Then he invites me and Jimmy to go and have dinner with him at the main table! I say, 'We can't do that, Bobby. We don't want to invade your privacy. We're just so happy to meet you.' And Bobby says, 'Well, give me a business card.' He ends up sending Jimmy and I a picture in the mail. It was just incredible that he was so kind to us."

Fifteen years later, Joe gets a job as head instructor at the brand-new PEAC Sports Academy in Toronto. Among the first boys he trains are Doug Gilmour's kids, Jake and Tyson; Malcolm and Jordan Subban; future Stanley Cup–winning goalie Jordan Binnington; Islanders first-rounder Josh Ho-Sang; and the youngest player at the academy, a scrawny kid from Newmarket named Connor McDavid.

"Connor doesn't stand out at first, because he is mostly competing against kids much older than him," Quinn says. McDavid's a '97, and the rest are born between 1992 and 1994. "But I learn quickly that he wants to master the game. Most of the other guys get tired of the drills and want to have some fun. But Connor has to keep going until he has it mastered. And after we're done on the ice, he goes home and does everything over and over again in his garage on Rollerblades. His dedication and attention to detail are extremely rare for that age."

"I just love doing those drills. I still do them today," McDavid says. "They translate so well to games."

By his second year in the academy, McDavid is holding his own in scrimmages against legitimate prospects three and four years older than him.

The academy team goes to a tournament at Gonzaga High School near Toronto in 2009. Many of the top Ontario Hockey League draft prospects are there.

"Connor is wide-eyed seeing some of these players who are 6-foot, 200 pounds, and he is just 12 years old," Quinn says.

"I am just so much smaller than everyone," McDavid says. "These guys are about to get drafted in the OHL, some of them first-rounders. I am definitely intimidated."

"I tell him, 'Don't worry. They can't hit you when you are moving pucks to space,'" Quinn says. "And sure enough, Connor leads the tournament in scoring and we win it, beating St. Michael's College, a team with a half dozen OHL first-rounders, 7–4 in the final. I think Connor gets five or six points in that game. He just keeps cycling in and out of the corners, just like he does now, and he has so much speed, no one can touch him."

Doug Gilmour eventually convinces Joe to start his own hockey training company, which he calls Power Edge Pro (PEP). And Bobby Orr's agency hires PEP to work with its prospects.

When Orr walks into that arena that day in 2010, Joe is running the prospects through his specialized drills and a scrimmage. The ice is jammed with top junior talent. But Orr can't take his eyes off the little guy.

"I'm watching him skate circles around everyone, and I'm saying, 'Holy mackerel, who is he?'" Orr says. "Here Connor is, years younger than all these other guys, and he's just amazing! His hands are incredible, his skating, his edges—I have never seen anything like it."

McDavid gets to meet Orr after the skate.

"He puts this little headlock on me," McDavid says. "I remember thinking I can't believe how strong he is."

The day Bobby meets Connor is also the first time Joe Quinn has seen Bobby since that night at the golf tournament almost two decades earlier.

"Bobby comes down to the boards and says to me, 'Jeepers, this training is hard. I don't think I could have done it in my time,'" Quinn says. "And I'm thinking to myself, 'Are you kidding me? You're Bobby freakin' Orr!' It's crazy, isn't it? I meet my idol at that golf tournament, and he is everything you want your idol to be. And then, all these years later, I help introduce him to Connor McDavid."

Joe eventually shows Bobby the photo they took together that night in Smiths Falls with his friend Jimmy.

"Bobby looks at it and says, 'You used to look like Robert Redford . . . What happened?'" Joe laughs. "He has this great, dark sense of humour."

Joe's company still works closely with Wasserman/Orr Hockey. And Joe still idolizes Number 4.

When it comes time for the McDavids to pick an agency to represent Connor, they invite Bobby over to their home in Newmarket.

"My mom is cleaning the house like crazy, but only the parts Bobby is going to see," McDavid laughs. "So, pretty much the front door to the dining room. Everything else just gets tucked away. You know moms. When you have hockey royalty over, we have to look like we're a nice, tidy family!"

When the visit is over, 14-year-old Connor tells his family Bobby is his guy. The rest of the McDavids feel the same way. They sign.

Today Orr watches Connor dominate the NHL. He is just as amazed as that first day he saw him.

Meanwhile, opposing defenders and goalies get to paraphrase Orr on a nightly basis, as McDavid blows by them. Maybe they don't say it out loud the way Orr did, but you can see it in their eyes.

"What was *that*?!"

Milbury's Solo Bag Skate

Dave Poulin and the Bruins Get a Lesson in Unconventional Coaching

The phone rings in Dave Poulin's Pittsburgh hotel room. His long-time roommate on the road, Rick Tocchet, answers. Tocchet makes a strange face and looks straight at Poulie. He hands the Philadelphia Flyers captain the phone.

"It's Clarkie," Tocchet says.

Poulie and Bob Clarke have been best friends for years, as teammates and training partners during Clarkie's final year in the league, and as golf partners ever since he moved into the Flyers front office.

"Back when we were teammates, Clarkie gave me a piece of advice," Poulie says. "He told me, 'If you ever get traded, and the first thing you ask is who you were traded for, then you don't really care that you've been traded. All you care about is what your value is.'"

And now Clarkie is the Flyers GM, on the other end of the phone, telling Poulie he's been traded to the Boston Bruins.

"He says to me, 'You've done some great things for our team, but we're going to make some changes. I've just traded you to Boston. You need to call Harry Sinden. Here's his number.' And I say, 'Nah, I don't need it. I'm good, thanks.' And I hang up without asking who I've been traded for. I fly back to Philly, and there is media waiting at the airport. They turn on their lights and cameras and say, 'Dave, what do you think of the trade?' And I say, 'What's the trade?' They all go, 'Clarkie didn't tell you?' And I say, 'Didn't ask.' I think that bothered Clarkie more than anything. That I turned his own advice on him."

Despite his indifferent exterior, Poulie is shattered. He has loved being the captain of the Flyers. And it cuts deep that his best friend decided he was the one who needed to go. He briefly ponders not reporting to Boston. His wife is in the midst of a high-risk pregnancy. They already have two other young daughters, and he's in the final year of his contract. But the Bruins are in first place, and they really want him. So he packs his bags and heads to Boston, to play for Mike Milbury.

Just a few weeks into Poulie's tenure as a Bruin, the team hits a mini-slump. They lose back-to-back games at home, then drop the first of a six-game road trip in Winnipeg. Milbury doesn't say a single word after the Jets game. The team flies to Vancouver, where the players are looking forward to a couple of scheduled days off before getting back on the ice.

"We land and Mike says, 'We're going right to the rink,'" Poulie says. "We're all like, 'You gotta be kidding me!' We're not supposed to skate for two days! We know we are about to get bag-skated. So we step out on the ice and he lines us up along the boards. Here we go. Then, one of the strangest things I've ever seen in hockey happens. Milbury says, 'I have the ice booked for three hours each of the next two days. I could crush you. But I don't think physical conditioning is your problem. There are some other things that are really bugging me, though. So, today I'm going to go one by one and tell you what's bothering me. And I'm going to skate for you.' We're all thinking, 'What the heck is going on?'"

He starts with Lyndon Byers, one of the toughest young players in the NHL. Milbury stands directly in front of him.

"Mike says, 'I absolutely love what you've brought to this team. You have a chance to be one of the best tough guys in the

NHL because you can actually play a little bit. But you've got to figure out when to fight, when not to fight. When it hurts the team, when it doesn't. And by the way, you are in the bars way too much. So, I'm going to go over and back twice for you.' And he skates as hard as he can, back and forth, across the ice! Mike is a former pro athlete, but he's already breathing hard. And he keeps going, right down the line, skating back and forth for every guy!

"Now he gets to me. He says, 'Three weeks ago, we traded for the captain of the Philadelphia Flyers. We were in Hartford, and I've never seen our locker room that excited. And some nights, you have been our best player, but some nights, your head is back in Philly. You're not a Flyer anymore! You do not wear orange and black! You wear *gold* and black! When you decide there's a Bruins logo on your jersey, we may have a chance to win the Stanley Cup. And for that, I'm going to skate for you.' And back and forth he goes!"

By this time, Milbury is halfway through the team, dripping sweat. The players are starting to get concerned about his heart. Then he gets to Craig Janney.

"Now, CJ is a really good player and we all love him, but he isn't in great shape. And Mike looks at him and says, 'You are the worst-conditioned pro athlete that I've ever seen in my life. You could be a great player, but you are 23 years old and in terrible shape. So, for you, I will skate nowhere.' And he goes right to the next guy! We feel awful for CJ because we love him, but we can barely contain our laughter."

On and on it goes, player by player. Finally, Milbury gets to Ray Bourque.

"We're all wondering what's he going to say for Ray. And he goes, 'I played with Number 4. He was the greatest defenceman in the history of the game.' And then he holds up his hand and wiggles his fingers and says, 'You are . . . what? Second? Third? Fourth all-time? You are definitely on the hand! One of the greatest ever. But you've still gotta throw that saucer pass up the middle of the ice, don't you? Ray-Ray Giveaway!'

"By this point, we're choking, just dying laughing. But we have to stifle it because Ray is so mad. I'm looking at him, and you can see his temperature going up and up. And then Milbury says, 'Now, I'm going to skate for you, Ray.' And off he goes. When it's over, he is bent over at the waist and can barely speak. He just says, 'If I see any of you in the next two days, I'll probably kill you. So get out of here.'"

And that's it. For an hour, the coach of the Boston Bruins bag-skates himself.

Three nights later, his Bruins beat the Canucks, 7–2. Ray Bourque has a goal and five assists.

"At one point, Ray looks at me after a goal and says, 'Ray-Ray Giveaway, my ass.'"

The Bruins go on to win the next three, and they bring home the President's Trophy for finishing first overall. Poulie has two theories on Milbury's motivation for the solo bag skate.

"He just knew how to get to us mentally," Poulie says. "Skating us back and forth wouldn't have made us any better. But this made us think about our faults. And he was right. My head was in Philly some nights. So it worked. It was genius, really."

And the other theory?

"I think he just needed a workout. And decided this would be more fun than the bike in the hotel gym!"

Cole's Goal

An Injury-Plagued Minor Leaguer Finally Gets His Moment

The 26-year-old NHL rookie stands alone at centre ice, 11 thousand fans buzzing in anticipation of what is about to happen. He takes a second to soak it in.

This is a goddamn moment right here! Cole Bardreau thinks to himself.

It would be for anyone in this position. But especially Cole. For a decade, he's been broken. Pieces of him, anyway. But at this moment, he's whole.

It's his shoulder first. He's 16, playing high school hockey for the Fairport Red Raiders in Upstate New York, when he tries to reverse hit an opponent and tears his labrum. The timing is awful. Cole is about to take part in USA Hockey's Final 40 camp, where they decide who will make it to the prestigious USA National Team Development Program.

"My shoulder is really bugging me at that camp, and I don't feel like I play very well," Cole says. "I don't belong with all these guys who are projected to be high draft picks: John Gibson, J.T. Miller, Rocco Grimaldi. I get called into the office at the end, and my dad and I are thinking I must be in trouble. There's no way in hell I can actually make it. And then they put a contract in front of me. Dad laughs and says, 'Sign that as fast as you can, and let's get out of here!'"

Cole has shoulder surgery after the camp, so he can be ready to head to Ann Arbor, Michigan, to join the program in the fall. He's still rehabbing when he tries to jump off a buddy's deck into a pool.

"Just being dumb kids, and the deck breaks, and I miss the pool and break my ankle," Cole says.

Surgery number two: screws inserted into his left ankle. When he gets to Ann Arbor, he has only been back on skates once.

"Our first practice is just a disaster," he says. "My ankle isn't right, and I'm a mess. We do this simple drill with half of us on each blue line, and you get 30 seconds in the middle to do whatever stickhandling moves you want. Everybody's watching. And I can't stickhandle. The puck is just flying off my stick. I feel so self-conscious. I just lose all my confidence."

It would take him the better part of two years to get it back. Along the way, he would change from skilled scorer to hard-nosed grinder.

That's the role he plays in the 2013 World Junior Championship in Ufa, Russia. He earns key minutes on the Grind Line with Blake Pietila and Ryan Hartman. The Americans win gold. Cole's confidence soars. It's his last year of NHL draft eligibility, and scouts are finally taking notice.

"That's the pinnacle of my career, coming out of World Juniors," he says. "I get back to Cornell, where I'm in my sophomore season, and I get three points in the first game back. I hadn't had three points in a game since minor hockey!"

In the second game, the hit comes from behind, always hockey's worst place. Cole's head hits the boards, then the ice. His first thought brings instant panic. He can't feel his fingers. The crowd falls silent. Cornell's trainer leaps off the bench and races across the ice.

By the time the trainer gets to Cole, he's on all fours. The sensation has returned to his fingers. The panic fades. He starts to think he's just injured his chest, maybe cracked a rib. And, well, he's a hockey player, so he begs back into the game. But that night, he doesn't feel quite right. The next morning, he goes straight to the campus medical centre for a precautionary X-ray.

"That's when the panic starts again," he says. "The images don't look good. I walk in with my book bag like a normal school day, and end on a spinal board in the back of an ambulance."

Cole has broken his C7 vertebra in two places. He's lucky not to be paralyzed. The first doctor who sees him says he'll need surgery and may never play hockey again.

"I'm 19 years old, and hockey is all I know," he says. "I break down in tears, my mom comes in, and she's crying."

"I walk into the room, and he doesn't see me," says Cole's mom, Debbie. "I have to walk back out. I lose all composure seeing him like that on the backboard, and I know if he sees my face at that moment, it will impact him greatly. So I try to compose myself before going back in. But it's awful to see your son like that. It changes your entire perspective on life."

The Bardreaus seek second, third and fourth opinions. One doctor, from Cole's hometown of Rochester, New York, takes the fracture images to a conference in Florida. Doctors there decide the injury is nearly identical to one suffered by former Carolina Panthers receiver Steve Smith. They put Cole on the same rehab program Smith followed. No surgery. He will wear a stiff neck brace for four months, 24/7.

"At the end of those four months, [the doctor] tells me I have no more risk of recurrence than the guy sitting next to me in the locker room," Cole says. "I'm determined to play hockey again."

There is much work to be done first. When he takes off the neck brace, it startles him.

"My neck is as skinny as my arm," he says. "It's a long road back."

The NHL Draft passes quietly, devastatingly. No one is taking a flyer on a kid in his last year of eligibility who just broke his neck. Cole stays on campus all summer, working out, regaining his strength. By fall, he's ready. Three minutes into Cornell's first exhibition game, he scores short-handed. He finishes with four points. He's back.

And then, in the second game of the regular season, Cole is killing a penalty late in the game when he collides with his teammate coming out of the box.

"I land on the bottom and immediately feel something go," he says. He's torn the medial collateral ligament in his knee. "That's a tough pill to swallow. But I just put my head down and rehab . . . again."

Enough, right? Enough pain for an entire career? Maybe a lifetime? But Cole's not done. Not even close.

A week after he returns to the lineup, he tears the MCL in his other knee. And at the start of the following season, his senior year, he breaks his foot again. It's borderline comical—unless you're Cole, and hockey is all that matters, and it just keeps breaking your heart, along with numerous other parts.

Finally, his luck turns, if only briefly. After the foot heals, Cole plays the rest of his final season at Cornell injury free. He turns more heads. The Philadelphia Flyers offer him a contract.

He starts the next season with their American Hockey League farm team in Allentown, Pennsylvania, the Lehigh Valley Phantoms. Cole's a pro now, eager to put his bad-luck past behind him. And then, in the third game of the season, an opponent's skate slices his wrist, severing a tendon.

"I lose feeling in my hand right away," he says. "I take my

glove off and blood is spewing everywhere. I think I'm going to lose my hand."

An ambulance rushes Cole to hospital, and doctors are able to prevent any permanent damage.

This is the point where you start to wonder if maybe this isn't meant to be. Maybe Cole should be proud of his gold medal, of coming back to earn that pro contract, and just . . . find some other dream. I wonder it aloud to him.

"Never," he responds without hesitation.

Another rehab, another comeback. He goes on a heater in his return and wins AHL Rookie of the Month.

"There's some chatter from scouts that finally I'm a legitimate prospect to make the Flyers," he says.

He trains harder than he ever has. Maybe too hard. In the middle of summer, he feels something pop in his groin. He requires double sports hernia surgery.

"This one stings," he says. "I remember Flyers assistant coach Riley Cote telling me he really thought I had a good shot of making it."

This is the first time Cole really struggles to bounce back. The entire season is basically a writeoff. The doubts finally creep in. He goes to see Dr. Jarrod Spencer, a sports psychologist in the Lehigh Valley who has worked with a number of hockey players.

"I never believed in it," Cole says. "But once I get past my ego and go see him, he really saves my career. I'm able to release all my emotions and frustrations about everything that has happened."

In 2017, now in his third year with the Phantoms, he gets into a fight with Toronto Marlies forward Dmytro Timashov and breaks his hand. There is also a small cut in his knuckle. No big deal, until it gets infected. And then it's a very big deal.

"I would take my broken neck over this injury any day," Cole says. "I have six surgeries, two more infections and two PICC lines in my arm giving me drip-line antibiotics eight hours a day for six weeks. Twice. Any time I would get touched, let alone slashed, there's a shooting pain through my arm. I just can't play hockey."

Doctors end up fusing two joints together. Cole can no longer move his right index finger. He has 12 screws and two plates inserted.

"My hand is just mangled now," he says. "It's the first time I start to feel a little cursed. All the other injuries healed. But this never goes away. It affects my stickhandling, and I'm worried about getting in any sort of scrum or fight, which is part of the game when you're a grinder."

Through all the pain, Cole's parents never ask him to quit hockey. They know their boy too well.

"I'm more worried about what his life is going to be like in 20 years with all the injuries," Debbie says. "I wonder why, after all he has been through, he continues to play like he's 6-foot-5, 250 pounds (Cole is 5-foot-10, 185). It baffles me. It's just not in him to be cautious."

It's now the summer of 2019. Cole is a free agent. He's about to turn 26. No longer a prospect, just another veteran trying to find a job. When he hasn't been hurt, he has shown potential at every level. The New York Islanders see that. They show the most interest, so he signs.

That fall, he's sent to the Islanders' AHL team in Bridgeport, Connecticut.

"I've come to terms with the fact the NHL may never happen for me," Cole says. "I'm just happy to be healthy and playing hockey."

On October 19, 2019, Cole takes the game-day skate in Bridgeport, then drives to the train station to pick up his girlfriend, Elle. At the exact moment Elle walks off the train, Cole's phone rings. It's Bridgeport's coach, Brent Thompson.

"We have to get you to Columbus," he says. "You've been called up. You're playing in the NHL tonight."

The break of a lifetime for Cole. Not so much for Elle. He

drops her off at another train station so she can head back home. (Elle understands. It's kind of a big day.)

Cole races to Kennedy Airport. Coach Thompson warns him that if he doesn't make it in time, he'll be sent right back down. He doesn't even have time to get a suit. He'll travel to his NHL debut in a sweatshirt and joggers. He's suddenly living *The Amazing Race.*

He gets there too late. The flight has left. Cole is crushed for a moment, but, luckily, finds another plane that will get him to Columbus in time.

"The flight is mostly empty. I have a row to myself," he says. "And it's in those two hours it hits me. I break down. I smile. I laugh. All my emotions come pouring out. It just sinks in that after everything I've been through, I'm finally there."

Cole feels sheepish walking into his first NHL dressing room in sweats, but it beats never walking in. The Islanders players greet him warmly. He sees his jersey hanging in his stall and beams.

They make him take the mandatory rookie lap during the warm-up, where the rest of the team holds back while he skates alone. "I'm sweating bullets for that because I know it's coming," he says. "I don't even take a shot because I'm worried I'll completely miss and embarrass myself."

It doesn't take long for Cole to get his "Welcome to the NHL" moment.

"My first shift, we are pinned in our own zone for about a minute," he laughs. "I'm just chasing the puck all over the place, thinking, 'This is going to be a long night.'"

But Cole settles in, even gets a few chances. He plays 15 shifts, 8:54 of ice time, and the Islanders win, 3–2, in OT. On the flight home, he finally checks his phone. There are endless messages from family, friends, old teammates. They know what this night means.

"It's funny. All I ever wanted was to play one game, one shift in the NHL," he says. "I went around the dressing room after, thanking the guys, saying, 'Okay, you can send me down now. I can die a happy man.'"

The Islanders don't send Cole down. They have injuries, and he's shown enough to stay a little longer. He gets his first point, an assist, against the Flyers. The Isles win the first six games he plays.

His seventh game is November 5, 2019, against the visiting Ottawa Senators. Near the end of the second period, Cole intercepts a pass in the neutral zone.

"It's the end of a shift and I probably should go off," he says. "But I think I have a chance to steal it, and sure enough, it gets thrown right to me and I have a breakaway."

He gets pulled down from behind, and the referee signals for a penalty shot.

"Right away, my nerves are shot. It's a 1–1 game, so it's important. I go to the bench to take a sip of water, and all the guys are rattling off what I should do. Our assistant coach says, 'Shoot low blocker.' I'm already freaking out and don't want to overcomplicate things, so that sounds like a good idea. And then I'm standing at centre ice, and the crowd is roaring, and everything that I went through to get here hits me . . ."

This is a goddamn moment right here!

You can't do dramatic flashback montages in books. If you could, we'd see the torn shoulder, the broken foot, the broken neck, the tears (in his knee), the tears (in his eyes), the severed tendon, the sports hernias, the foot (again), the mangled hand.

Cole and his countless scars, visible and not, slowly start to move up the ice. He starts left, cuts back in as he crosses the blue line and shoots.

"And I miss my shot," he says. "Craig Anderson is giving me that blocker side—a trick to make me shoot there, because he slides back over just as I'm shooting. But he kind of overplays it, and because I miss my spot, it hits the inside of his pad."

At first, Cole loses sight of the puck. But as he skates by the net, he watches it slide through Anderson. And trickle in.

Cole lets out a primal scream and almost doubles over.

He's mobbed by the entire Islanders team when he gets back to the bench.

"They don't care who I am, that I've only been there now for a few games," Cole says. "I am part of their team. It's really special how genuinely happy they are for me."

When he sits back down on the bench, he is shaking. Cole is just the seventh player ever to score his first NHL goal on a penalty shot. His Islanders win, 4–1.

He calls his parents, separately, after the game. Scott and Debbie split when Cole was nine. Scott picks up the phone and just keeps saying, "Holy shit!" over and over. Succinct and eloquent, considering what his son has gone through to get here.

Debbie watched the penalty shot with her hands over her eyes, peeking at the last minute.

"I think I had missed every breakaway and shootout I've ever taken, so I don't blame her," Cole laughs.

"A moment like that is such a gift to a mom," Debbie says.

Cole would play two more games with the Islanders before being sent back to Bridgeport.

"It still stings being sent back, because I realized up there that I can play at that level," Cole says. "But even if I never make it back, I'll always have that night, that goal. It made everything worth it."

The Great Stamkos Car Heist

Chris and Steven Stamkos, Steve Yzerman and the Two Jags

Long before Steven Stamkos becomes one of the best goal scorers of his generation, one coach tries to turn him into a checker. Actually, he's just a fill-in coach. The real guy couldn't make it that day. So this glorified temp decides the most talented kid on the team needs to play the shutdown role.

"You go out and shadow that guy, and don't let him get away from you!" the coach tells Stamkos. And the kid listens. He shadows the other team's superstar all over the ice. But after two periods, Stamkos is fed up and gives the coach an earful.

"Why am I the only guy chasing him around?" he complains. "I want to play hockey! C'mon, Dad!"

Yes, the coach is Steven's father, Chris. Steven is five years old. The player he's been shadowing all game is P.K. Subban.

"P.K. is a year older and is way bigger than everyone, and he's just dominant," Chris remembers. "They beat us, 6–2, in the round-robin, and P.K. scores a hat trick and is in on almost every goal. And Steven can skate like the wind, so I figure having him shadow P.K. is our only shot in the quarter-finals. We still lose, 3–2, but he does a great job. I just think it's hilarious that he's smart enough at five to figure out he's the only guy out there chasing P.K."

Little Steven forgives Dad for that one. It's what happens 20 years later that Chris may never live down.

Tampa, January 2013

STEVEN: *So, one of my perks of playing in Tampa is that there is one car dealership here that hooks a few guys up with cars. I get a nice dark blue Jaguar. Usually, when my parents are in town, I let them use that car and drive it to the games.*

This seems like a much better idea than a Ford Fiesta rental from Enterprise.

CHRIS: *We're down visiting for a few days, and we drive the car to the game and park it in the lot they have for the families, players and executives. It's a great night. The Lightning win and Steven plays really well. We visit with him for a few minutes after, and then leave the rink to head back to his house. We have another couple with us, and I take a quick trip to the bathroom and tell them to meet me at the car. Everybody leaves their keys in the car in that parking lot, so we get in, and off we go. It's about a 15- or 20-minute ride to the gated community where Steven lives. I reach up to press the security clicker on the visor to open the gate, and it isn't there. So, I'm a little confused. But I figure he must have just taken it out and put it in his car. No big deal. Security knows us and lets us in. I pull into the garage behind Steven's house, and then I look down at the console and see some sunglasses that aren't mine. Then I see some documents and papers that aren't mine. And it hits me: This isn't Steven's car! Oh my God!*

Looks like the long-awaited sequel to *Gone in 60 Seconds* is finally here. Large popcorn, please!

STEVEN: *After the game, I'm usually one of the last ones out of the room. So, it's about an hour after and I go check my phone and I see that I have a bunch of missed calls from Liz Silvia, who is Steve Yzerman's right-hand woman. I'm thinking, "That's weird. Why would I have a call from her at this time of night?" So I call Liz, and she says, "Steven, I think your dad took Steve Yzerman's car."*

CHRIS: *What have I done?! I realize it almost right away, because I know that Yzerman has pretty much the identical car to Steven. So, I'm sitting there in the garage saying, "I just stole the GM's car!"*

I mean . . . it could have been worse. It could have been . . . no, actually, the GM is the single worst person it could have been.

STEVEN: *I'm panicked and haven't put two and two together yet, so I call my dad and say, "What the hell are you doing? Liz said you took Steve's car?"*

CHRIS: *By the time Steven calls me, I've already called Kevin, the security guy at the arena, and confessed my crime. Kevin calls Liz, Liz calls Steven, Steven calls me to ask me, "What the hell did you do?" I say, "Don't worry, son, I'll drive it right back!"*

STEVEN *[chuckling]: Well, it was a nice run in Tampa. But I guess I'm getting traded.*

Hockey has a long history of parents wanting to get their kids traded. But this is a novel approach.

CHRIS: *I head back to the arena with my friend Mario and I say, "Mario, if we get stopped by the cops, we're toast! I have no ID on me. I've left it in the other car. I'm driving a Jaguar that belongs to the GM of the hockey team, who also happens to be a Hall of Famer! We're going to jail if we get stopped!"*

This could have taken a whole *Thelma and Louise* turn here. I'm a little disappointed it didn't.

CHRIS: *Luckily, we make it. And it turns out Yzerman has taken Steven's car home when he realizes I've taken his. So, he comes back and we swap cars, and he is really good about it. I say, "Steve, I'm so sorry." He says, "No problem." And then I can't help myself. I say, "Steve, I have to tell you. I used your directory and made a few trades." He laughs, thankfully.*

STEVEN: *The whole thing is hilarious now. Dad's been my biggest supporter my whole life, so I'm not mad at him. I mean, it's an honest mistake. It was at night, and the cars are pretty much identical. And I think it's actually a proud moment for Dad. He gets to tell the story to all his buddies.*

He still does. It's one of his buddies who tells me about it.

CHRIS: *That was the lockout-shortened year. The Lightning were rolling until that night, and then didn't end up making the playoffs. I run into Yzerman again late in the season, and he says, "You should have made those deals."*

The Night Wick Went Blind

Hayley Wickenheiser
Makes a Painful Mistake

To the countless young hockey players who idolize her, Hayley Wickenheiser is puck perfection. On Canada's national team by age 15, she has four Olympic gold medals and seven World Championship gold medals. She is the first woman to score a goal in a men's professional league (Finland, 2003), and a first-year-eligible Hall of Famer. Oh, and she played softball in the Olympics, too. Legend.

She's so legendary, in fact, that it rattles rookies to share the ice with her on the national team.

"The first time I suit up for Canada and get to play with Wick is the Four Nations Cup in Lake Placid," says Tessa Bonhomme. "I can't even speak to her, I am so overwhelmed to be on her team. We are playing the Americans, and I get a penalty on a terrible call. My first game, and I'm in the box, staring at the coach, thinking I'm going to get benched. Then Wick gets a penalty and we're down five-on-three. Now we're in the box together.

"I've never spoken to her. I just take a seat so she has her space, because she's just giving it to the ref. There is literally foam coming from both sides of her mouth. I'm sitting there, thinking, 'This is your moment. Just say something to her!' So I say, 'That was a bullshit call!' And she just looks at me, then stands by the door for the rest of her penalty. I feel like an idiot. What a terrible time to say something. Maybe I should have offered her water or something. These are things you think about in the box with the GOAT!

"Now my penalty is about to end, and Wick is blocking the door. What do I say? 'Excuse me, legend, but the rookie has to go out first?' She's such a competitor, I really think she is going to jump on the ice for me. Thank God, there is a whistle with a few seconds left in my penalty. I stand up and try to figure out a way to tell her I need to get past her. So I say, 'Do you think the coach is going to tell me to go to the bench or go on the ice?' She doesn't say anything, but she gives me a little nod towards the bench. My first real moment with Wick. One little nod, and I figure we are now best buds forever! It's amazing how you can remember every detail when it's one of the great ones. I bet Wick doesn't remember a second of that."

Tessa's right: she doesn't. But the GOAT was a green kid once, too, with her own "I can't believe I did that" tale.

It is Wickenheiser's second season with the Canadian national team. She is just 16, playing in the final of the Pacific Rim Challenge against Team USA.

After two periods, the game is tight. The tournament is on the line.

"We come off the ice after two, and our dressing room is like a shoebox. We're all crammed together in this little community. There are a couple of full spray bottles on the table," Wick says.

"I always like to pour water all over my face after a period. My teammates can all attest to the fact I usually have snot flying out of my nose or spit or some form of something gross all over my face while I'm playing. I'm pretty disgusting during games."

(Guess Tessa wasn't kidding about Wick foaming at the mouth in the penalty box.)

"So, I grab a spray bottle and I just spray it all over my face like I always do. And in a couple of seconds, I go, 'Oh God, that's not water!'"

Uh oh. The spray bottle is rubbing alcohol.

"My face is on fire and I can't see anything! France St-Louis, who is our veteran at the time, and Stacy Wilson jump up and grab a bunch of water bottles and basically do the old chemical face wash, dipping my head over the garbage can, running water over my face endlessly. After a few minutes, I kind of start to see again and the stinging goes away. Still, my eyes are really messed up."

But she's Hayley Wickenheiser and it's a championship game. Zero chance she sits. Wick takes her regular shift for the entire third period.

You know how, when we try to remember significant moments, we often say, "It's a little fuzzy"? Well, for Wick, it literally is.

"I can make out shapes and I can tell the difference between my teammates and the other team, but everything is blurry," Wick says. "I really have no idea if I accomplish much, but somehow we win the game. It is one of the finest moments of stupidity in my career. But I gave the girls a good laugh. They weren't real surprised. I get so focused during a game, I'm pretty oblivious to everything going on around me."

Wick's memory bank is overflowing with unforgettable moments from countless gold medal wins. But that one will forever be . . . a blur.

Wes McCauley's Toughest Call

The NHL's Most Beloved Referee
Gets in Trouble with Mom

The young defenceman gets called into his coach's office and takes a seat across the desk from him. He's not sure where the conversation is going, but the first thing he hears excites him.

"There were scouts at the game on the weekend," says Dave Farrish, head coach of the Fort Wayne Komets of the International Hockey League. "And they brought up your name."

Wes McCauley perks up. It's 1995. He's 23. After four solid years at Michigan State, and the thrill of being a late-round draft pick of the Detroit Red Wings, Fort Wayne is his fourth team in three seasons of pro hockey. He's starting to question his future in the game.

"Oh yeah?" Wes responds to his coach. "That's good to hear."

Understatement. This is the moment every minor leaguer waits for. Someone has finally noticed his potential. This is it. This is the break!

Wes slides to the front of his chair, eager to hear more. Coach Farrish finishes his thought.

"Wes, we all think that, with your bloodlines, you'd make a really good referee."

Wait . . . what?

"I guess that's the moment I first start to think about offici-ating," Wes laughs. (Laughs today, I should clarify. Not so much then.)

The bloodlines Farrish refers to come from Wes's dad, John, a respected NHL official for 15 years. During the 1979 Challenge Cup, a series between NHL All-Stars and the Soviet Union national team, John gets punched in the eye by a fan. He strug-gles with depth perception after, and retires two years later, while Wes is still a young boy. So, Wes never dreams of following in his dad's footsteps.

"I never really thought of my dad as a referee; he was always a coach to me," McCauley says. "In 1978, he was the assistant coach of Canada's field lacrosse team. They beat the US, 17–16, in double overtime over in England to win the World Championship. I was six and carried the flag—I was the mascot of that team. I got a World Championship ring just for carrying the flag! Those are the memories I have with my dad, much more than from his officiat-ing. From the time I start playing hockey, my dream is to *play* in the NHL, not to ref there."

So, even after hearing his coach's advice that night in Fort Wayne, Wes decides to give playing one more shot, with a team in Milan, Italy.

"After that season in Milan, I realize that Dave Farrish is right," Wes says. "I'm not getting to the NHL as a player, so I may as well give officiating a try."

His first phone call is to Andy Van Hellemond, who encour-ages Wes to sign up for an Ontario Hockey Association officiating school in Guelph. A different NHL dream is born.

We're all the better for Wes's career shift. He has become hockey's most respected, and most entertaining, referee. His dra-matic live-mic calls are the stuff of legend.

"After reviewing the play . . . the call on the ice . . . STANDS! We got a good goal!"

"Both guys . . . five minutes each for . . . FIIIGHTINGGG!" (He accompanies this with a rapid one-two combo punching gesture for effect.)

"It's a kids' game, right?" Wes says. "The moment you take the kid out of you when you're playing or officiating a sport, that's the day you have to get out of it. I know I get a little loud on the microphone sometimes, but I have fun."

Wes wants everyone to have fun. On January 18, 2020, in Ottawa, he kicks the Flames' and Senators' starting centres out of the opening faceoff so brothers Matthew and Brady Tkachuk can take the draw.

"I put myself in their shoes, and their parents' shoes," he says. "My younger brother Blaine played college hockey after I did, and my parents are gone now, but I thought, 'Wouldn't it have been cool for them to have watched us take a faceoff against each other?' And I know all the Tkachuks are at the game."

Matthew and Brady take the draw, as their parents, Keith and Chantal, beam from the stands. It's a great moment.

Although the McCauley brothers never got the chance to face each other as players, they do share the ice early in Wes's refereeing career.

In 1998, Wes moves from his hometown of Georgetown, Ontario, to Cincinnati, Ohio, to get pro officiating experience. The Cincinnati area is a hotbed of minor-pro hockey, with AHL and IHL teams there, an ECHL team in nearby Dayton, plus pro teams in surrounding cities like Louisville, Lexington and Indianapolis.

Two years later, Wes's younger brother Blaine graduates from Lake Superior State and signs with Dayton.

"Dayton is about a half hour from Cincinnati, and Blaine isn't making much—maybe $300–$350 a week—so I tell him to come live with my wife and I," Wes says.

Wes gets to referee Blaine's first professional game. He has since done Stanley Cup finals, World Cups, the biggest games in hockey, but still calls that night the highlight of his career.

"It's really special, and he actually behaves, which is nice," Wes chuckles.

You see, Blaine is a bit of a wild card. He racks up 255 penalty minutes in his rookie year in Dayton, including a bunch on another night when his brother is wearing the stripes.

"Blaine's the kind of player who plays right on the edge," Wes says. "And this particular night, he goes over it. Right from the first period. Blaine is agitated, irritated, just being a little . . . you know what. So I'm like, 'Blaine, slow down!' This is my third year as a ref. I know we have to bring down the temperature a bit. But in the second, Blaine just decides to grab someone and start a fight. The instigator gets an automatic ejection, so I do what I have to. I throw my little brother out of the game."

Blaine leaves the ice without a fuss, and when it's over, he is waiting for Wes outside the referee's room. Little bro needs a ride home.

"Not much is said, really," Wes says. "The car ride is definitely quieter than our usual ones. We get home around 11. My first son, Riley, had been born a few weeks before. So, I'm trying not to make any noise, and Blaine just goes downstairs to his room. The house is dead quiet."

The silence is broken around a half hour later, when the phone rings. It's Mom.

"She just lays into me!" Wes laughs. "It's one of those conversations with your parent where you don't get to say anything. She just says, 'You can't be kicking out your little brother! He's trying to establish his career! He's gotta play to move up! You're supposed to be taking care of him!' So, now I've clued in. Blaine doesn't say anything to me after the game, and then gets home, goes downstairs and calls Mom to tell her I've thrown him out!"

When Mom is done with her rant, Wes finally gets to explain.

"I say, 'Mom, I had no choice! It's the rules! I don't think Blaine told you the whole story. He called you, didn't he?' My mom says, 'That's not important,' and starts going off on me again. But by the end of the conversation, she tries to turn it into a lesson, as moms do. She says, 'If you can throw your brother out of a game, you can call a penalty on anyone. If they deserve a penalty, call the penalty.' I'm thinking, 'That's what I was trying to tell you!' It's just one of those hilarious calls that could only come from your mom."

After they hang up, Wes walks straight to the basement door. He hesitates for a second, not wanting to wake his son or his wife, Bethany, upstairs. But he can't help himself. He opens the door, and yells:

"I can't believe you called Mom!"

Then he shuts the door and goes to bed. Referees, and older brothers, always get the last word.

Dumb and Dumber

Two Stories about Ray Ferraro Getting Smacked in the Head

———

The Atlanta Thrashers are awful.

This could be a blanket statement for most of their 12 years in the NHL, but in this case we're specifically referring to November 20, 1999, the 18th game of their expansion season.

The Thrashers are down, 2–0, after one period to the Sabres in Buffalo. They take four penalties in the first, and coach Curt Fraser is livid.

"Curt comes into the locker room and yells, 'No more penalties! We can't be short-handed anymore!'" says Ray Ferraro. "He basically begs us to just stay on the ice."

Ray is a 16-year NHL vet in 1999, with more than 1,000 games and 340 goals on his resumé. He'd been in Los Angeles the previous four seasons and loved it (most do). But after two knee surgeries, and back-to-back 6- and 13-goal seasons, the Kings weren't interested in re-signing him. He desperately wanted to play for a contender, to get one last shot at his first Cup, but there weren't any bites. So, Ray signed in Atlanta, trying to extend his career a few more years with the fledgling franchise. Just 18 games in, it already feels like a long season. And it's about to get longer.

"It's my first shift of the period, right after Curt has lost his mind with us not to take more penalties," Ray says. "Right off the faceoff, their centreman pushes the puck through my feet and tries to go around me. I try to stop him, but I trip him, and I get a penalty literally seconds into my shift. So, I'm sitting in the penalty box and I look across, and Curt is just staring at me, shaking his head. I'm mad at myself, and mad at Curt for giving me the look. So, I throw a couple of expletives in his general direction. Because I know he's going to bench me."

Especially when Buffalo's Stu Barnes scores on the ensuing power play, making it 3–0 Sabres. Ray is prophetic. From the moment his ass hits the bench, it remains glued to it.

"I sit there for the entire second, and most of the third. By this time, I'm sitting down by the backup goalie, talking to him, because I know I'm not going to get back in the game. But with three minutes left, we're down, 4–1, and we get a power play. We pull the goalie and Curt yells my name to go on for the goalie and be the sixth attacker. I don't even have my chinstrap on. I jump on the ice. I skate right into their zone, somebody shoots it, the rebound comes right out to me and I score. We end up getting one more, but lose, 4–3. So hey, I get benched but I score, so I salvage something out of the night."

Ray figures he's out of Fraser's doghouse for now. Until the plane ride back to Atlanta.

"I'm watching a movie—*Dumb and Dumber*, appropriately enough," Ray says. "I have these headphones on, and Curt comes up from behind me and rips them off. He says, 'Did you swear at me tonight?' And I'm like, 'No, not a chance.' And he says, 'I'll ask you again. Did you swear at me tonight?' And I say no again, even though I did. Curt says, 'The coaches were just watching the game video, and we saw you swear at me from the penalty box, from the little camera in the penalty box!' I look around, and all our tough guys are sitting around me—Matt Johnson, Kelly Buchberger, Ed Ward, Steve Staios—and all of a sudden, everybody is looking out the window. It's awkward. And I'm thinking Curt might throw me out the window!"

Like Denis Lemieux in *Slap Shot*, Ray "feels shame." He tries to call Fraser the next day, but the coach doesn't respond. And sure enough, at the team's next practice, Ray is on the fourth line.

"This is a Thrashers team that is going to win 14 games. I'm 35 years old and on the fourth line. It doesn't get much lower."

Ray's purgatory lasts several weeks, until another fateful Fraser intermission rant.

"We are up, 1–0, and they score twice late in the second to take the lead. Curt is really frustrated, so he comes in and takes a stick and smashes it against the wall and breaks it. Then he throws the end of the stick. Well, it hits one of the cement crossbeams, comes back and hits me on the side of the head! And right away, I go, 'Owww.' Kelly Buchberger just starts giggling. Curt feels terrible. He must have apologized 57 times. He wasn't trying to hit me, or anyone. Well, after that, I'm off the fourth line! I'm on the power play! I'm back!"

Not many times in life is a projectile to the melon considered a lucky break. But Ray makes the most of it. He rebounds to score 19 goals that season, and 29 the next, his best goal total in a decade.

"All the boys in that room still tell me that stick to the side of the head saved my career and gave me another three years in the NHL," he laughs.

Ray would retire in 2002, after a terrific 18-year, 408-goal career. And that should be the end of this story. Except it turns out that Ray's head isn't quite safe yet.

He never did get to that elusive Cup final. But in his second career as a broadcaster, he makes it there every year. (He's the best analyst in the game, by the way.) During the 2011 Canucks–Bruins series, we are broadcasting from a building across False Creek in Vancouver, looking back at the arena. It's a gorgeous spot, built for the 2010 Olympics, with floor-to-ceiling glass windows and a huge patio overlooking the water. We are on the set, about to go live on *SportsCentre* before Game 7. It's a huge night. The Canucks have a chance to end Canada's long Stanley Cup drought.

Ray is inside, getting a bit of makeup before hustling to join us outside on the set. When he's in a hurry, Ray has Olympic race-walker speed. Unfortunately for Ray, but fortunately for this book, he forgets about the floor-to-ceiling windows and walks right into one. His nose is split wide open.

As supportive buddies tend to do when a much-loved team-mate is gushing blood and cursing, we laugh like it's a scene from . . . well . . . *Dumb and Dumber*. Because of the makeup, there is an imprint of Ray's face on the glass. No one takes more glee in this than TSN Insider Darren Dreger, who tapes a re-enactment on his phone and shares it on social media.

Ray is taken to the hospital for stitches. But like a true gamer, he is on the post-game panel, live.

Most remember that night for the Bruins win, and for the riot that followed in downtown Vancouver. But we remember Ray's swollen, stitched-up face. The wounds are fresh, and little bits of blood and guck ooze from them as he brilliantly dissects the Bruins' 4–0 win.

And like Kelly Buchberger back in that Thrashers dressing room, Bob McKenzie and I stifle giggles the entire show.

Laila's Gift

A Little Girl Battles for Her Life as Her Favourite Team Battles for the Cup

———

Like most beautiful stories, this one begins with a taco.

It's October 27, 2018—Halloween Costume Night in St. Louis. The Blues are hosting the Chicago Blackhawks. A little girl dressed as a taco stands near the Blues bench, holding up a sign that reads: COLTON, CAN THE TACO GET A STICK PLEASE?

Truth is, the stick is already a lock. The girl's mom has secretly called in a favour. She knows the team chiropractor and tells him her little taco will be there for the warm-up, hoping for a stick from her favourite player, Blues defenceman Colton Parayko.

Sure enough, after his warm-up skate, Parayko hands the taco his stick and tells her to unwrap the tape on the blade. He's autographed it for her. She screams.

We see moments like this every night in hockey. A player gives a young fan a stick or a puck. Their face lights up. It's a few seconds of magic. We all smile. Then it's over. Time to watch the game.

Except this time, it isn't over. This time, it's the beginning. Of a fight for a life . . . and for a Cup. And of a story about the remarkable bond between a little girl and a team.

Laila Anderson has loved the St. Louis Blues forever. Forever is 11 years for Laila. But given what she has been through, it feels a lot longer.

"Hockey is in my blood," Laila says. "My dad is from Minnesota, and my mom knows a bunch of the Blues alumni, so I was basically born to love the hockey team from the city I live in. And that's St. Louis."

Blues broadcaster Kelly Chase is the first player Laila falls for, even though he's done playing eight years before she's born. His is the first jersey she wants. But Mom can't find a Chase jersey anywhere in St. Louis. (Laila wants this fact included, just to chirp Chaser. So, yeah, she really does have hockey in her blood.)

"Mom had to find a jersey and iron CHASE on the back," Laila laughs.

On August 14, 2014, she is a perfectly normal nine-year-old girl (except maybe for the Chase obsession) when her grandparents take her out for dinner at an Italian restaurant. Laila starts to feel sick, and throws up in the bathroom. Her head throbs.

"I go to pick her up, and she's just in an awful condition," says Laila's mom, Heather. "But she feels better in the morning, so we figure it's the flu. But it keeps happening. A couple of weeks later, she's riding in the car with her dad, and all of a sudden, she stops answering him. She's staring off into space. She tries to speak, but can't get her words out. And when she gets out of the car, she collapses."

These episodes continue, on and off, for the next 14 months. But no one can figure out what is wrong with Laila Anderson. She is misdiagnosed multiple times and put on countless drugs. Nothing works.

Finally, they cut out a piece of her brain. In recovery after the biopsy, she seems to be in a spell, repeating the same thing over and over for an entire day: "Kelly Chase is my favourite . . . I need to be tough like Kelly Chase."

Chase comes to visit, and he brings a friend: Blues forward Alex Steen. "Laila is so smart—an adult in a kid's body," Chase says. "So, I figure the best guy to bring is the smartest guy on the team, and that's Steener. He has kids, he's incredibly thoughtful, he doesn't want any attention. And she has a huge impact on him." Heather records the visit on her cellphone. Laila's conscious now, and her eyes are dinner plates. She hugs her beloved Blues.

"That visit changes everything," Heather says. "She's had 65 stitches in her head and she feels like she looks like Frankenstein's monster. But then those two show up. Kelly's been beaten up a few times. Steen is missing his teeth. They tell her, 'You're part of the Tough Guy Club.' After that, she names her scar after her doctor. She's proud to show it to everyone. Her whole attitude changes."

But the biopsy brings no answers. The family is crestfallen, and desperate. Finally, a young blood doctor named Julia Warren, still a fellow, approaches Heather.

"She says, 'I can't get Laila out of my head. Do you mind if I run a few tests?'" And I go, 'Of course. Whoever fixes my kid wins. That's the deal.'"

Dr. Warren wins. She diagnoses Laila with hemophagocytic lymphohistiocytosis, or HLH, a rare, life-threatening disease where immune cells grow out of control and attack the body. She is just the 15th child ever to have HLH only in the brain.

And now a parent's mind races. Why? Is she going to die? How do we fix our little girl? The answers aren't easy. They need to find a bone marrow donor. Fast. And she will need chemo—heavy chemo—to stop the damage to her brain. When they tell Laila, she responds with three words.

"Let's do this."

Tough Guy Club.

Laila is 11 days into her first round of chemo when she attends that Halloween game and Parayko gives her his signed stick. Two nights later, St. Louis Children's Hospital holds a Halloween event at a local theatre where patients get to go trick-or-treating. Laila comes as the taco again, obviously. When the doors open, she sees every Blues player, and they're all in costume. They recognize her from the game and tell her she's their new good luck charm. They've just won, 7–3, only their third *W* of the season.

"Then I see Colton, dressed as a basketball player because he's 6-foot-6," Laila says. "And he gives up his entire night to make sure I have the best time possible. He carries my bag, my drink . . . He spends the whole evening with me. He's just a really special person."

Laila has always been all-in on the Blues. Now the Blues are all-in on Laila.

"She is just so easy to talk to," Parayko says. "Super-happy, witty, appreciative, wise way beyond her years. Everything about her is so impressive."

The season rolls on. The Blues struggle. Laila continues her treatment, waiting and hoping for that bone marrow donor.

"I have the doctor in my contacts as 'Bone Marrow Guy,'" Heather says. "And I'm driving one day, and those three words appear on my screen as my phone rings. He says they have found a 10-out-of-10 match, and that person is excited to donate. I just pull over and cry. Some random stranger has agreed to save my kid's life."

She calls Laila.

"And I call Chaser right away," Laila says. "Because he's the first one I need to tell."

"Tears are running down my face, but I don't let her know that," Chase says, his voice cracking. "After all the shit she's been through just to find out what was wrong with her, I'm just so damn happy for her."

On January 2, 2019, Laila goes into isolation, to be blasted with chemo. They need to tear her immune system down to nothing before the bone marrow transplant. This is the beginning of her climb back.

On the same day, the Blues are in last place, 31st out of 31 teams in the NHL. It would be their final day in that position. This is the beginning of their climb back.

"I'm not sure people realize how crazy this story is," Heather says. "It's absolutely insane . . . the parallels."

Laila's love of the Blues gets her through the chemo and months in isolation. They tell her she can have nothing in the room. But Mom sneaks in a Blues sticker, then another. Soon, there are three giant Blues fatheads in the room. The nurses aren't happy, but they allow it, because they know what it means to their patient.

Laila has the transplant on January 24. Two doctors have to manually pump three bags of bone marrow into her. She puts Chase's number on one bag, Steen's on the second, Parayko's on the third.

As Laila fights for her life, her Blues start winning. They do the near-impossible, climbing from last place into a playoff position. Laila remains in isolation the entire time, watching every second of every game.

"She's an inspiration to us the entire run," Parayko says. "The guys in the room are constantly asking how she's doing. On one of my visits near the end of the season, she says to me, 'If you can make it to the third round, I should be able to go.' I'm like, 'Okay, no pressure at all.'"

But after three months in isolation, Heather knows Laila can't wait that long.

"When they make the playoffs and are playing Winnipeg, I ask the doctor if there is any way she can go to Game 3, the first game in St. Louis," Heather says. "And he says there is no chance she can go from being around zero people to 18,000 in a germ-infested arena. I say, 'What if she wears a mask? What if she wears gloves? What if I put her in a suite that has glass around it? What if we sanitize everything?' Finally, he says, 'All right, fine.'"

Heather takes a video of the moment she tells her daughter she can go to the game. Laila breaks down. Someone from the Blues posts it later. It goes viral.

Laila leaves isolation for the first time in four months to go see her Blues. She wears gloves and a mask. They bring her in through the back to avoid the crowd. The suite she sits in is completely wiped down. And in the middle of the game, there she is, on the big screen. The crowd goes nuts.

"Just to be there and see my boys play is everything," Laila says.

She keeps improving. The Blues keep winning. "Gloria" keeps playing. They beat Winnipeg . . . then Dallas . . . then San Jose. Now it's June, and they're headed to Boston for Game 7 of the Stanley Cup final. It's the most far-fetched Movie of the Week ever. Except it's real.

The doctors have allowed Laila to go to more playoff games in St. Louis, but none on the road. On the day before Game 7, Heather pulls over in a Starbucks parking lot and shoots one more video. She tells Laila she has to ask her a few questions for the media. It's a beautiful sunny June day.

HEATHER: *If you could watch the game anywhere in the world tomorrow, anywhere in the world, where would you watch your boys play Game 7?*

LAILA *[firmly]: Boston.*

HEATHER: *What if I told you the Blues called, and they want you at the game?*

LAILA: *What? How?*

HEATHER: *The doctor said it's okay.*

LAILA *[instantly sobbing]: No, he didn't. Mommy, no, he didn't! Oh my God! I'm going to Boston?! I love you.*

You know the rest. With Laila in the crowd, the Blues beat the Bruins, 4–1, in Game 7 of the Stanley Cup final. It's their first-ever title.

"I just know, the whole game, they are going to win," Laila says. "At the end, my whole body is hanging over the rail, watching the clock tick down—three . . . two . . . one—and they all go hug Binnington. It's surreal! They bring me up a championship hat and shirt, and then they say, 'Laila, you're coming down on the ice.'"

"We see Steen first, and he just stops in the middle of an interview, drops the mic and comes to hug her," Heather says. "And then Colton sees her and just drops to his knees and slides into her and starts hugging her."

"Just to know how hard she had battled and then to see her that happy, lifting the Stanley Cup with me—it will always be one of my favourite memories," Parayko says.

At the parade a few days later, the Blues carry Laila onto the stage as the crowd chants her name. LAILA gets engraved on the inside of their Stanley Cup rings.

The morning after the players receive the rings, the doorbell rings at the Anderson house. It's Parayko and Steen with one final gift.

"Alex pulls out this box," Laila says, "and it's a ring . . . for me. They worked their whole lives for that Stanley Cup ring, and for them to put my name on it, and to give me one? I can't tell you what that means."

In December 2019, Laila meets the donor who saved her life. His name is Kenton Felmlee, a 19-year-old student at the University of Kansas. He doesn't follow hockey. He knows nothing about Laila's story when he agrees to donate.

"She has been such an inspiration to St. Louis, but she is just as inspiring to me," Kenton says. "And she's gotten me into hockey. I wear my Blues Stanley Cup Champions sweatshirt pretty much every day."

Damn. How many heroes can fit into one fairy tale?

Laila is now back to being a (somewhat) normal 12-year-old. She goes to every Blues game she can. Chase, Steen and Parayko aren't just idols anymore; they are friends for life.

There is a long road ahead medically, but Laila has a real chance to live a long, healthy life—and to tell her kids and grandkids someday about the time her boys came from last place to win the Stanley Cup. And how she was battling right there with them. Part of the Tough Guy Club.

Torts and the Bus to Nowhere

Coach John Tortorella
Teaches Marty St. Louis and the
Lightning Some Hard Lessons

Martin St. Louis learns early in his time with John Tortorella in Tampa that there are two different versions of Angry Torts.

There is Loud Angry Torts. He's the "I guess that's what I'm saying, Brooksie" guy you see on the *SportsCentre* top 10 lists. (Torts hates that we always show those clips, by the way. Not as much as he hates "The Quiz," but same ballpark.)

And then there is Quiet Angry Torts. Not as well known as the other guy, QAT can teach you a lesson in a completely different way.

Let's start with Loud Angry Torts, the guy you're more familiar with.

It's 2005, the season after the lockout. The Tampa Bay Lightning are the defending Cup champs—two years running thanks to the cancelled season. Marty St. Louis is coming off a career-defining, 94-point Hart and Art Ross Trophy–winning tour de force. And he's just signed his first big contract: six years, 31.5 million dollars.

"I've always been the guy who talked about being underpaid, and now I have this big contract that I have to live up to, and I'm really struggling," St. Louis says.

On November 10, 2005, with the Lightning at home against the Rangers, Torts benches him.

"We're tied 1–1, and I actually scored the goal," Marty says. "He calls me into his office after the second period and shows me a clip of something I did wrong. I think he's nitpicking. I just want him to leave me alone. My confidence is already low enough. Then, in the third, he short-shifts me and sits me. The Rangers score four, and we lose, 5–2."

Marty fumes on the bench. As soon as they get off the ice, he charges towards Torts's office.

"I come storming in, and he's lying on the couch outside his office," Marty says. "So, I wave my thumb towards his office and say, 'Can I talk to you?' And he gets up and says, 'Did you just fucking thumb me?' And I say firmly, 'I just want to talk to you in your office.' And he says it again. 'You just fucking thumbed me!'"

"I think I tell Marty to shove that thumb up his ass," Torts laughs. "He thinks he's going to walk in my office and get the best of me?"

Before long, Nigel Kirwan, the Lightning's video coach, is between the two men. Marty has flipped Torts's Hulk switch. Loud Angry Torts is turning green and growing.

"Nigel is pushing me out of the office, and Torts is behind Nigel and we're yelling at each other, and it's like one of those scraps where both parties are pretending they want to fight but neither one really wants to," Marty laughs. "I finally leave and say angrily, 'Come and get me when you're ready to talk!'

"So, I go shower up and sit on the couch in the players' lounge. All the players are asking if I'm okay. I say, 'I told him to come get me when he's ready, so I'm staying here until he comes!' But everyone is leaving for the plane! And all my close friends—Freddy (Modin), Vinnie (Lecavalier), Richie (Brad Richards), Andy (Dave Andreychuk)—are all laughing and making fun of me, saying, 'Marty, he ain't coming.' Sure enough, he doesn't come. And I'm sitting there, all by myself, like an idiot. Finally, I have to run to make the plane, tail between my legs."

"There's no way we're having that meeting," Torts says.

By the next day, Marty is feeling a little sheepish and goes in to apologize.

"And Torts says, 'What are you apologizing for? It's over.' That's the best thing about him. He's fiery, but sometimes it's just to see your reaction. There's never a grudge."

Marty grows to understand and appreciate Loud Angry Torts. But it's Quiet Angry Torts that catches all the Lightning off guard. On February 9, 2007, they lose, 5–0, to the Rangers at Madison Square Garden. The next morning, the Lightning are scheduled to dress at MSG, then take a bus across town to practice at Chelsea Piers. The players put on all their gear and are sitting in the dressing room. They are told there will be a team meeting at 10:30 a.m.

So, they sit. And sit. It's 10:40 . . . 10:50 . . . 11 o'clock. The Lightning don't have a captain at this point, so the three alternates—St. Louis, Richards and Lecavalier—finally go into Torts's office to see what is going on.

The coach isn't even dressed for practice. He's just sitting there in his suit.

"I decided I was going to sit and see how long it would take them to come in," Torts says. "I'm sweating, because I don't feel comfortable being late for anything. And my GM is sitting on the bus, waiting for us! But I'm determined to make my point. Finally, the three stooges decide to poke their heads in."

Richards vividly remembers Torts's calm, sarcastic delivery.

"He looks up and says, 'Oh, you're ready now? Sorry, I didn't know you were ready. You weren't ready last night, so I just figured you wouldn't be ready this morning. So, you're ready now? Okay, get on the bus.'"

And off goes the Lightning team bus through midtown Manhattan. Quiet Angry Torts sits in the front, saying nothing. The players are expecting a long, hard bag skate when they arrive.

But when the bus finally pulls up at Chelsea Piers, the door doesn't open. The bus just sits, idling. Torts doesn't move. All the players can see is the back of his head.

"I tell our bus driver, Rocky, to just drive around the Chelsea Piers parking lot, and then go back to MSG," Torts says.

"We're all sitting there, wondering what the hell is going on," Marty says. "And then the bus just turns around and drives back through the city. We just drive around Manhattan all morning."

"We must have been sitting in our equipment for three hours," Richards says. "We figure out his message pretty quick. 'You wasted my time last night. I'm going to waste yours today.'"

Quiet Angry Torts is a hilarious evil genius.

Richards and Torts will have a very public falling-out when they are reunited in New York, with the Rangers, years later. But time passes. And time heals. At a reunion of the Lightning's Cup-winning team in 2017, the two chat and mend fences.

"I love those guys," Torts says. "We were learning together back then, so I had to send messages when needed. We always moved past it. But you know what I found out at that reunion? I always thought I had this really disciplined team that never went out. Now they tell me they were out every night! I had no clue. They were all laughing at me. So I'm glad I made them sit on that bus!"

Richards and St. Louis still laugh about "Are you thumbing me?" And their bus ride to nowhere.

Loud Angry Torts. Quiet Angry Torts. They know both versions helped them win a Stanley Cup.

Cuthbert's Other Golden Call

A Broadcaster Makes the Most
of His Big Break

Niedermayer regroups. Crosby over the line ... Sidney Crosby can't bust in. Up with it again ... He's on the ice with Iginla. Iginla ... Crosby ... scores! Sidney Crosby! The Golden Goal! And Canada has once-in-a-lifetime Olympic gold! —CHRIS CUTHBERT, FEBRUARY 28, 2010

Two decades before the call of a lifetime, Chris Cuthbert is a young game host for *Hockey Night in Canada*. It's 1988—coincidentally, the same year that Canada hosts its first Winter Olympic Games, in Calgary. Chris is hosting a first-round playoff series between the Edmonton Oilers and Calgary Flames. But he sees a window to chase his real dream: play-by-play.

"Hard to believe now, but some of the playoff series are not on TV in 1988," Chris says. "*Hockey Night* decides it's going to do drop-ins during intermissions on some of the games it isn't covering. One of those is Washington–New Jersey. And it strikes me that all of those games are on opposite nights to my series, Edmonton–Calgary.

"I call Don Wallace, the executive producer, and ask if I can go do play-by-play for those few minutes that they plan on dropping in to that series. He thinks it's strange, but says if I'm willing to do red-eye flights back and forth, they'll use me. I know he thinks I'm crazy. My wife thinks I'm crazy. I *am* crazy!"

So, minutes after Esa Tikkanen's three assists lead the Oilers past the Flames, 3–1, in Game 1, Cuthbert races to the Calgary airport to catch a red-eye across the continent. He gets into Washington the next afternoon and is off to the rink.

The plan is simple: during the intermissions of the Boston–Montreal series, *Hockey Night* will send viewers to Washington for about three minutes of that game, called by Chris.

"I don't do much prep," he says. "Basically, I just know the players who are going to be on the ice. But then, around 5 p.m., I have a panic attack because I have not prepped the way I'm supposed to. So I summon my 'high school/college cramming for a test' mode. But I don't have resources. You can't fire up the internet in 1988. All I have is a couple of team media guides. So I go to the front of the Washington guide and start reading. The second bio is Sam McMaster, the assistant GM of the Capitals. And for some reason, I still don't know why, I read it. It's information there's no way I will ever need."

There isn't room at the Capitals' old rink in Landover, Maryland, for Chris to have a typical play-by-play booth. So, they just stick him in the crowd. He has a chair and a folding table behind one of the sections.

"They move me during the anthem because we're blocking one of the aisles," Chris says. "Good thing we're only doing a couple of minutes of play-by-play later, because we are really flying by the seat of our pants."

The producer on site is Jim Hough, who will tell Chris when he is on the air. For now, Chris sits alone at his table in the crowd, watching the game and practising a little so he's ready when they come to him.

Then, about seven minutes in, Hough's voice is suddenly in Chris's ear: "They're coming to you." Chris is confused.

"Jim is about the most low-key producer anywhere," he says. "There is zero anxiety or emotion in his voice. But the other game isn't in intermission yet . . . so I'm not sure why I'm on. I start calling the game, and we keep going. And going. And going! Finally, we go to commercial. I say to Jim, 'I guess we come back next intermission?' And he says, 'No, we're coming right back after the commercial.' So, I just keep calling the game."

For the entire period, Chris does both play-by-play and colour commentary, because he has no analyst. He isn't even sure he's actually on the air. He guesses the *Hockey Night* producers might be testing him, making sure he's ready when his three minutes do come.

"I haven't done anything like this since Saskatchewan junior hockey in '79–80, with the Yorkton Terriers, where you call the games by yourself," Chris says. "I get really confused late in the period, when I give a score from the Montreal–Boston game. And in my head, I'm saying, 'Why am I on TV doing this game when the other game is still going on?'"

What Chris doesn't know is that there has been a major power failure in Quebec. An emergency generator in the Montreal Forum is keeping the lights on and the game going. But CBC doesn't have power to get the TV signal out. So, the entire nation is watching Chris Cuthbert do the Capitals–Devils game, alone in the stands in Washington.

When the period ends, there is no panel to throw to, no fluffy taped features to fill the time. Chris has to do the intermission himself. Hough scrambles to find a guest for him—Sam McMaster.

Valuable broadcasting lesson: read the media guides.

Chris still figures he'll be sending viewers back to Montreal eventually. But it never happens. He calls the entire second period, and now must fill another intermission, this time by interviewing Capitals forward George McPhee, a scratch that night.

When a broadcaster does a live interview, he has two voices to listen to. One, of course, is the person he's interviewing. The other is the producer, talking to him in his earpiece. And in this moment, it leads to *Three Stooges*-style confusion.

107

"George and I are chatting just before we come on air, when Jim says in my ear, 'Remember, you're talking to Mike McPhee.' So I correct him, saying, 'It's *George* McPhee.' And Jim says, 'What did I say?' I answer, 'Mike.' But at that exact same moment, George, who doesn't know me at all, asks me my name. So, when I say 'Mike,' he thinks I'm answering him. So, George proceeds to call me Mike the entire interview!"

They never get power back in Montreal, so Chris/Mike calls the rest of the game, a 3–1 Capitals win.

"I get off the air and say to myself, 'What just happened?' There is no feedback, no cellphones, no Twitter, nothing. Jim and I get in the car for the long ride back from Landover, and I ask him, 'Have our careers just ended?' And Jim, again with his monotone, no-panic voice, says, 'I'm not sure.' I feel like I had done my best under the circumstances, but . . . I just don't know."

He takes the red-eye back through Toronto to Calgary, and when he gets to his hotel room, the phone is lit up. Chris had shown his bosses, and all of Canada, that he was made to do play-by-play.

"For the first time in my life, it's my 15 minutes of fame!" Chris says. "There are tons of messages, thankfully all positive. TV columnists want to talk to me. It's crazy. I get to the rink, and Wayne Gretzky and Glen Sather even come up to me. I actually have to go and hide in the studio at the rink because I need to get away from everyone."

The adrenaline rush from all this attention lasts until the third period of Game 3, when Chris's mind and body realize they have been awake for three days.

"I am fading and just need to get to bed," he says. "Then Jari Kurri scores with four minutes left to force overtime. For a host, that means you have to fill another intermission. I don't have a chance of making any sense. I'm done. I try to say something going to a commercial, and the producer, Larry Isaac, comes in my ear after and says, 'I don't know what language you are speaking, but I haven't heard it on this show before.'"

Mercifully, Gretzky scores eight minutes into overtime. Chris's 72-hour shift is over. He would go back to the other series a couple of more times, but in a much smaller role.

"My job in Game 5 is to do a brief synopsis of the series and interview the seven-year-old who sang the anthem," he laughs.

Cuthbert had done some play-by-play for *Hockey Night* before that fateful night in Washington, but most consider it the night he was "discovered." By the early '90s, he's one of hockey's premier voices. And in 2010, in Vancouver, he is *the* voice of the definitive hockey moment of a generation.

"Until the Golden Goal, that night in Washington was the most memorable night of my career," Chris says. "I'm terrible with dates, but the one I can always give you is April 18, 1988. Not important in hockey history, but probably the most important night of my career."

The Carjack Comeback

Jon Cooper and Dustin Tokarski

Coach Jon Cooper feels like he's in a *Slap Shot* sequel.

He's watching his minor-league team in a full-scale brawl. This, after getting to the game late because he spent the day at the police station with his goalie. Oh, and it's about to get *waaayyy* crazier.

Things had been going so well. A rising star in the coaching world, Cooper had won back-to-back championships with the St. Louis Bandits of the North American Hockey League, moved to Green Bay and the United States Hockey League, winning another title there, and then guided the Norfolk Admirals, Tampa Bay's AHL farm team, to the 2012 Calder Cup championship. Three leagues, four rings, in six years.

Shortly after sobering up from the Admirals' celebration, Cooper is on the move again.

"We're the toast of the town in Norfolk, and then, two days after the parade, they announce we're relocating," he says. "I'm moving from Virginia Beach to . . . Syracuse?"

Cooper is still getting used to the new town four months later, as his Syracuse Crunch (one of hockey's great team names) prepare to leave for a big early-season road game in Binghamton—or "Bingo," as they call it in the minors.

Both rosters are full of soon-to-be NHLers. Cooper's defending champs have names like Tyler Johnson, Ondrej Palat, Richard Panik, Vladislav Namestnikov and Brett Connolly. Binghamton, Ottawa's farm team, has Mark Stone, Mika Zibanejad, Jakob Silfverberg, Mike Hoffman, Mark Borowiecki and goalie Robin Lehner.

Bingo is about an hour away from Syracuse. The team bus is scheduled to leave at 2 p.m. The Crunch hold a quick morning skate, then Cooper heads home to grab some rest before leaving for Bingo. It's a big game. The NHL is in a lockout, and Lightning coach Guy Boucher has come down to watch the team.

"I'm getting dressed and ready to leave for the bus when my phone rings," Cooper says. "Our GM, Jim Sarosy, says, 'You need to get down here right now! Dustin Tokarski is in the police station!'"

Cooper races over. His starting goalie is indeed there, but not arrested, just rattled. Tokarski has just been carjacked at knife-point.

The 23-year-old former Canadian World Junior hero they call "Ticker" lives in a downtown apartment complex with a gated garage. The bad guy sneaks in and waits. When the goalie gets into his car to go to the rink, the assailant comes at him with a knife.

"So Ticker is like, 'Holy shit!'" Cooper says. "And he jumps out the other side and runs. Unfortunately, in that moment of panic, he leaves the keys in the car. And the guy steals the car, smashes through the gate of the complex and is gone."

Cooper comforts his shaken goalie at the police station, while trying to figure out how they're going to make the team bus in five minutes. They decide Boucher will go to Bingo with the team. Cooper and Tokarski will find another ride when they finish at the station.

"They locate the car, but now it's a police chase," Cooper says. "So, we ask if we can just file the report and leave. But the officer tells us if they can catch the guy right now, Ticker can just ID him, then he won't have to come back. It will count as a positive ID in court. So, we decide to wait it out.

"Well, they chase this guy all over Syracuse, and eventually he gets on the highway and they put the tire strips down to stop him. We're getting a play-by-play of this at the police station. Ticker is saying, 'Oh man, that's my car! He's gonna wreck my car!' And the cop is like, 'Sorry, bud, that's how we have to stop him.'

"Sure enough, it works. Now they have to drive Ticker 30 minutes out of town to ID the guy! I wait for him at the station, and it takes forever. I'm checking my watch every 30 seconds. Finally, they get back.

"Now it's 4:30. We have a 7:00 game. I'm like, 'Guys, let's get going!' And they say, 'We just have to do the police report.' I'm dying. It's like the old *Dragnet* show, this guy typing out the report using his index finger . . . tap . . . tap . . . tap. It's taking an eternity! Plus, Dustin Tokarski is a popular player with the local team, so he's drawing a crowd. Pictures are being taken. Now it's 6 o'clock and I say, 'Guys, we have to go right now! We have a game in an hour!'"

Sarosy, the GM, picks the pair up at the police station at 6:05. Fifty-five minutes till game time—a 60-minute drive to Bingo.

"We race down the highway, and we miss the exit to the rink," Cooper continues. "So we're like, 'Just stop the car and we'll run!' I can't miss the start of this game. We jump out and sprint across the road, all the way to the arena. We run in while the anthem is on. I say, 'Ticker, obviously you aren't playing tonight. Just sit in the locker room; don't even get dressed.' It had already been a rough day for him. So, I sprint out there. In Binghamton, you have to walk on the ice to get to the bench. I had been getting into my suit, half-assed, on the ride there, and now I'm walking on the ice during the anthem, tying my tie on the bench."

Cooper can feel his team collectively wondering, "WTF happened? Is our goalie all right?" He tries to assure them everything is okay, but it's not the ideal bench buzz as the puck drops.

Sure enough, six minutes into the second period, it's 5–0, Bingo.

"We're getting killed," Cooper says. "Riku Helenius is our

goalie, and Robin Lehner is in net for them. Lehner looks like a box lacrosse goalie. He's huge and all pads—you can't see any mesh behind him. Riku is a good goalie, but he's the opposite. He looks like a field lacrosse goalie, this tiny figure in a huge net. And he isn't getting any help. It's just a bad night for us."

So the Crunch decide to . . . Crunch.

"Our team has the attitude that if we can't beat you on the scoreboard, we'll beat you up," Cooper says. "So, halfway through the game, Lehner covers up the puck and our Jared Nightingale comes in completely late with his stick and basically stabs the goalie. He shouldn't, but he does. And it's a full-scale line brawl. Robin Lehner, at the time, is a very tough guy with a temper who is willing to go with *anyone*. And at our end, Riku just wants out of the net. So, Riku races from the other end of the ice, right at Lehner. I'm pretty sure he's thinking, 'I'm about to lose this fight, but it's 5–0 and I really need to get out of this game!'"

Not the most rational plan, but it works. When the brawl ends, Helenius and Lehner are both ejected. Cooper has no goalie.

"Holy shit, we've told Ticker he didn't have to dress!" Cooper realizes. "So, I yell at the trainers to tell him to get ready. This poor guy gets carjacked at knifepoint, his car tires get destroyed in the police chase, he has to ID the carjacker and then sprint to the game, and now we have to stick him in the middle of a 5–0 blowout brawl fest."

Cue the Great Carjack Comeback.

Corey Conacher scores: 5–1.

Mark Barberio: 5–2.

Brett Connolly: 5–3.

Ondrej Palat: 5–4.

J.T. Wyman: 5–5.

And, 3:44 into overtime, Richard Panik. The Crunch win, 6–5.

"Just unreal," Cooper says with a laugh. "I've coached in a lot of different leagues and seen a lot of crazy things. But nothing quite like that day."

Ticker ends up on the TSN ticker a few months later, traded to the Montreal Canadiens. That very same season, Tampa fires Guy Boucher and names Cooper as his replacement. The carjacker is also on the move, to jail, after pleading guilty.

Tokarski's stat line for that fateful day will never be matched: 34:14 played; 14 shots; 14 saves; one carjacking at knifepoint; gets the *W* and player-of-the-game honours.

The Reps

Stories from NHL Agents

A wise insider once taught me that if you really want to know how a player feels about something, ask his agent. The reps see the parts of the game we seldom do: contract negotiations, family complications, trade demands. I asked six prominent NHL agents to tell me their favourite story about recruiting young stars, getting deals done, or their craziest clients.

Pat Brisson and the Comedian Coach

Pat Brisson and his client are sitting on the patio at the Loews Santa Monica Beach Hotel in Los Angeles, trying to negotiate a contract with St. Louis Blues GM Ron Caron. Brisson's player is up to his usual tricks.

"He starts sticking these long blades of grass up his nose!" Brisson laughs. "And Prof Caron, as we call him, doesn't see very well, so he doesn't notice. We're having this serious conversation about a contract, and now his nostrils are full of grass. And he keeps saying, 'It sure is dry around here.' Finally, Caron notices and starts laughing. And he just can't stop. He has to get up and walk away from the table. That's what Bergie does to people. He's crazy."

"Bergie" is Marc Bergevin. To most of us, he's a very serious, very professional NHL general manager. But to his friends, he is one of the funniest guys the game has ever seen.

When the 2004–05 NHL lockout hits, Brisson and his partner, J.P. Barry, put together a team of their clients for a European tour. The roster includes the likes of Brendan Shanahan, Marty Brodeur, Dominik Hasek, Sergei Fedorov, Anson Carter, Tie Domi, Luc Robitaille, Daniel Brière, Rob Blake and Sergei Gonchar.

"Bergie is in his last year as a player. He's about to retire," Brisson says. "And I tell him I want him to come on the trip. He says, 'Great!' But then I say, 'Bergie, I don't want you to play! The only way you are coming on this trip is if you coach! I need someone to entertain these guys.'"

For 17 days, through seven countries and 10 games, Bergevin is a one-man travelling stand-up act. He wears costumes into the dressing room for his pre-game speeches. In Norway, he's Julius Caesar. Another night, he's a Godfather-like mob boss, smoking a cigarette, speaking in a full Brando accent.

"One place had mascots, and I stole their outfits and wore them in the room," Bergevin laughs. "Just wanted to add a little humour on a long trip."

"Another game, he curls up in the stick bag and gets the trainers to carry it into the middle of the room," Brisson says. "All the players are saying, 'Where's Bergie?' They unzip the bag and he gets out, wearing only his underwear."

It's not just in the room. Bergie is a human Netflix comedy special, available on demand, round the clock. On one flight, he spreads yogurt all over the glasses of Brisson's father, Frank, as he sleeps. Poor Frank wakes up and his entire world is cloudy. And smells like bacterial fermentation of milk, with a hint of strawberry.

Maple Leafs star Mats Sundin is supposed to join the team for just two games. After his first night with Bergie, he says, "I'm staying for the rest of the trip. I'm not missing this."

"Bergie was the perfect hire," Brisson says. "If that trip were a movie, you couldn't have cast a better guy for the role. The lockout wasn't fun for anyone, but those 17 days, the players got to fly around Europe, playing hockey and laughing their asses off at their coach."

Jeff Jackson and the Small Kid from Chicago

Jeff Jackson is a teenager in the early '80s, playing hockey in Newmarket, Ontario. He has a good friend and teammate named Jack Doak. The two lose touch, as teenage teammates often do. But 30 years later, Jackson, now an NHL agent, is scouting at a tournament in Toronto.

"I'm standing in the lobby of the rink, and I see this guy, and we're staring at each other, and he says, 'Jeff?' And I say, 'Doaker?' Turns out he's an assistant coach for one of the teams. And we reconnect."

Doak's son Aidan is playing hockey at a prep school in Chicago: Lake Forest Academy. And before long, Jackson's old buddy is pushing him to sign one of Aidan's teammates.

"Every time Doaker texts me or we see each other, he talks about this unbelievable kid I have to rep," Jackson says. "My first question is, 'How big is he?' And Doaker says, '5-foot-6.' I'm like, 'There is no way I'm going to rep him. That's just too small.' Doaker keeps nudging. 'You have to see him, he's really fiery, and all he does is score!' It becomes a joke between us. He just won't leave me alone. But there is no way I'm going all the way to Chicago to see this little guy play."

Jackson finally agrees to look at some video of the kid. There are some great plays on it. But it's Chicago high school hockey. He still isn't sold.

Doak has become good friends with the kid's parents, and they are coming up to visit him in Port Perry. They ask Jackson for a favour.

"They call me and say, 'Look, I know you aren't interested in representing our son, but could you meet us for a coffee and maybe give us some advice?'" Jackson says. "So I say, 'Sure,' and we meet at a Second Cup in Burlington. They walk in. He's really short. His parents are short. So, there's no way he's going to grow. I figure I'll spend a half hour with them, and that will be that."

Two hours later, they are still talking. And Jackson knows he's going to represent Alex DeBrincat.

"He has this sparkle in his eye," Jackson says. "There's just something about him. I love him and his parents, Dave and Tracey, right away. I come home and say to my wife, 'I'm going to rep this kid.' And I call Gags (Dave Gagner), Bobby (Orr) and Ricky (Curran) and say, 'I want to take a flyer on this guy.' At worst, I figure he plays junior, gets some points and might be able to play in Europe."

DeBrincat signs as a free agent with the Erie Otters in the Ontario Hockey League. The first time Jackson sees him play is at a summer development camp.

"In the first scrimmage, he scores six goals," Jackson laughs. "Connor McDavid [who plays for the Otters and is also repped by Jackson and Wasserman/Orr Hockey] is standing there with me, and he says, 'This kid can play!' I wink and say, 'He's going to play on your wing.' I didn't actually believe that. I figure maybe he's just getting lucky. But sure enough, he scores 51 goals his rookie season on Connor's wing. And 51 and 65 his next two years."

DeBrincat gets drafted by Chicago in the second round, scores 41 goals in his second NHL season, and signs a three-year, $19.2 million contract.

"We hit the jackpot with Alex as a player and a person," Jackson says. "He is the only guy I've ever signed that I didn't watch play multiple times. It just shows . . . sometimes you take a chance. You never know."

Pat Morris and the $1.8 Million Putt

Pat Morris's client is getting restless. It's four days into free agency and the player isn't close to getting the deal he wants. He would love around $1.5 million a year, preferably for three years. (Sorry, no names for this one. Future negotiations may be at stake.)

118

"My player gets offered three years at 1.2 million by one team, and I tell him not to take it," Morris says. "But now he's getting nervous. He's pissed at me because I don't have anything else yet. Finally, I get an offer from another team: three years at 1.5 million per. It's a really good deal. But before we sign, I circle back to the first team. You know when you call a guy and you can tell he's on the golf course? Well, this GM is definitely in the middle of a round."

Their conversation goes like this:

MORRIS: *I have an offer and my client is going to sign in five minutes. But I thought I'd check back with you first.*

GM: *What's the term?*

MORRIS: *Three years.*

GM: *What's the number?*

MORRIS: *I'm not telling you the number. That's not appropriate.*

GM: *Can you give me a hint?*

MORRIS: *Well, you might want to have a two in it.*

GM: *Hang on a sec. I have to putt.*

Moments later, Morris hears cheering. A few seconds later, the GM is back on the line.

GM: *Made it! I'll offer him three years at 2.1 per. Will that get the deal done?*

Morris restrains himself from yelling, "Hell yeah!" He calls his client. The player can't believe it. He's elated and takes the deal.

"I'm pretty sure the GM forgot what he offered July 1," Pat laughs. "He was so happy he made the putt, he just felt generous."

Émilie Castonguay and Sid Serendipity

The trailblazer stands in Le Colisée de Rimouski with tears in her eyes. She's watching her life come full circle. She is here for her client, Alexis Lafrenière, the best junior player in the world. But she's also here because of the other man they are cheering for tonight.

Émilie Castonguay is 19 when she follows her heart. Buys a plane ticket to Minnesota to watch Sidney Crosby at Shattuck-St. Mary's. She's not some superfan. She just wants to see him play hockey in person.

"I had seen interviews and video of him since he was very young," Castonguay says. "I am just so amazed by his talent. I need to see him play live. And when I watch him, I know in my mind that someday I want to work with athletes who are that determined. I want to help them achieve everything they want."

She has always loved the game. Just months after going to watch Crosby at Shattuck, Castonguay is off to Niagara University in Buffalo to play NCAA hockey. She captains the Purple Eagles her last two years. But she's a third-liner and already knows her future lies off the ice. Law school in Montreal follows. The first dream is to be an NHL general manager. She convinces Montreal Canadiens GM Pierre Gauthier to mentor her. Picks his brain endlessly.

"Pierre says that I always take the player's side in all our conversations, so maybe I should go that way," Castonguay laughs.

So, she does. Finds some part-time work with Momentum Hockey, a new player agency in Montreal. Hustles. Does whatever it takes to learn the business. She joins Momentum full time after law school. Castonguay becomes one of only two female player agents certified by the NHL Players' Association.

When Momentum gets to pitch a young phenom named Alexis Lafrenière and his family three years later, Castonguay leads the presentation, along with fellow agents Olivier Fortier and Chris Daigle. Lafrenière signs with Momentum.

Now, it's September 27, 2019, and Castonguay is in Rimouski, Quebec, where Alexis plays. She is standing and cheering with the crowd, holding back tears, as the Océanic retire Sidney Crosby's jersey.

"When I would be home on break from school at Niagara, I would make the six-hour drive to Rimouski to watch Sid play," Castonguay says. "I became an agent because of him. And then, somehow, when Rimouski has only a small chance to win the draft lottery and get Alexis, they do! Now we're representing him. I'm watching our player, who may go first overall in the NHL Draft, just like Sid. And I'm standing there, as they retire Sid's jersey. It's crazy. I can't help but start crying. Sometimes, you put things out in the universe, you work towards them and . . . they happen."

Lafrenière scores the overtime winner in front of Castonguay and Crosby. Of course. The agent doesn't meet Sid that night in Rimouski. She still hasn't. There have been opportunities. But she wants to wait.

"I don't want to just say, 'Hi, Sid,' and 'Bye,'" Castonguay says. "I want to sit and have an actual conversation with him. To just say thank you, and tell him he inspired me to do this."

Judd Moldaver and the
Awkward Auston Introduction

Auston Matthews had been warned about guys like this. It's 2011. He's 14, and he's starting to get courted by agents.

"My dad says to me, 'Auston, during this process, we're going to meet some guys that will just be full of it. You and I will talk after and say, 'Yeah, forget that guy.'"

Now Auston's in an arena parking lot in Los Angeles, listening to a guy named Judd try to talk Spanish to his mom and thinking, "Yup, here's one of those guys Dad was talking about."

Judd Moldaver spends a lot of time speaking with players and their families in his early years in the sports agent business. Ron Filion, the coach of the Arizona Bobcats, tells him he needs to come watch this kid Auston Matthews play.

"I trust Ron's hockey opinion, so if he tells me come see a guy, we go," Moldaver says. "I'm sitting in the stands, and you can tell right away Auston is a special player. He does this one move in the second period where he opens up his legs and uses his body in a way that is really sophisticated for a kid his age. And I'm thinking, 'Wow, this kid is different.' But it's not like I'm the only one who knows that. It isn't complicated to see that he is something special."

Before the tournament, Moldaver contacts Brian Matthews, Auston's dad, to say he'll be there. They meet inside, and the conversation drifts into the parking lot.

"They are calling Auston 'Papi,' and I knew his mom, Ema, is Mexican and Brian is also fluent in Spanish," Moldaver says. "My mom is Honduran, and I speak a little Spanish, so I think that might help them warm up to me. I kind of black out during these types of meetings. I'm trying to be myself, but I'm not sure what I'm saying. I just hope they don't think I'm crazy!"

Ummm . . . well . . .

"I'm thinking, 'What the hell is with this guy?'" Auston says. "Judd grabs my stick and starts twirling it around, asking me what my flex is. He's talking a million miles an hour, trying to speak Spanish. We get in the car after, and I'm pretty sure this is exactly the kind of guy Dad was talking about. So my dad says, 'What did you think?' And I go, 'Uh . . . I don't know. What did you think?' And Dad says, 'I love him! He's awesome!'"

"He just walked up and introduced himself in the rink," Brian Matthews says. "The more we talked, the more I liked him. Once we got to the parking lot, it was done for me. He was our guy."

He still is.

"So much for first impressions," Auston laughs. "Judd is family now. He's my brother, not my agent. I trust him with my life."

Allan Walsh and the Elias Sweepstakes

The 2004 NHL lockout is hard on everyone. But no one more than New Jersey Devils star Patrik Elias. He contracts hepatitis A playing in Russia and ends up in a hospital in the Czech Republic for a month.

"He almost dies," Allan Walsh says. "It takes him half of the next year to recover."

Elias fires his agent that same year and hires Walsh as he approaches unrestricted free agency in the summer of 2006.

"I go into my first meetings with Lou Lamoriello, the Devils' legendary GM, and the thing with Lou is he is always prepared and gets to the point fairly quickly," Allan says. "He just gives you a number, and that's usually it. There's a lot of integrity behind the offer. But Lou won't give us a number. We talk in February, March, April . . . no number. Patty calls me and asks what's going on. I tell him, 'We're not going to get a number from Lou until June 30.'

"Lou has said many times, 'If you have time, use it.' He knows what he's doing and he's going to wait until the last moment to give us an offer."

June 30 is the day before Elias will become a free agent. Walsh isn't off by much. Lou gives an offer in the last few days of June. It's $32 million over six years.

"I remember Lou saying to me, 'The team isn't doing well financially, and that's as far as we can go,'" Walsh says. "Well, that's nowhere near what we're thinking. We want something in the 40s. So, we aren't really in the same universe."

So, Elias goes to market. The free agent frenzy begins at noon on July 1. Walsh's phone starts ringing immediately. One of the first callers is New York Rangers GM Glen Sather.

"Glen says, 'Elias, what are you looking for?'" Walsh says. "I respond, 'Glen, that's not how it's going to work. You have to make an offer.' And Slats goes, 'All right, all right. Here's the deal: I'm very interested. You go do whatever you need to do. Get all your offers from all the other teams, but don't do anything! And after you've got all your offers, come back to me and tell me what you've got on the table and I'll tell you the best I can do.' I say, 'Okay, fine, Glen. Speak to you later.'"

The phone keeps ringing. Los Angeles makes an offer. So does Montreal. And Toronto. Around mid-afternoon, Walsh gives Sather a call. (The following is Walsh's version of the conversations that day with Glen Sather and Lou Lamoriello, from his notes and memory.)

SATHER: *Where are you at?*

WALSH: *No, Glen, where are you at?*

SATHER: *What are your offers?*

WALSH: *No, Glen, you make me an offer.*

SATHER: *All right. I'll make you an offer that's going to knock your socks off! I want this guy. But I don't want you going around shopping my offer. Does he want to be a New York Ranger?*

Walsh and Elias have talked about this. Returning to New Jersey is his first priority. But New York City is close to home and is his clear second choice.

WALSH: *Slats, we aren't playing games. Patty had his final conversation with Lou. They've moved on and we've moved on. There has been no communication with Lou since last night.*

124

SATHER: *Okay. I'll give you six years, 42 million. But I'm taking you on your word that you're only going to talk to Patrik and no one else.*

Remember, New Jersey's offer had been $32 million over six years.

WALSH: *Slats, you've been fair. I'm going to call Patrik.*

Walsh calls Elias. Elias says, "Wow, that's a strong offer. That's the one. Call him back and finish it off." Walsh calls Sather back and they work out contract structure and a signing bonus. Elias agrees to it. So, Walsh calls Sather back one last time.

WALSH: *Okay, Slats, we have a deal on dollars, terms, structure for each year, salary versus signing bonus. Now, obviously, we want a full no-move for the entire six years.*

SATHER: *No fucking way I'm doing that.*

WALSH: *What do you mean you're not doing that?*

SATHER: *I didn't give Wayne Gretzky a no-move clause! I never gave Mark Messier a no-move clause. And I'm not giving Patrik Elias one, either!*

WALSH: *Slats, there was no such thing as no-moves back then! You're asking Patrick to jump the river and leave the New Jersey Devils to sign with the New York Rangers. And you're not going to give him a no-move?*

SATHER: *I'll get on the phone and give Patrik my word that I will never trade him. But there is no way I'm putting it in a contract.*

125

WALSH: *Slats, I want you to think carefully about this. Do you really want me to call Patrik and say you won't do this?*

SATHER: *All right, fine. I'll do a 10-team limited no-trade.*

WALSH: *It has to be a full no-move.*

SATHER: *Okay, I'll give you 12 teams.*

WALSH: *It has to be a full no-move.*

SATHER: *You call Patrik and tell him I'm going to pay him 42 million dollars, but he's not getting a no-move.*

Walsh hangs up and calls Elias to tell him the Rangers won't give him a no-move. "What?!" Elias says. There is a long pause—10 seconds, then 15, then 20. Finally, Elias says, "Call Lou."
Walsh calls Lamoriello.

WALSH: *Lou, I'm going to tell it to you straight. We have a deal in principle with the New York Rangers. And we've agreed on terms, we've agreed on the number of years, we've agreed on the total dollar amount.*

LAMORIELLO: *How much?*

WALSH: *Six years. Forty-two million.*

LAMORIELLO: *Wow.*

WALSH: *But Slats will not give Patty a no-move. And Patty instructed me to call you.*

LAMORIELLO: *Allan, don't do anything. I'm going to call my owner. Give me 10 minutes.*

True to his word, Lamoriello calls back in 10.

LAMORIELLO: *I talked to my owner. We can do the 42 million. But I gotta do it over seven years, not six. I'll give you a full no-move clause for the entire contract. But I need you to not go back to the Rangers with this.*

Walsh calls Elias. He urges him to take the Devil deal. He knows Patrik's heart belongs in New Jersey.

Now it's the end of the day. Walsh keeps getting calls from media, asking him to confirm that Elias has signed with the Rangers. Walsh hears that Rangers management is already celebrating in New York. He calls Lamoriello back and finalizes the deal with the Devils.

LAMORIELLO: *Allan, I've got Marie here. She's going to type up the contract. But it has to be signed now!*

It's already the middle of the night in the Czech Republic, where Elias lives. Lou keeps calling Walsh to tell him the contract is coming soon. And Sather keeps calling, trying to get Walsh back on the line. Finally, the contract gets faxed to the Czech Republic. Elias drives to a hotel in the middle of the night to sign it and fax it back. He's staying a Devil.

Walsh calls Sather.

WALSH: *Glen, we had a deal. But you wouldn't give Patrik the no-trade. So, we started speaking again to New Jersey, only after you refused to give him a formal no-move. And we have now signed with New Jersey.*

SATHER [*after a couple of seconds of silence*]: *So, you lever-aged my deal to get the deal you wanted all along from New Jersey. He never wanted to come to New York.*

WALSH: *Slats, if you would have agreed to the no-move, Patrik would be a New York Ranger right now.*

SATHER: *Not the first time someone used me like that. Not the last.*

[*Click.*]

Patrik Elias would spend the rest of his career in New Jersey. Walsh would do many more deals with Lamoriello. "After that day, we developed a strong relationship," Walsh says. "Lou is honest, straightforward and gets right to the point."

Even Sather simmers down over time, and they eventually work together again. Walsh has great respect for both legends. And misses those days.

"Negotiations like that don't really happen much today," Walsh says. "The whole business has become more academic, much more numbers-oriented. There just aren't the personalities anymore."

I Gotta Feeling

Tessa Bonhomme and the
2010 Olympic Gold Medal Game

On a street corner, a deal is going down. The dealer shows up on a bike to meet the two buyers. Cash goes one way; the package goes the other. The buyers now have to smuggle the package past tight security to its destination. Somehow, they pull it off. They find the girl they know will take care of the goods until they're needed. If they're needed. That's the tricky part. She stashes them away, swearing secrecy.

No, this is not season 5 of *Narcos*. It's February 25, 2010, in Vancouver—the day of the Olympic gold medal game in women's hockey.

The buyers are Britt Bonhomme and Ryan Morrissey, the sister and cousin of Team Canada defenceman Tessa Bonhomme. Ryan has been working at the bobsleigh track up in Whistler during the Games. He's hitchhiked down to watch Tessa play the biggest game of her life.

Ryan and Britt want something special for the Canadian women if they win. So, they phone a cigar store and order enough for the whole team. But there's no time for the pair to get to the store and back, so the cigar store owner sends the shipment with his son on a bicycle. He meets Ryan and Britt at a designated street corner outside the rink. They sneak the cigars inside and hand them over the glass to Canada's third goalie, Charline Labonté. They're quietly hidden away without any of the other players or coaching staff seeing. Everybody knows it would be a horrible jinx if they did.

At about the same time, Tessa and her Canadian teammates are taking the ice for the warm-up. Tessa's heart is pounding. Her eyes are saucers.

"I've never seen this many people for a warm-up," she says. "The buzz around the arena is crazy. I'm suddenly really nervous. So, I take a knee next to Jayna Hefford. I look at her and just say, 'Holy shit.' And she just looks back at me and says, 'I know, right?' Here is a legend, who has been at every Olympics with women's hockey, and she feels exactly the way I do. So, I realize it isn't just me. This moment really is beyond every dream we've ever had. We *should* feel this way. That really helps me. I have the best warm-up of my life."

In the room after the warm-up, everything seems familiar again to Bonhomme. Cherie Piper is playing DJ and the music is pumping. Jenn Botterill is dancing. Hayley Wickenheiser is dead serious, rubbing her hands together, talking to herself quietly, as she always does.

"And I just have this Zen moment," Tessa says. "Everything is going to be okay. We've been better than the Americans all year, and today is not going to be any different."

But as the team leaves the room, they get chirped. Hard.

"There's a handful of players from the American men's team in the hallway outside our room," Tessa says. "They are giving it to us, saying, 'Aren't you going to be embarrassed losing the gold medal in your home country?' I'm so mad, because I'm thinking, 'Where the hell are *our* guys?' And then we turn the corner, and they are all there! Jonathan Toews, Mike Babcock—all of the boys are lined up along the hallway to cheer us on as we take the ice. Now we're beyond pumped. There is no way we are losing this game."

As they are about to step on the ice, the Black Eyed Peas song "I Gotta Feeling" is blaring through the arena.

I gotta feeling that tonight's gonna be a good night . . .

Team Canada forward Sarah Vaillancourt turns to her team and yells, "You're damn right it's gonna be a good night! Let's go *whiiiite!*" And the Canadian team charges the ice like a scene from *Braveheart.*

Despite her confidence, Bonhomme makes a mistake early, getting pickpocketed behind her own net by American forward Erika Lawler. On the bench, she stews.

"I kick the boards, slam my stick, drop an f-bomb," she says. "I'm just tearing a strip off myself, huffing and puffing. And then Kim St-Pierre kicks me in the back and I turn around and yell, 'What?!' And she says, 'Tessie, look around. Do you know how many people would kill to be in the position you are in right now? So, enjoy it and don't worry about one little mistake.'"

Many had expected St-Pierre to start the game. Instead, coach Melody Davidson goes with Shannon Szabados.

"So, here's Kim, who could be grumpy as hell on the bench because she doesn't get the start in the gold medal game, and instead, she's making me feel better."

As St-Pierre leads on the bench, Szabados shines on the ice. She is brilliant as Canada kills off a pair of five-on-three power plays. Emerging superstar Marie-Philip Poulin scores twice in the second period, and Canada is up, 2–0. The lead feels bigger than that to Tessa.

As time winds down in the third, Davidson puts Tessa and Carla MacLeod out for the last shift.

"All I can think is, 'I want the puck!'" Tessa says. "When I used to watch big games with my dad, he would always say, 'Why doesn't anyone get the puck after?' So I'm going to grab it."

But in the final couple of seconds, as Canadian players are

already pouring off the bench to celebrate, American forward Hilary Knight winds up to take a shot, and Bonhomme tackles her.

"The buzzer goes, and I just throw off all my gear and start celebrating, and totally forget about the puck."

Tessa has dreamt of this exact moment her entire hockey life. Jumping on a pile of teammates after winning Olympic gold. Real life doesn't go as well as the dream.

"I'm a little late to the pile," Tessa says. "I'm ready to jump on, and I'm going for it! All you are going to see on the top of that pile is my long last name and number 25! But someone falls off and stands up, and I clip her feet as I'm jumping. I just fall right on top of Botts [Jennifer Botterill] and face-smash her. So we are face to face, and we're both laughing and crying, and she says, 'This is the best ever!' And all I can say is, 'I failed my jump!'"

When Tessa first made Team Canada, she hugged Davidson. The coach is not a hugger, and told her, "If you want to stay on this team, stop hugging me."

So, of course Tessa has hugged her every time she gets on the team bus, all year. (Don't ever tell a hockey player if something bothers you.) Now, as the players celebrate their gold, they hear Davidson's voice coming towards them. "Bring it in, girls!"

Tessa turns around, and Davidson is running towards them, arms wide open, ready for the biggest group hug in hockey history.

Back in the dressing room, the smuggled-in cigars are waiting in Tessa's stall. She has no idea they were delivered before the game by her sister and cousin. She figures they are from Hockey Canada, and that, as the unofficial president of the team's social committee, she's been nominated to distribute them.

"I'm wearing these wild Canada shutter shades I'd gotten from a fan during the medal ceremony. I traded a stick for them. So, I'm wearing these shades, carrying this box of stogies, and I see the prime minister, Stephen Harper. I say, 'Mr. Prime Minister, care for a stogie?' And he goes, 'Absolutely!' I look at him and say, 'Not gonna lie, I don't know what to do with these things. I've never lit one before in my life.'

"And so the prime minister snips it and shows me how to light it. I still have this photo of the PM holding my medal with a cigar in his mouth, and I'm wearing these shutter shades. It's nuts. I always say, 'That's the guy who taught me how to handle a cigar!'"

The cigars would end up becoming one of the Olympics' silliest controversies. Once the building is empty, the players go back on the ice for photos—cigars, beer and champagne in tow. It's supposed to be a private moment of celebration. But some of the photos get to the media, and the Canadian players take heat for smoking cigars on the Olympic ice—and acting, well, not polite-Canadian enough.

"We just wanted to celebrate in the place that we won," Tessa says. "That rink was ours. We owned it. They were cool photos. It's funny how it was portrayed."

Later, the players arrive at Canada House and are immediately ushered backstage. Actor Donald Sutherland is there to introduce them to the crowd. As he tries to put on the Team Canada jersey they have handed him, he dislocates his shoulder. He drops to a knee in pain. And then the Canadian icon calmly pops the shoulder back in himself, puts the jersey on and grabs the mic.

"He strolls onstage like nothing happens and introduces us," Tessa laughs. "What a legend!"

Apparently, it isn't just Canadian hockey players who are tough.

Tessa still hasn't seen her family. As she gets on the stage, she scans the crowd.

"For whatever reason, I can see this little sea parting in the middle of the crowd as people are coming through. It's my sister, who is five feet tall, dragging my dad! I just jump into the crowd and start running towards them. I give my dad my medal and hug my sister. We're all squished like sardines. I have this digital camera around my wrist. Some guy says, 'Let me take a picture.' And it's the best picture. It's me with my arm around my sister and my dad. Dad, who never even cried when his father passed, has tears in his eyes. He's wearing my medal. And my sister and I have the biggest shit-eating grins. Then I see my mom and finally get to hug her and thank her. They have sacrificed so much for me. This moment means everything."

Cousin Ryan, the other half of the cigar-smuggling team, is also there. Tessa has saved a stogie for him. He lights it up. And Tessa's two families—relatives and team—have the party of a lifetime.

Tonight's gonna be a good, good night . . .

Whit, Bugsy and the Overbooked Private Jet

Ryan Whitney and the 2006–07 Pittsburgh Penguins

A team desperately trying to win a game for a gravely ill team-mate—it's the perfect formula for a tear-jerker of a sports movie...unless, of course, that player isn't dying, but is just missing a road trip, and the team wants to win so he can come to the rookie party.

That's how much the 2006–07 Pittsburgh Penguins love Ryan "Bugsy" Malone.

The Pens are a team on the rise. Sidney Crosby is already the face of the NHL in just his second season. Rookies Evgeni Malkin and Jordan Staal have joined him to form the best trio of young centres the league has seen in ages. Marc-André Fleury is a budding star in goal. And veteran Sergei Gonchar leads a defence corps that also features a 23-year-old South Boston kid and future podcasting legend/vodka mogul named Ryan Whitney.

"I love that team," Whitney says. "And everyone on the team loves Bugsy Malone! He's just one of my all-time favourite team-mates. Everyone wants to hang around with him. One of the great pranksters. He steals three pairs of my dress shoes that season. One he nails to a locker, so I have to wear sandals on the plane. One he spray-paints fluorescent blue. I actually get a lot of compliments on those. And one he puts a dead mouse in. But I love him. And can he go! The boys go out for drinks with him and think they can keep up, and they are completely destroyed the next day. Meanwhile, Bugsy's fine. We'd say, 'You got Bugsied!'"

On one episode of *Spittin' Chiclets*, Whitney's crazy-popular podcast, he ranks Bugsy first on an all-time list of "Guys I want next to me in a bar fight."

But Bugsy isn't there for Whitney—in the bars or on the bench—when the Penguins head to Philadelphia for the start of an early-season four-game road trip. Bugsy has been injured in a fight with Rostislav Klesla of the Columbus Blue Jackets a few nights earlier, and is forced to stay back in Pittsburgh to heal.

He's missing history.

Malkin has sat out the first four games of his rookie season with an injury of his own. He finally makes his NHL debut on October 18, against New Jersey. Late in the second period, he scores his first NHL goal on a gorgeous feed from Whitney. (Technically, Whitney tries to poke in a loose puck in front of Martin Brodeur, whiffs, and Malkin jams it home. Whatever. Primary assist for Whit.)

The next night, Malkin scores the tying goal in the third against the Islanders (from Crosby and Whitney), and the Penguins win, 4–3, in overtime (Gonchar, from Whitney). He scores again in his third game, and his fourth (from Crosby and Whitney). So, to summarize, Malkin has scored in his first four NHL games. And Whit is on an apple tear.

Malkin's fifth game is in Philadelphia, the first stop on the Bugsy-less road trip. He scores on a power play in the second (Whitney gets the second assist), Crosby has a hat trick, and the young Pens have won four in a row.

"Now we're off to LA and we are all pumped up," Whitney says. "Malkin has goals in five straight, and it's been 89 years since anyone scored in their first six in the NHL! Plus, the night after the game in LA is our rookie party."

Right before the game, head coach Michel Therrien and assistant Mike Yeo decide to dangle a carrot before their young team.

"They tell us that if we win the game, Bugsy can fly out for the rookie party!" Whitney says. "That is just unheard of! If a guy is injured, he has to stay at home. So, we're like, 'What?!' And the guys love Bugsy so much, we know we gotta win this game. We're all fired up. It's like a Game 7!"

And Malkin delivers.

"What does Malkin do?" Whit says, excitedly/rhetorically. "He scores in the first period to tie the record! A goal in each of his first six games!"

The Penguins still trail, 3–2, in the third when another rookie, Noah Welch, scores to force overtime. Less than three minutes in, the Penguins get a four-on-three power play. Crosby feeds Gonchar at the point. Gonchar fires, Dan Cloutier makes the save, and . . .

"Malkin snipes the winner!" Whitney exclaims, as if he's doing play-by-play. "We go nuts! Seven goals in six games! He's already a superstar! And the whole bench is going bananas knowing that Bugsy is getting flown out by the coaching staff to be part of the rookie party!"

Needless to say, a whole colony of Penguins get Bugsied the next night.

Remarkably, that's not even Whit's best story from that season. Three months later, he gets named to the YoungStars Game over the NHL All-Star Weekend in Dallas, along with Malkin and Staal. Crosby, of course, will play in the "real" game.

"I'm fired up, because I'm having a great year and anyone who makes the game gets a first-class ticket," Whitney says. "Life is great! But then I hear that I don't even need the first-class seat because Mario Lemieux has a private jet to take us all there. Even better! Are you kidding me? Don't even have to go to the main airport. I get to fly on a PJ with Sid and Mario!

"Now, naturally, I am the most insignificant person of the bunch. But it doesn't matter. Well, what happens? I show up and I'm in the hangar, waiting to get on the plane. I see Mario and his wife. I see Sid and his parents. I see Malkin and Staal. And I'm like, 'I wonder how big this plane is?' Well, wouldn't you know, there isn't a seat left for me!"

But there is no way Whit is missing out on his "PJ" flight to Dallas with Sid and Mario.

"So, I have to sit in the bathroom!" he laughs. "I sit in the bathroom the whole flight. And when people have to take a piss, I just get up out of my seat and hang out for a little bit, and when they go to sit back down, I go back to the bathroom. And believe me, I don't give a shit! I'm on a private jet with the legend Mario Lemieux! What a moment!"

Whitney would play nine more seasons in the NHL, but none would match the magic of 2006–07.

Until maybe 2019, when his podcast blows up and Whit gets a vodka named after him. Now an entire generation can get "Bugsied" on Pink Whitney.

Mario and Sid had no clue they were in the presence of another legend on that jet. Sitting behind them, on a toilet seat.

LA (Not So) Confidential

Broadcasters Gord Miller and Keith Olbermann Chase the Gretzky Trade

Gord Miller is 18 years old, and looks 13, when he first interviews Wayne Gretzky. He blows it.

"I'm working for CBC Radio in Edmonton and have to get post-game sound, which I've never done before. The Oilers beat Minnesota and Wayne has a big night. I have this little tape recorder and I stick it in Wayne's scrum. I come out after and realize I hadn't taken the pause button off. I have nothing! I have to go back in.

"Wayne is now by himself, and I'm terrified. I say, 'Hi, Wayne. I work for CBC. I'm really sorry, but I messed up and didn't record your interview.' At some point, he says, 'Just go ahead and ask your question.' And then I realize I'm 18 years old, talking one on one with Wayne Gretzky! And all I can think to say is, 'Good game.' That's my question: 'Good game.' What a disaster."

Five years (and four Oilers Cups) later, Miller ends up landing another Gretzky one on one—next to a pool at a Los Angeles mansion. Before that interview, he'll slide Gretzky an envelope containing $500. Just part of one of the wildest weeks of Miller's career.

Keith Olbermann is 21 when he gets assigned to cover hockey at the 1980 Olympics in Lake Placid for UPI Radio. His job is to report on an American team that isn't expected to do much. But when they start to win, the cub reporter gets replaced by his boss, Sam Rosen (the future voice of the New York Rangers). Olbermann's new assignment is to sit in the stands, holding a microphone to gather crowd noise. As Al Michaels of ABC is yelling, "Do you believe in miracles?" Keith is already rushing outside to record the celebration.

Eight years later, Olbermann is a rising star in television in Los Angeles. Here, hockey is usually buried deep in the sportscasts. Until one summer day, when the phone rings in his office, and the caller has a really good story to tell. In fact, a Great One.

=====

In the summer of 1988, the Edmonton sports scene is buzzing. The Oilers are a dynasty. The Eskimos are defending Grey Cup champions. Local boy Kurt Browning is the best male figure skater in the world. And Canada's version of a royal wedding is about to take place: Wayne Gretzky is marrying actress Janet Jones.

"It's a crazy time to be a sportscaster in Edmonton," says Miller. He's 23 by this time, and looks 16, but he's an established reporter/anchor with CBC Edmonton.

In the weeks leading up to the wedding, Wayne Gretzky's brother Glen tells Miller that there is trouble between Wayne and the Oilers' ownership. Chris Cuthbert, Miller's colleague at CBC Edmonton, is hearing the same thing.

"As it turns out, the issue was that Wayne Gretzky had signed a personal-services contract with Oilers owner Peter Pocklington that had land deals and all these other things in it, and the NHL didn't like that. They outlawed those deals. So, in the early '80s, the Oilers had to restructure Gretzky's contract. And he would become an unrestricted free agent in the summer of 1989. We kept hearing rumbles that he was interested in exploring that."

Cuthbert gets a phone call from one of Gretzky's close friends, Eddie Mio.

"Eddie says there is a real chance Wayne is going to be traded," Cuthbert says. "And Eddie's not happy about it at all."

So, Cuthbert and Miller start digging. One of the rumours they hear is that the Vancouver Canucks are chasing Gretzky. In one of his suit pockets, Miller finds a business card for a young executive with the Canucks named Brian Burke. They had met at a game that past season. Miller calls the Canucks' assistant GM and asks if there is anything to the rumours.

"I call and say, 'Hi, Mr. Burke, I'm Gord Miller from Edmonton. We met in the press box—' and he interrupts and says, 'Is there a question here?' That pretty much still defines our relationship. So I say, 'Yes sir, we're hearing the Edmonton Oilers might trade Wayne Gretzky and the Canucks might be interested.' And instead of telling me to get lost, Burkie says, 'It's not us; it's the Kings. And here's the deal: it's Jimmy Carson, Martin Gelinas . . . ' He pretty much has the whole thing!"

"We are concerned because there is this big buzz in the Vancouver marketplace that we are going to get Gretzky," Burke says. "So Pat Quinn, the Canucks' GM, tells me, 'Get it out there that he's not coming here. We don't need that disappointment.' I say, 'Who should I give it to?' And Pat says, 'Whoever calls you first.' Gord calls me first."

Miller and Cuthbert decide they have enough to report that the Oilers are seriously considering trading Wayne Gretzky to the Kings. It's part of their sportscast one early August night.

Today a story like that would go viral in seconds. But in 1988, there is no internet, no social media, no cellphones and, apparently, not a lot of people paying attention to the CBC Edmonton sportscast during summer vacation. Because the story gets picked up by . . . well . . . nobody.

"I think most people just laughed it off as ridiculous," Cuthbert says.

"Bob McKenzie still bugs me about it," Miller says. "He says, 'You and Chris must have been pretty big deals back then, because you broke the biggest trade in hockey history and no one noticed!'"

A few days later, Miller flies to Los Angeles. If the deal does go down, he has to be there.

"I'm told that whenever the Kings do an announcement, it's always at what is now the Sheraton Gateway Hotel. So I book myself in there. But nothing's going on. It's quiet. I would learn years later that, on Sunday afternoon, Kings owner Bruce McNall calls the house Gretzky is staying at in LA, and a kid answers the phone. McNall says, 'I need to speak to Wayne Gretzky.' The kid, who is 11, says, 'He's sleeping.' And McNall says, 'Wake him up!' I know this because Alan Thicke told me. Gretzky was staying in his guest house, and the kid who answered the phone was his son, Robin."

Robin Thicke will later say that phone call inspired his sexy hit song "Blurred Lines."

(Editor's note: This is a blatant lie for a nonsensical joke. We apologize.)

Miller knows none of this on that August Sunday in 1988. So he sits. And waits. For a trade he's still not sure will happen.

=====

That same Sunday, Olbermann is finishing off a week's vacation and getting ready for his last few shifts at KTLA. He has just signed a new contract at rival TV station KCBS.

"They offered me a raise of seven times what I was making," Olbermann says. "Those were the glory days of local news and sports. I go in to work on Monday, and I'm boxing up stuff in my office when the phone rings. This guy says, 'I just overheard Bruce McNall claiming he's traded for Gretzky!' And I say, 'Sure, whatever.' I don't think much of it. These rumours have been circulating around LA the last few days.

DARRYL
Sidney Crosby (aka "Darryl") brought the Stanley Cup back to Rimouski in 2017 and celebrated with his old Océanic roommate, Eric Neilson. (ERIC NEILSON)

FIXING RAZOR
The late Ray Emery with Matt Nichol, the trainer who helped him make it back to the NHL, after Emery won the Stanley Cup with Chicago in 2013. (MATT NICHOL)

BIZNASTY'S LAST DANCE
Paul "Biznasty" Bissonnette celebrates a Calder Cup win with the Ontario Reign in 2016, before two torn ACLs end his career.
(AMERICAN HOCKEY LEAGUE)

NOODLES, THE PUFFIN AND THE REPORT CARD
Jamie "Noodles" McLennan starred with the Lethbridge Hurricanes in junior before being drafted by the New York Islanders and fighting a mascot in Newfoundland.
(LETHBRIDGE HURRICANES)

(KENDALL COYNE SCHOFIELD)

THE FASTEST-SKATING GIRL

Kendall Coyne Schofield changed the perception of women's hockey when she held her own against Connor McDavid and other NHL stars in the fastest skater event at the NHL All-Star Weekend in 2019. (EZRA SHAW/GETTY IMAGES)

THE ACCIDENTAL TAUNTER
Mike Johnson after scoring a goal with the Toronto Maple Leafs during the
1999–2000 season. We don't believe anyone got mad at him for this celebration.
(GRAIG ABEL/GETTY IMAGES)

"WHAT IS THAT?"
Bobby Orr and Connor
McDavid during NHL
Draft Week in Florida
in 2015.
(ELIOT J. SCHECHTER/NHLI)

MILBURY'S SOLO BAG SKATE
Dave Poulin and his twin daughters, Taylor (*left*) and Lindsay (*right*), after he was traded to Boston and witnessed coach Mike Milbury's legendary solo bag skate. (DAVE POULIN)

COLE'S GOAL
After overcoming a broken neck and numerous other career-threatening injuries, New York Islander Cole Bardreau beats Ottawa's Craig Anderson for his first NHL goal, on a penalty shot, in 2019.
(NEW YORK ISLANDERS)

THE GREAT STAMKOS CAR HEIST
Steven Stamkos and his father, Chris, are still best friends despite Chris's mistakenly stealing Tampa GM Steve Yzerman's car. (CHRIS STAMKOS)

THE NIGHT WICK WENT BLIND
Hayley Wickenheiser found a way to win, even when she couldn't see for an entire period.
(DAVE SANDFORD/HHOF-IIHF)

WES McCAULEY'S TOUGHEST CALL
NHL referee Wes McCauley has become a fan favourite (except for the night he angered one fan—Mom—for kicking his younger brother out of a game).
(JEFF VINNICK/NHLI)

LAILA'S GIFT
St. Louis Blues superfan Laila Anderson, dressed as a taco, meets Colton Parayko at a team Halloween party, and celebrates a Stanley Cup win with him seven months later. (HEATHER ANDERSON)

THE CARJACK COMEBACK
Syracuse Crunch goalie Dustin Tokarski poses with police officers after being carjacked, hours before leading his team to a stunning comeback win. (JON COOPER)

I GOTTA FEELING
The moment when Tessa Bonhomme finds her father, Doug, and sister, Britt, in the crowd after winning gold at the 2010 Olympics in Vancouver. (TESSA BONHOMME)

THE 30TH BRONCO
Former Humboldt assistant coach Chris Beaudry (with his daughter, Emily) has found peace after battling addiction and unimaginable grief following the bus crash that killed 16 members of his Broncos family.
(CHRIS BEAUDRY)

THE LONE RANGER (FAN)
Steve Levy (with longtime ESPN partner Barry Melrose) covered his beloved New York Rangers' Stanley Cup win in 1994, and has covered every Cup final since. (STEVE LEVY)

TIMING IS EVERYTHING
Brad Richards overcame the embarrassment of being late to his first team bus ride and helped Canada win the 2004 World Cup of Hockey (with his dad, Glen, his mom, Delite, and his sister, Paige).
(DELITE RICHARDS)

THE ACCOUNTANT
Scott Foster was destined to be a Blackhawk from age six. Three decades later, he goes from beer leaguer to Chicago hero when he comes in as an emergency goalie on March 29, 2018, against the Winnipeg Jets. (*LEFT*, JOHN HUS; *RIGHT*, CHICAGO BLACKHAWKS)

THE KID WHO WON EVERYTHING
After winning the Memorial Cup and World Junior gold, Robert Thomas celebrates a Stanley Cup victory with his dad, Scott, his mom, Debbie, and his brother, Connor, in 2019. (SCOTT THOMAS AND DEBBIE WAECHTER)

RONAN'S RIDE
John Ronan with daughter
Camryn in Evansville, Indiana,
the last stop on his seven-year
minor-league hockey odyssey.
(JOHN RONAN)

**THE CASE OF
THE MISTAKEN
McCREARY**
Wayne Gretzky poses
with referee Bill
McCreary (*far right*)
and his officiating crew
during the second inter-
mission of the Great
One's final NHL game,
on April 18, 1999. (BILL
McCREARY)

**TUCKER AND THE
WRATH OF THE MIGHTY
QUINN**
Darcy Tucker (*left*) wor-
shipped Pat Quinn, even after
the legendary coach scolded
him for taking a bad penalty
(while they shared a Scotch).
(TORONTO MAPLE LEAFS)

"CAN YOU BELIEVE IT?!"
Jordan Eberle, the "worst player" at Canada's summer training camp, scores the tying goal with 5.4 seconds left in the 2009 World Junior semifinal against Russia.
(ANDRE RINGUETTE/HHOF-IIHF)

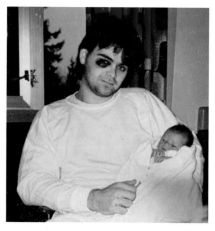

THE DRAFT EMAIL DISASTER
TSN Insider Darren Dreger has broken countless trades, including one by dropping his phone at the 2011 NHL Draft.
(DARREN DREGER)

BUTCH'S BATTLES
Garth Butcher with his New Year's baby, Matt, born in 1987. The black eye is courtesy of Edmonton Oilers tough guys Jeff Beukeboom and Marty McSorley, whom he fought in the same game a few nights earlier. (GARTH BUTCHER)

CUATRO POR PAPI
Auston Matthews holds
the pucks from his
four-goal NHL debut
against Ottawa, a game
witnessed by his proud
parents, Brian and Ema.

CARLO'S COMMUTE
Carlo Colaiacovo raced home from Europe to witness the birth of his son, Leo, then raced back to play hero in a playoff game. (CARLO COLAIACOVO)

THE APPRENTICESHIP OF JIM McKENZIE
Jim McKenzie was a naive rookie with the Moose Jaw Warriors in 1986–87. He'd learn a lot in his 14 NHL seasons, including who Dave Brown was.
(MOOSE JAW WARRIORS)

CAMMI'S FLAME
When Cammi Granato carried the Olympic torch through Lake Placid in 2002, she had no idea she would also carry it up the stairs to the cauldron during the Opening Ceremonies in Salt Lake City.
(CAMMI GRANATO)

HULLY
Brett Hull and Kelly Chase shared an occasional (!) beer during their six years as road roommates with the St. Louis Blues. **(KELLY CHASE)**

BOBBY MAC VS. TRETIAK
Future TSN Hockey Insider Bob McKenzie during his playing days. He'd later get one chance at glory: a shootout attempt against Russian legend Vladislav Tretiak.
(BOB McKENZIE)

JONNY HOCKEY
"The Butterfly Child," Jonathan Pitre, meets his idol, Sidney Crosby (with Matt Cullen), for the first time, after a game in Minnesota.
(TINA BOILEAU)

THE GOLDEN GOALIE
Robert Luongo celebrates with his family after winning gold at the 2010 Olympics.
(PASQUALINA LUONGO)

THE BOY WHO CAME FROM AWAY
Yamen Bai, a Syrian refugee, fell in love with hockey when he arrived in St. John's, Newfoundland. Generous Canadians bought him equipment so he could play.
(MICHAEL DOYLE)

"A few hours later, the phone rings again. It's a different guy, who says he was over at LA Country Club and Bruce McNall burst into the clubhouse and told them to all buy Kings tickets because he's traded for Wayne Gretzky!' Twenty minutes later, another caller says, 'Hey, I just saw Bruce McNall and—' I interrupt him and say, 'And he told you he just traded for Wayne Gretzky, right?' And he says, 'Yeah! He mentioned something about Jimmy Carson and a lot of money.'"

Olbermann can't decide if he's being pranked, or if Bruce McNall is running around with a megaphone, announcing the biggest trade in hockey history to all of Los Angeles County.

Then he gets one more call. This one comes from a guy who claims his ex-wife signs the cheques at McNall's company. He puts her on the phone. She tells Olbermann she has personally cut the $15 million cheque for Peter Pocklington, and that Wayne Gretzky is now an LA King. She gives him all the details of the deal. Olbermann does a little work to verify her identity and then says to his bosses, "I think we have the Gretzky trade." He goes on the air at 10 p.m. on KTLA, reporting the deal.

Tuesday morning, Gretzky holds his tearful news conference in Edmonton, and then flies to LA to be introduced by the Kings. Miller has gotten good advice: it will happen at his hotel, the Sheraton Gateway.

"Perfect!" Miller says. "So, I go back to the hotel and there's a message from the front desk. My Visa card is over its limit. I think I only had about a thousand-dollar limit. I'm thinking, 'I'm going to get kicked out of here, and be on the street, with no credit card and no money, trying to cover the biggest story of my life.' So, I'm negotiating with them, trying to stay in my hotel, as Wayne walks in with Mike Barnett, his agent, and Craig Simpson. They walk in as I'm pleading with the guy at the front desk. And Wayne goes, 'What's up?' So, I tell him my issue and Wayne takes $500 cash out and puts it on the front desk to cover it. And then he says to me, 'You're a shitshow.'"

Gretzky holds his news conference, and agrees to do a one-on-one interview with Miller the next day, by Alan Thicke's pool. But Miller figures that before he does the interview, he had better pay Gretzky back.

"My office wires me $500 from Western Union, and I give it to Wayne before the interview in an envelope," Miller says. "I have regrets from that interview because Wayne kind of laid it out to me that he didn't really want to be traded, but I didn't follow up as well as I could have. The next day, in the Edmonton paper, they have that story."

Still, at 23, Miller has covered the trade of our lifetime. He joins TSN two years later and becomes one of hockey's top play-by-play voices.

Olbermann goes on to fame at ESPN and MSNBC. "We submit our coverage of the Gretzky trade to the local sports-reporting Emmy Awards the next year. I lose to Fred Roggin, whose report was an exposé on Morganna, the Kissing Bandit. My girlfriend, my agent and I get up and walk out of the Emmys."

Miller has his own postscripts. "Alan Thicke would always say his kid made the deal happen. Brian Burke still says he made my career. And Gretzky says I would have been out on the street and missed the whole story if he didn't lend me 500 bucks!"

The 30th Bronco

Humboldt Broncos Assistant Coach
Chris Beaudry

It's the Nipawin assistant coach who calls him first. Asking if he is okay, if everyone is.

Chris Beaudry is confused by the question, thinking, "Why wouldn't I—*we*—be okay?"

He isn't on the bus, you see. Nipawin, Saskatchewan, where the big game is that night, is closer to his farm than Humboldt, the town he coaches in. So, he is driving there, meeting his team at the rink. Chris is 15 minutes behind the bus when he gets the call. The Nipawin coach has heard there has been an accident.

"When he tells me, I figure it's a blown tire, maybe a moose, not a big deal," Chris says. "And then I come upon the scene and I see it. And instantly, this massive feeling of cowardice comes over me. I want to run. I want to hide. The first time I call my wife, I tell her to hide everything in the house with a Broncos logo on it. I can't be this person anymore. This can't be my life. This can't be real."

You need to know something now. This is a story of unbearable pain and grief. A story of not one but two horrific bus crashes. And one young hockey coach, unfathomably tied to both. But it's also a story about finding a way back, out of the darkness. And if

145

you have been there, or are still there, maybe it will help. That's why the coach is telling his story. I'd want to know that first. Otherwise, the rest is too hard.

=====

Chris Beaudry is terrible at hockey. Worst kid on the ice. He's 12, just moved from Calgary to a farm in Saskatchewan, and can barely skate. Baseball had been his thing in Alberta.

"I'm brutal," he says with a chuckle. "Pure ankle bender, hands of stone, awful. I start in pee wee and just get destroyed, because I never lift my head up. But I just love it."

By bantam, the skating comes, along with some muscle, and Chris starts to find joy in running other kids over. He becomes a scrapper, making room for the skilled kids to do their thing. Makes him feel worthy on the team. It also has some side benefits.

"When I am 16, there is this big wrestling event on TV, and my buddy and I really want to go watch it. So we look at each other on the bench and say, "Let's just fight on the draw. We just grab two guys right off the faceoff and get kicked out. We shower, dress and are back on the farm in time to watch wrestling before the game is even over. Brilliant plan."

The young fighter is also a drinker. Hardly rare for a fun-loving farm boy on the prairies. But Chris drinks a lot. He drinks to feel happy, because he has stopped liking himself sober. He now believes he was an alcoholic by 14. This is all adult self-reflection, of course. Back then, he's just a good Sasky boy, playing hockey, drinking with the boys, having a time.

Chris is smart enough to realize early that a pro hockey career isn't an option. Farming is his future. His dad gives him his first cow at 12, and by the time he graduates high school, he has six. He's a full-time grain and cattle farmer the day after graduation. But the game still calls him. So, after a few years away, he comes back to try coaching.

He's 24, in his first year as an assistant with the Naicam

Vikings of the Wheatland Senior Hockey League, when their team bus stops by the side of the highway.

"So many tiny moments, decisions, can change everything," Chris says. "We are playing in Kenaston in the senior men's provincials, and we have rooms booked at the Imperial Bar. Somehow, it gets double-booked—first time in the Imperial's existence, I'm sure. So, after our game, we decide to go stay in Saskatoon. A few miles out of the city, I ask the bus driver to pull over, just so everyone can take a leak. And while we are sitting on the side of the highway, flashers on, we get hit."

A car strikes the bus at 130 kilometres an hour. Both the driver of the car, apparently distracted, and its passenger are killed instantly. A number of Vikings players on the bus are injured. Chris is hurt the worst. He is standing near the front when the car hits and is launched into the air. When he comes to, his body is halfway out the front door of the bus. The most severe of his injuries is compartment syndrome in his right leg, where the muscle won't stop swelling. To avoid amputation, doctors cut the leg open and let the muscle swell outside the body.

"The pain is so bad. They tell me I'm in shock," he says. It takes him a year to fully recover.

"I am already drinking enough before the accident. But now I am the guy who said, 'Hey, let's stop the bus.' For the longest time, I tell myself I killed those people. If I had said, 'Stop' a mile earlier or later, maybe it doesn't happen."

The guilt leads to more drinking. And the injury adds painkillers to his addiction equation.

"I am over-prescribed and I just keep taking them for months. It spirals fast. I'm a complete mess. I have episodes where I just lose it and smash things. Look through old tapes of 'Rider [Saskatchewan Roughriders] games, and you'll find me getting hauled away by police."

Rock bottom comes in the ultimate cliché location: Vegas.

"I go down for a hockey tournament and I'm drunk and

high and in a club, paying a deejay $100 a song to play George Strait over and over. It doesn't make everyone at the club very happy. Apparently, they don't want to hear another round of 'Troubadour.' Heated words are exchanged, and now I am being chased by a bunch of angry men and women. I just start running, out of the club and across the street. I just miss by inches being plowed over by a bus. A few blocks down, I sit down on a curb and say, 'What am I doing? I just spent seven hundred dollars to hear "Troubadour" played seven times. I lost four grand at the table. What the fuck has happened to me?' So I see a cab and jump in and just yell, 'Airport. Let's go.' I don't even go get my stuff. I just fly home."

It's April 5, 2014. The last time Chris Beaudry drank or used.

Through Alcoholics Anonymous and a book called *The Mindful Athlete* by George Mumford, he comes to understand his demons and how to fight them.

"I realize that I would beat myself up all day whenever something would go wrong. I'd be, 'Yeah, you deserve that. You're a fucking loser!' When I'd have a bad crop because of the weather, I'd think, 'This is God getting back at you for being such a piece of shit.' The pills and the booze and that lack of self-esteem had made me a train wreck. But as soon as you become aware of those patterns—you realize, 'Okay, my drinking was a pattern, my thinking is a pattern'—now we can start to implement change."

As Chris recovers, he starts coaching again and lands a spot on the board of a Junior A team, the Humboldt Broncos. He takes a hockey analytics course and has to interview a range of people for it. One of them is Broncos coach Darcy Haugan. The two bond instantly.

"He just thinks the way I think," Chris says. "Now that I am sober and have a new outlook on life, his thoughts mirror mine. That wins aren't the most important thing in hockey. That you don't develop prospects, you develop *people*. And when you have good people, the wins follow."

In 2017, Darcy hires Chris to be one of his assistants, with an arrangement that will let him continue to farm.

"Darcy is just such an honest guy, no bullshit coach answers for anything," Chris says. "And everything is fun. We would be in the middle of a serious hockey discussion and some Billy Idol video comes on and everything halts. We're suddenly singing old tunes. This is a daily occurrence with him.

"I steal my coaching motto from the book *InSideOut Coaching*, by Joe Ehrmann. He writes, 'I coach boys to be men of empathy and integrity who will lead, be responsible, and change the world for good.' That's what Darcy and I want. And he wants someone who has an understanding of addictions. You are coaching 17- to 20-year-old boys. We know that not everyone is a saint. Drugs and alcohol are a factor in junior hockey. But this team is so close, there are enough good people, that the guys who have issues find their peers within the room. Nothing ever comes to us. That is very rare. It's a very close team."

Chris becomes tight with a bunch of the Broncos. In Bryce Fiske, he sees a little of himself—a fun-loving kid with a mischievous side. Jacob Leicht and Morgan Gobeil are among those he had coached years before in the SaskFirst Hockey Program. He loves all the players. They are his younger brothers.

===

And now he sits alone in a fire truck, where they have told him he must stay. Staring out the window at the unimaginable.

"I can see people being moved, some being lined up and covered, others rushed off. These are my boys, but I'm too far away to be able to tell who is who."

His mind stops functioning rationally.

"There are these green bags everywhere, the sod from the truck that hit the bus. But I keep thinking, over and over, 'Why are there so many hockey bags?' I just can't piece anything together. None of it makes any sense."

That feeling of cowardice that hit him as he came upon the scene stays with him the whole night. He goes through the motions—"pretending," he calls it—doing what the police ask, identifying the injured at the hospital, consoling the broken at the church.

And then, at 5 a.m., the coroner calls. He asks Chris to come to the morgue. They need him to identify the bodies. He is the only one left to do it.

"That was when the cowardice flips, and I realize I have a job to do. My sister comes with me. The first few bodies are the ones the doctors have been able to clean, and they just get progressively worse. And I go through these different stages of shock. This feeling of coldness comes over me that won't leave me for months. I take straight hot-water baths and not feel any heat. Just a chill through my whole body for weeks.

"I remember seeing Conner Lukan, who is one of the toughest kids I ever met, and he doesn't even look hurt. And I am looking at him, thinking, 'Get up, Conner. Help me. You're fucking fine. I need you. I don't want to do this alone.' I really believe he is just lying there, waiting for me to come and get him up. That's the denial part of grief."

One of the last bodies Chris sees, we know now, is Parker Tobin's. But the coroner tells him it is Xavier Labelle's.

"I say, 'No, it's not. This isn't Xavier.' But they insist from everything they've gathered that it has to be. So, I start to think it's my mind again. Everything is mixed up. This must be part of that."

Days later, it's revealed the two players have been tragically mixed up. Tobin has passed away. Labelle is alive.

Sixteen members of the Broncos family die in the accident:

» Tyler Bieber, a 29-year-old play-by-play announcer from Humboldt, Saskatchewan;
» Logan Boulet, a 21-year-old defenceman from Lethbridge, Alberta;

» Dayna Brons, a 24-year-old athletic therapist from Lake Lenore, Saskatchewan;
» Mark Cross, a 27-year-old assistant coach from Strasbourg, Saskatchewan;
» Glen Doerksen, a 59-year-old bus driver from Carrot River, Saskatchewan;
» Darcy Haugan, the team's 42-year-old head coach, from Humboldt, Saskatchewan;
» Adam Herold, a 16-year-old defenceman from Montmartre, Saskatchewan;
» Brody Hinz, the team's 18-year-old statistician, from Humboldt, Saskatchewan;
» Logan Hunter, an 18-year-old forward from St. Albert, Alberta;
» Jaxon Joseph, a 20-year-old forward from St. Albert, Alberta;
» Jacob Leicht, a 19-year-old forward from Humboldt, Saskatchewan;
» Conner Lukan, a 21-year-old forward from Slave Lake, Alberta;
» Logan Schatz, a 20-year-old forward from Allan, Saskatchewan;
» Evan Thomas, an 18-year-old forward from Saskatoon, Saskatchewan;
» Parker Tobin, an 18-year-old goalie from Stony Plain, Alberta;
» Stephen Wack, a 21-year-old defenceman from St. Albert, Alberta.

Thirteen others are injured, many seriously.

Chris wanders, "zombie-like," in the days after. A few of the Broncos parents ask him to gather items from their boys' stalls in the dressing room. He searches for something, anything, that might bring someone a smile.

"As I'm leaving, I look up and see this 'Believe' sign above the door leading out to the ice. Darcy had brought the team together a month before the playoffs and told them, 'You guys gotta believe you aren't a fifth-place team. Because when we believe in ourselves, we can't be stopped.' We found this old piece of the boards that we cleaned up and wrote 'Believe' on it with a big Jiffy marker and hung it above our door. So, the day after the accident, I get a rink worker to come in and remove the sign. You aren't supposed to take things out of the room, so I sneak it out the back door under my jacket."

Chris brings the sign to the waiting room of the intensive care unit, where the families have all gathered. He tells them what the sign meant to the team. And what it means now.

"I tell them I believe everyone is going to get out of this hospital. Everyone is going home, and we will pass this sign around until they all go home."

And that's exactly what the Broncos and their families do. One by one, as the injured boys heal.

On the outside, Chris is trying to play the role of inspirational coach. "Be strong and lead," like Darcy would have. But he feels out of body, floating helplessly through various stages of shock.

"I kind of came up with this idea that shock is like a math equation," he says. "Your grandpa dies, 10 people reach out. You maybe feel shock for half a day. A parent dies 20 years before they should, 50 people reach out, and you feel shock for a few days. A child dies, a thousand people reach out, and you feel shock for weeks. Well, we had millions of people reaching out, and this shock lasted in different stages for months and months and months."

For that shock, he is forever grateful.

"I know thoughts are real. I know love is real. I know compassion is real. And there were millions of people sending out thoughts, love and compassion. And I have to send a thank you to all of them, because they kept me in shock. A mind can break in a situation like that. A heart can't. And their love, compassion and thoughts kept my mind from breaking."

Five months after the accident, the Broncos hold a ceremony for the victims and survivors of the crash after the team's home opener. Twenty-nine banners are unveiled, one for each Bronco on the bus.

Chris, the 30th Bronco, stands arm in arm with the surviving players at one end of the rink—watching, sobbing.

He's still lost. But in the months that follow, the shock, anger and endless grief start to fade, ever so slowly. Chris begins to breathe again.

He meditates. He uses the concepts he has learned in Alcoholics Anonymous and the coaching books he has read. He can now recognize when moments of anger and grief and the desire to drink and use are coming. And when he is aware of them, he can stop them.

"I just didn't want to feel that way anymore," he says. "I wanted to talk about it. I would go to AA and weird everyone out because all I wanted to talk about was death. So, my sister and a counsellor I was working with created a group to share grief. We call it Rise Together. We take the steps that Elisabeth Kübler-Ross set up for grieving, and we add shock to it. We set it up like an AA meeting. You can just bare your soul to people."

The group isn't just for the Broncos family. Anyone going through grief can come. But several relatives of those who died in the crash show up. Chris holds nothing back.

"I could talk to moms and tell them what it felt like, being the first person who knew their boy to see them after they passed. And they would tell me their stories. I was taking that pain from the pit of your stomach, putting it right in front of your face, and you're looking at it. And that, to me, is moving through grief. And just like in AA, what I found is I would learn something about myself from someone else's story. Someone would say a phrase that would just click—'That's what I'm feeling right now! That's what's happening with me and what I can't get past.'

"I would hear that from people who had lost family members 20 years ago, 10 years ago, five years ago, and we kept hearing that it will get better. And that helped give us hope. Maybe it's a month away. Maybe it's a year away. But someday I'm not going to feel like this 24 hours a day. Maybe at first, it'll still be 23 hours and 55 minutes. But that's going to be the best fucking five minutes I'm going to live. And then I'm going to stretch it out farther and farther."

Chris has been through hell. The years of self-loathing. The drinking and drugs that came with it. The horrific coincidence of two team bus accidents. But he knows that the families who lost sons, daughters, husbands and dads—and the boys who were on that bus and survived to remember it—went through worse. And are still going through it. He wants to make it clear he would never try to tell their story. Only his own.

And for right now—because *right now* is all Chris Beaudry believes in—his story ends like this:

"I'm gonna be okay."

The Lone Ranger (Fan)

ESPN's Steve Levy

It's early in the morning on June 20, 1999. The most controversial goal in Stanley Cup history has just been scored, and the guy about to talk about it on ESPN hasn't really seen it. He catches a glimpse of the play live, on a tiny five-inch black-and-white monitor in the bowels of the rink. But then, instantly, he has to switch into work mode. Now he's about to interview the hero, who probably—maybe? . . . arguably?—shouldn't have been the hero. Except the broadcaster doesn't know that yet. Nor does the hero.

Wait. I've already confused you. So, hold that scene for a moment, and let's flash back to the early '80s.

Steve Levy is a hockey-crazy high schooler on Long Island, New York. A boy in love with the wrong team.

"I'm a diehard Rangers fan," Levy says. "And that isn't easy on Long Island. My four years in high school are the years of the four Islanders Stanley Cups in a row! I'm a total outcast, the only Rangers fan in the whole school. The Nassau Coliseum is 15 minutes from me. And yet, all I want to do is jump on the train and go meet my dad in the big city. My Rangers are just awful, losing to the Islanders every year. So, that's my childhood. Wearing my Carol Vadnais jersey everywhere. An outcast Rangers fan."

The Lone Ranger (fan) studies broadcasting and applies for a play-by-play job with the Rangers' farm team in Binghamton, New York, while still in college.

"I come eighth on their list," Levy laughs. "Not even kidding. The job would have paid 12 grand a year, working year round, doing sales in the off-season. You room on the road with the bus driver, which my mom has an issue with. And none of it matters because I finish eighth!"

Yet, somehow, the kid who can't come close to securing a small-town gig ends up landing a job in New York City with WNBC radio, rare for a budding broadcaster right out of college. He would eventually do updates on the legendary *Mike and the Mad Dog* show at WFAN radio and anchor at WCBS-TV.

"Never having to leave New York, it's unheard of on air. It's the luckiest, flukiest thing ever," Levy says.

It's neither luck nor a fluke. The kid from Long Island is a natural at sports broadcasting, no matter what they think in Binghamton. In 1993, he gets a job with ESPN. The timing is perfect. A year later, his beloved Rangers are on a historic playoff run.

"I go to the 'Messier guarantee' game as a fan with my friends. I'm at the 'Matteau, Matteau, Matteau' game as a fan," Levy says. "Then ESPN assigns me to cover Game 7 of the Cup final! The dream! I'm going to get to see my Rangers lift the Cup!

"But I don't. I never see it. Because you have to be downstairs in the Rangers dressing room with 10 minutes left on the clock. And then it gets worse. I'm there to interview players, and we get Adam Graves, who had a brilliant season and is maybe the third or fourth most important member of that team. He's standing there, waiting for me to go on live with him, and *SportsCenter*, being what it is, with different sports priorities, isn't coming to me.

"So, we're waiting. Five minutes. Ten minutes! And poor Graves is just standing there, instead of celebrating the first Rangers Cup in 50 years! Champagne is flowing everywhere. My producer, Tom McNeeley, keeps saying, 'They're coming, Steve.

SportsCenter knows you have him.' But they don't come. And we're in the middle of Cleveland Indians highlights! So, I'm just dying, mostly out of respect for Graves. And then Graves takes my microphone, puts it down, leans over and whispers to me, 'Hey, I know how important this night is for you, too.' It just blows my mind. How does this guy, who just won the Cup and is waiting for an eternity to do an interview, have any idea who I am and what my background is? It's just unbelievable. Just the classiest guy."

Finally, *SportsCenter* comes to Levy and Graves. Hours later, when his TV work is done, the long-suffering Rangers fan from Long Island gets to drink from the Cup.

"Highly unprofessional, but worth it," he says.

The most memorable story of Levy's long career would also come during a post-game interview in a Stanley Cup–winning dressing room. Which is where we started this tale.

The now-veteran ESPN host is in the Dallas Stars room. They have just beaten the Sabres, 2–1, in triple overtime to win the Stanley Cup in six games. And Steve is going live with the post-game celebration.

"I would usually cover the winning locker room, and the deal back then, when we had the broadcast rights, is that you have to be in the room early, depending on how big the lead is. If it's a three-goal lead, you have to be in the winning locker room with 15 minutes left. A two-goal lead, 10 minutes. A one-goal lead, five minutes. Well, this one is triple OT, so I've been down there a while."

One of sportscasting's sad secrets is that, just because you are covering the biggest games, you don't always get to witness their endings. Most Super Bowls I cover, I watch the first 55 minutes from the stands, but I see the final, pivotal moments on a small monitor hanging in the bowels of the stadium, while I wait in a cattle line to rush onto the field.

All Levy knows is that Brett Hull has scored the Cup-winning goal, the one he barely saw, and he's about to interview him live.

"And then, in my ear [piece], I hear our reporter Al Morganti in the Buffalo locker room saying that the Sabres are going nuts because Hull's foot was in the crease. And now Brett Hull is beside me, the hero of the game, I'm getting him first, and I'm about to start my interview.

"So I say, 'Hully, I have to ask you this. The Sabres are saying your foot was in the crease.' And Brett says, 'No way, Steve. No chance!' And in those days at ESPN, we don't have a monitor. But we're on a podium and the guys next to me—I believe it's *Hockey Night in Canada*—do have a monitor. So, we're on camera on ESPN, live, and I'm pointing at *Hockey Night*'s monitor. We're both staring at the monitor on live TV, watching the replays for the first time. Brett says, 'Look, Steve, my foot's not in the crease! It's not in the crease! Oh yeah, it's in the crease.'"

Levy feels awful that he is the guy to dampen the greatest moment of Hull's career. Then again, Hull doesn't really care. They aren't taking his Cup away. He just gives a "too late now" shrug and goes off to get doused with champagne.

"I still feel like that is one of the darker days in the history of the Cup final," Levy says. "With the way the rules were called then, there is no way that should have counted. Brett and I have talked about it over the years, how I was the guy who told him the crowning achievement in his career probably shouldn't have counted, but he's forgiven me. It's funny; to this day, at odd places in Buffalo, like some AAA Buffalo Bisons baseball game, you will get people holding up signs that say, 'NO GOAL!'"

Levy now covers a bunch of sports for ESPN. In 2019, he calls his first *Monday Night Football* game. But a big chunk of his heart is still with hockey.

Every June, he's back in whatever NHL arena they are handing the Cup out in, reporting with his long-time partner, Barry Melrose. The eighth-place finisher in the Binghamton Rangers' play-by-play auditions, ready to go live.

As soon as the baseball highlights are over.

Timing Is Everything

Brad Richards's World Cup Hiccup

Brad Richards is in full panic mode. He paces outside the elevator on his floor of the Fairmont Château Laurier hotel in Ottawa, pressing the down button over and over, sweat dripping through his suit—the second one he's put on this morning. A great night out with one of his idols has quickly morphed into the worst morning of his hockey career.

"I think I'm having a heart attack," Richards says. "I'm about to look like the biggest idiot ever in front of some of the best hockey players in the world. Everything is unravelling."

The timing of Richards's terrible, horrible, no-good, very bad day is curious, as it comes right in the middle of his wonderful, incredible, never-bad, really awesome year.

It is September 2004. Two months and change ago, Richards led the Tampa Bay Lightning to their first Stanley Cup. He won the Conn Smythe Trophy as playoff MVP. Now he has been named to Canada's World Cup team, along with his teammate and one of his best friends, Martin St. Louis.

"Even though we've just won the Cup, we are still kids, and not used to being around these stars. If you play in an Original Six market, you have famous alumni around, coming in the dressing room. I'd see that later in my career in New York, Chicago and Detroit. But not in Tampa. So, when we get to camp for the

World Cup, we aren't used to being around all these superstars."

It gets real—fast. At Canada's first practice, Richards and St. Louis are put on a line with Mario Lemieux.

"We are just shitting ourselves," Richards says. "We just can't believe we're playing with Mario. We get the first-line rush on a fresh sheet of ice and Marty toe-picks and falls, and I throw this terrible pass right into Mario's feet. Just horrible. It's a simple drill, and we're just a mess for the first three rushes. Mario is like, 'What's wrong with you guys? Settle down.' We looked like some beer leaguers who had won a contest to practise with Mario Lemieux."

"I keep saying to Richie, 'I'm so nervous. I can't do this,'" St. Louis says. "And after we missed about three straight passes, I skate up to Mario and say, 'Mario, I'm so sorry.' And he says, 'Just relax, kid.' Richie and I eventually settle down, but man, did we feel stupid."

A couple of days later, Team Canada is set to fly to Columbus, Ohio, to play a pre-tournament game against Team USA. Canada has five lines for the tournament, and the coaches tell Lemieux, St. Louis and Richards that they can sit the first game out.

"Marty and I still have to go to the game, but Mario doesn't—he is just going to stay and hang out with the prime minister or something," Richards says. "I mean, he's Mario. But the night before the trip, Mario says to us, 'Let's go out.' Marty and I are like little kids, we're so excited."

"Mario says, 'Meet me in 30 minutes in the lobby,'" St. Louis adds. "Richie and I start high-fiving in the elevator! We're going bar-hopping with Mario Lemieux!"

"It's just the best night," Richards says. "He has this cool hat on, just a legend. I would stay out until nine in the morning if he wants to. In the end, we just have a few beers, nothing crazy, but what a great time."

The next morning, Richards has a 6:45 a.m. wake-up call for a 7:30 bus ride to the airport for the flight to Columbus. Critical fact for this story: most hockey teams and hockey players are militaristic with their schedules. And Richards is a loyal soldier.

"Being on time is everything to me," he says. "I'm the kind of guy who has to always be early," he says. "I had Torts [John Tortorella] as coach since my rookie year, and he insisted we be 10 minutes early to everything. Every meeting, every bus. And it stuck with me."

Richards's Team Canada roommate, Kirk Maltby, goes down for breakfast, but Brad figures he'll just grab something on the plane. Since he isn't playing that night, he's not concerned about getting his proper pre-game meals in.

"I have this new suit that I got just for the World Cup," Richards says. "I haven't even tried it on. So I lay it out and put my passport in the pocket and jump in the shower. I'm not really hungover or anything, but I guess I'm a little foggy from our night with Mario, because I'm running a few minutes behind. No biggie, though. I'm fine.

"I get out of the shower and put on my suit, and I can't get the belt through the loops. It isn't the right size belt for the suit. And now it's almost 7:20 and I'm starting to rush a little, because I should be down there by now. So, I'm struggling with the belt and the loops, and then . . . *riiiiiip!* I tear the suit right down the seam, all the way to my ass! Now I'm panicking. I grab another suit and sprint down and get there at 7:28. I'm the last one. Everyone is on the bus. It's our first game together, so everyone is ready to go."

Richards is already embarrassed. The team has been on the bus for a while, and there is only one seat left—near the very back, right in front of his idol, Joe Sakic. So he does the walk of shame past a who's who of Canadian hockey. But at least he isn't late.

Then, as the bus begins to pull away, one of the team officials yells, "Everybody got their passports?" Richards grabs for his suit pocket, and . . . uh-oh. When the first suit ripped, he left the passport in it.

161

"My heart just sinks," he says. "I can't stop this bus with the best players on the world on it because I'm an idiot and forgot my passport. Maybe I just won't say anything and it'll be fine . . . I'll somehow get through customs. But if I don't, that's even worse. Oh God, I have to do this. I have to stop the bus."

And so, the Conn Smythe Trophy winner sheepishly gets out of his seat and says, "Sorry, guys, I forgot it." He can't even look at Sakic. He keeps his head down as he sprints past Scott Niedermayer, Jarome Iginla, Martin Brodeur . . .

"It's my first time in an environment like this, playing for Canada at this huge event, and I'm a total embarrassment," he says. "This is our first bus ride as a team. There is nothing worse than this. It would be bad enough on your own team, but at least they know you and would know you've never done it before. But these guys don't know me. They are probably all thinking, 'Who is this absent-minded assclown?'"

Associate coach Ken Hitchcock is the first to chirp.

"Hitch says, 'There's always one idiot,' or something like that, and I just want to crawl under the seats and disappear. I run back in the hotel, and the elevator is taking forever. I'm in a full sweat. I still get shivers talking about it."

The bus waits. Richards eventually gets back on it. Then the real ribbing begins.

"They are all over me the whole day," he says. "Gretz is relentless. 'You win a Stanley Cup, and now you make your own rules!' he keeps saying, always laughing, but non-stop needling. I mostly tune them out because I am so mad at myself. I am just in a bubble the whole day, going over this calamity of events. I am completely mortified for three or four days."

The rest of the tournament goes much more smoothly for Richards. He and St. Louis only get to play one pre-tournament game with Mario. Lemieux ends up on the left wing with Sakic and Iginla for most of the tournament. Simon Gagné plays with Richards and St. Louis.

Richards gets four points in six games, including a key assist on a Lemieux power-play goal in the semis. Canada wins the World Cup, beating Finland, 3–2, in the final.

"The whole thing is just amazing. I'm 24. To win the Cup, and then two months later to get to play with some of your idols wearing the Team Canada jersey, and to win that tournament. Unreal."

Oh, and he was the first one on the bus to that final. Fifteen minutes early.

The Accountant

Beer Leaguer Scott Foster's
14 Minutes of Fame

On a Saturday night in February 2020, a 42-year-old former Zamboni driver named Dave Ayres comes in as an emergency backup goalie—an EBUG—for the Carolina Hurricanes against Toronto. The Hurricanes win, 6–3. Dave is an instant legend. But he is quick to point out that he has practised with the Leafs dozens of times, knows all the players, all their tendencies. He isn't some random beer leaguer who has never seen an NHL shot. Still, Dave becomes a celebrity, appearing on countless talk shows, telling his story over and over.

So, we won't tell it again.

This is the story of another EBUG, one who really *was* a random beer leaguer who'd never seen an NHL shot. He didn't do the talk show circuit. After his 15 minutes of fame (14:01, actually), he turned down most interviews, preferring to return to his quiet life. And keeping much of his story to himself. Until now.

The accountant walks his little girl to school, and gets mobbed in the drop-off area. All the other kids want his autograph. Morgan giggles, loving the attention her daddy gets. He feels awkward, embarrassed. He tries to downplay it, tries to explain to the other parents that he's not really who the kids think he is. I mean, he is that guy. But he's not really . . . well, it's complicated. He's spent months trying to help his daughters understand the difference between their dad and the real Blackhawks.

"But Daddy, you were a Blackhawk!"

How do you explain the nuances of one of the craziest Cinderella stories in NHL history to a five-year-old?

He sighs. Smiles. Concedes.

"You're right, sweetie. For one night, Daddy was a Blackhawk."

Daddy *is* a Blackhawk. From the very beginning. Scott Foster is six years old when he plays on his first hockey team, the Point Edward Blackhawks. Point Edward Arena sits underneath the Blue Water Bridge in Sarnia, Ontario, three hours west of Toronto. The Blackhawks have the same colours and same logo as the NHL team. Legendary foreshadowing.

In most minor novice house leagues, a different kid plays goal every week. Many of them hate it. They stand awkwardly in their oversized pads, crying, begging their parents to rescue them. Not Scott. He instantly loves the feel of the equipment, the thrill he gets from diving on the ice to make a save. He gets a shutout.

"I'm hooked," Scott says. "I stake my claim to the net right after that game. And I haven't left the crease since. My parents still have this photo of me in all my equipment, proudly wearing my Blackhawks jersey."

They actually have two now. But we're still 30 years away from that part.

"We have this video of him from when he's really little, just learning to skate, and he's holding his stick halfway down, like it's a goalie stick," Scott's dad, Greg, says. "So it's clear from the beginning where he belongs."

"I get my first set of goalie gloves for Christmas and don't take them off for a week," Scott says. "I buy a set of pads from this older kid down the street. I pay his dad one dollar for them. They are these old, brown-leather, deer hair–stuffed pads. They soak up every bit of water on the ice. I can barely lift my legs. But I don't care. They are the best things I've ever had."

For the next 15 years, Scott's only dream is to play in the NHL. He excels in minor hockey. Plays Junior B. Gets a scholarship to Western Michigan. But after barely seeing the ice his last two years there, he realizes it's time for real life. He gets a master's degree in accounting and moves to Chicago with his girlfriend, Erin, a track star he met at WMU.

Johnny's Icehouse has the best men's beer leagues in Chicago. Goalies are in high demand. Scott fills out a "free agent form," and the calls come fast. He subs in one night for a team whose goalie can't make it. In the dressing room afterwards, the team's manager says he'll cut the other goalie immediately if Scott agrees to stay. Beer-league managers are ruthless. He ends up playing for a couple of teams. It's decent hockey, full of ex-college and minor-pro players.

Life is good. Scott marries Erin in the fall of 2009. He gets a green card, works for a couple of different firms. They have a baby daughter, Morgan. Johnny's gives him his hockey fix, a couple of nights a week.

In October 2015, Scott and Erin go for dinner and a movie—*The Martian*—to celebrate their anniversary. Erin is expecting their second daughter, Wynni, in a few weeks. Date nights are about to get scarce.

"We're in the middle of the movie, and his phone just lights up," Erin says.

"I get this email from 'Mark Bernard, Chicago Blackhawks,'" Scott says. "What?"

Six months earlier, Scott watched his beloved Toronto Maple Leafs play the Florida Panthers on TV. Panthers goalie Roberto Luongo was injured and taken to hospital. His backup, Al Montoya, also went down. Luongo ended up rushing back to finish the game. It prompts the NHL to create a rule requiring teams to have a list of EBUGs available for every home game. The Blackhawks are scrambling to put together their list. They call the guy who runs Johnny's, and Scott's is one of the names he gives them.

"I never believe this is my path to the NHL," Scott says. "I just figure it's going to be a fun fact that if seven goalies get hurt, I'm on this list to maybe go to the rink."

Scott's only contact with the Blackhawks is an annual email asking if he still wants to be on their EBUG list. But in 2017, he gets a different email. The rules have changed. Now the NHL wants an emergency goalie in the rink for every game.

"My first reaction is, 'I'm done with this,'" Scott says. "I have a job and two young daughters. I don't need this. It's gone from a cool story to an actual time commitment."

He starts to type back: "Sorry, no longer interested." But Erin stops him.

"I say, 'Are you crazy? Of course you are doing this!'" Erin says. "I travel all the time for my job, and he does a lot of the child rearing. I call him SuperDad. So why should he not get to do something he loves?'"

The new person handling Chicago's EBUG list is Meghan Hunter, GM Stan Bowman's assistant. Scott recognizes her name and asks, "Are you the Meghan Hunter that is the niece of Mark and Dale Hunter . . . Ron Hunter's daughter?" She is. The Hunters are from the area where Scott grew up. Meghan's dad ran summer conditioning skates Scott took part in. He hated them. Couldn't walk afterwards.

This tiny detail is just a footnote in Scott's story. Or maybe it's everything. Because when Scott says that yes, he'll come to some games to be an EBUG, Meghan gives him first choice of the games he wants to do.

Scott picks 15 games. For his first 14, he is basically a fan with a free ticket and a good parking spot.

"I get to park down where the players park, which is cool," he says. "Frankie, the parking attendant guy, grabs my gear, and I just take the elevator right up to the press box and eat popcorn and watch the game. I sit right behind Blackhawks goaltending coach Jimmy Waite, who doesn't even know I'm there. I just sit and wait for the food to come out in the second intermission. Always love a cup of peanut M&Ms."

March 29, 2018, is like any other never-gonna-play game day for Scott. He works his normal 9-to-5 shift, sitting in his cubicle, crunching numbers. He takes the Green Line train back to the Oak Park station, hooks up a little trailer to his bicycle, picks up his daughters from daycare and rides home. When Erin gets back from work, Scott throws his gear in the car and begins the 25-minute drive to the rink. He's on the 290, almost at the United Center, when his phone rings.

It's Kyle Davidson from the Blackhawks. He says, "One of the goalies might be hurt, so you may be downstairs tonight. We'll meet you at the loading dock."

Scott's heart starts to beat a little faster. This time, Frankie, the parking guy, rushes to grab his gear.

"I can feel he has some urgency, and they're trying to confirm my last name—I guess for the sweater," Scott says. "Now they're taking me down through the building, telling me Anton Forsberg is definitely out. I'm the backup. My head is spinning. I've never even been down here by the dressing room before."

Scott signs a one-day contract, an unpaid amateur tryout. "They can never say I was a salary cap problem," he laughs.

Mike Gapski, Chicago's trainer, asks him if he wants to warm up in the weight room.

"I'm like, 'Nope, I'm good.' I play beer league. We have a three-minute warm-up after the Zamboni gets off. Those dynamic warm-up days are over for me. Gappy's like, 'Ohhh-*kayyy* then.'"

He takes Scott into the Blackhawks dressing room. His sweater is already hanging in a stall: FOSTER 90.

"It's unbelievable," he says. "I haven't had my name on a sweater since college. Not sure how I feel about number 90, but I'm not going to complain."

One by one, the Hawks players come over to say a quick hello. Patrick Kane, Brent Seabrook, Patrick Sharp . . .

"I remember welcoming Scott, but we're really not paying much attention to the emergency goalie," Sharp says. "The big story of the night is Brent Seabrook's 1,000th game. So we're just excited for him."

"I really want to take pics, but I resist," Scott says. "I shove my phone up the arm of my chest protector, in case I get a chance later."

One Blackhawk notices Scott's Western Michigan bag and comes over for a chat. His name is Jordan Oesterle, a young defenceman and fellow WMU alumni. Besides that, Scott blends quietly into the background. With Forsberg's injury, rookie Collin Delia is about to make his first NHL start. Add that to Seabrook's 1,000th, and the emergency goalie dressing will likely just be a cute footnote in the game reports after.

The Hawks decide Scott will watch the game from the players' lounge, adjacent to the dressing room. If a goalie takes a warm-up or sits on the bench, and then is forced into the game, he has to play right away. This way, if the worst happens, Scott at least will get a warm-up.

"When they tell me I won't be sitting on the bench, it's crushing," he says. "I've never said this before in my hockey career, but I was dying to sit on that bench. Just to watch a game from there would be amazing."

He listens to coach Joel Quenneville's pre-game speech, then retreats to the lounge. The other injured Blackhawks are there—captain Jonathan Toews, goalies Corey Crawford and Forsberg—all in their suits. Scott is in full gear.

"I probably could have taken off the top part, but this is probably the only time I'm going to wear this sweater, so it's not coming off all night. I somehow have to get a photo in it."

Scott makes small talk with the other players and stands for the anthems, which gives the vets a chuckle. He turns down a meal. Still too nervous. He'll regret that later. He hasn't eaten since before lunch. And then he sits on a lounge chair and watches the game, just like at home. Except in full goalie gear, next to Jonathan Toews.

"Playing never even enters my mind," Scott says.

He misses a sign. In the second intermission, Scott returns to the dressing room to find Delia being fed sports drinks, fighting dehydration.

"It doesn't register with me," he says. "I'm still just thinking about getting a photo in the sweater."

Blackhawks equipment manager Troy Parchman tells Scott during the intermission that he can keep the sweater and socks after the game, but the team has to fly to Colorado right away, so they'll be gone quickly. "It just reminds me it's all coming to an end soon."

Six minutes into the third, Delia takes a shot and doubles over in pain. Patrick Sharp skates right over to him.

"I ask, 'Is it your knee?'" Sharp says. And Collin goes, 'No, it's cramps.' So I say, 'Well, drink some water because you aren't coming out. We don't have another goalie!'"

Technically inaccurate. The other goalie is staring at the TV in the players' lounge, in disbelief.

"I remember one of the guys making a joke about Delia getting hit in the crotch," Scott says. "But I know that's not what just happened. That's the moment it hits me. He's cramping! My heart starts to race. He's not getting up. The guys around me are going crazy. They realize this beer leaguer next to them might be going in. Toews would apologize to me later, saying he felt bad because he probably made me more nervous. But I don't even notice them. That room may as well have been dark and empty. I'm in my own world, just staring at Delia lying on the ice, thinking, 'Is this actually happening?'"

The answer comes fast. One of the equipment managers sprints into the room.

"You're going in!" he says. Scott doesn't move. The trainer has to repeat it a couple of times. "Foster, you are going in the game! *Now!*"

Scott snaps back to semi-consciousness and heads into the dressing room to grab his gloves, helmet and stick.

"I'm trying hard to look cool and composed, but inside my body, it's a disaster zone," he says. "I start freaking out when one of the equipment guys grabs my beer-league game stick, an old model left over from college a dozen years ago. I grab it from him. But when I realize it has a crack in the shaft, I grab my other stick that is also broken, but . . . less broken."

The accountant emerges from the tunnel and shuffles along the Blackhawks bench. Joel Quenneville is smiling, almost giggling. It's been a long season in Chicago. This is a much-needed distraction for everyone. Except Scott.

"I cannot comprehend a single thing that's happening," he says. "As I step on the ice, I realize I was going to go get my skates sharpened the night before, but didn't bother to. Now I'm skating to the net in front of 20,000 people, and my blades are not beer league–worthy, let alone NHL-worthy. Oh well, too late now."

Back at home, Erin has been watching the game with Scott's parents, who are visiting for Easter weekend.

"I'm sitting on the sofa with Scott's mom, and his father is in the lounge chair, and all of a sudden, Collin goes down. I'm like, 'Holy crap, he's hurt! Holy crap, Scott's going in!' My father-in-law is staring at the television, in shock."

"We are both in shock!" says Scott's mom, Christine. "We get Scott's sister and her family on FaceTime from New Zealand. And Greg just holds his iPad up at the TV so they can watch the game."

Erin sprints upstairs and wakes their oldest daughter, Morgan.

"It's a once-in-a-lifetime thing," Erin says. "I can't let her sleep through it. My heart is racing, my phone is blowing up. And Morgan is just staring at the TV, going, 'Why is Daddy on TV? Why is he wearing a Blackhawks jersey?' She's so confused."

Scott makes it to the net with his dull blades and cracked stick. A familiar face comes out to warm him up. It's Oesterle, his fellow Western Michigan alum.

"Jordan and one other player are taking shots, and every second puck is going in," Scott says. "I just can't get the cadence of how they are shooting. I think I stop six of 12. They say, 'Do you want more?' Which I think probably means, 'You really need more!' But I just say, 'No, let's just go.'"

"The guys on the bench are watching all these pucks beat him, and we're saying, 'Uh-oh,'" says Sharp. "No lead is safe."

It's 6–2, Chicago. There are 14 minutes left.

"I just want to face a shot, any shot," he says. "Then maybe my nerves will settle and maybe I can convince myself it's just hockey."

About a minute in, he gets one. Winnipeg defenceman Tyler Myers lets a wrist shot go from a terrible angle. It goes off Scott's stick, then his left pad. The stadium erupts.

Listen to the crowd as he makes his first save!
(PAT FOLEY, BLACKHAWKS PLAY-BY-PLAY VOICE)

Career save percentage: 1.000.

"He probably wouldn't have even bothered shooting from there on a real NHL goalie," Scott says. "But it's a really important moment to me, just to face a shot and save it."

A minute later, there's a turnover inside the Hawks blue line. Dustin Byfuglien steals the puck, turns and rips one towards the top corner. Scott gets a glove on it.

A Byfuglien takeaway . . . He shoots! And a save by Foster!

"Probably my biggest regret is that I don't catch that one," he says. "It would have looked really good if I snagged it. But I'll take knocking down a Byfuglien shot any day. At one point, he circles the net and I think, 'Man, that is one enormous human being.'"

Scott's nerves settle a little. But the TV time outs kill him. Too long to think, "Is this real? Am I playing goal in the NHL?" He makes a conscious decision not to go to the bench.

"There's no way I can handle having a conversation with anyone," he laughs.

With two minutes left, Jets forward Patrik Laine bursts down the right side and, as he gets below the goal line, backhands a perfect no-look pass in front. Paul Stastny is alone. Foster slides across the net.

Here's Laine . . . puts it in front . . . Save by Foster!

The Chicago bench erupts. Twenty thousand fans are going nuts—plus four more in the Fosters' home, and another three in New Zealand on the iPad.

"Every time the puck gets remotely near him, my heart stops," Erin says. "We are all in disbelief, just saying, 'Don't get hurt. Please don't get hurt.'"

With 1:25 left, Myers gets his second shot from the high slot. Scott is in perfect position, and it hits him square in the logo.

Here's a shot . . . Foster sucks up another one!

Seven shots, seven saves. The Jets don't get another one.

As the clock ticks down, the atmosphere feels more like a Game 7 than Game 78 for a team playing out the string. The buzzer goes. It's over.

Hawks win! Hawks win! And look at Scott Foster. He comes in and makes seven stops in a row to preserve a victory!

The accountant has a 14-minute shutout. Defenceman Connor Murphy is the first to get to Scott. The goalie looks at him, and just kind of shrugs.

"Connor has this huge grin on his face, and I just stare at him like, 'Well, that just happened.'"

He doesn't raise him arms. Doesn't fist-pump the sky. He just stands there, coolly, like he just won the Friday night game at Johnny's.

"That was the longest 14 minutes of my life," Scott says. "If you told me it took three hours, I would say, 'No . . . way longer than that.' I'm relieved it's over. It's hard to wrap my head around the magnitude of what just happened. Of going from Johnny's beer league . . . to the NHL."

Back at home, the Fosters can't believe what they've just seen.

"I think that's the proudest his dad has ever been," Erin says. "There are tears in his eyes, and the look on his face is just sheer joy. We are all cheering and crying. Except Morgan. She says, 'Can I go back to bed now?'"

Blackhawks director of media relations John Steinmiller stops Scott in the tunnel on the way off the ice.

"Stay here, Scott," Steinmiller says. "You're going back out. You're the first star."

And so, the little boy from Sarnia—the original Blackhawk, the kid who fell in love with the game and the position 30 years ago, who dreamed of this day until real life no longer allowed those kinds of crazy dreams—steps back on the ice, raises his cracked goalie stick to the crowd and smiles.

As he walks back towards the dressing room, Adam Rogowin, the Hawks' VP of communications, pulls Scott aside.

"I'm trying to find out if he's comfortable doing media," Rogowin says. "And all Scott says is, 'Do you mind grabbing my phone and taking a photo of me?' All he wants is a photo of himself in that Blackhawks sweater! I say, 'Buddy, I can get you a ton of action shots of you *playing* in your Blackhawks sweater!' I take the photo of him with my phone. I just think it's so cool that all he wants is that pic."

When Scott walks into the dressing room, it explodes with cheers. They give him a standing ovation and present him with their championship belt, given to each game's MVP.

"I just thank them and tell them how special it was," he says. "They probably block like 30 shots, with a four-goal lead in a meaningless game in late March. Guys like Duncan Keith, throwing their bodies in front of pucks for me. Unreal."

"Even I blocked a shot, which didn't happen often in my career!" Sharp says. "The crowd was going crazy, it was like we were back in the playoffs. We wanted it so bad for Scottie. Everyone wants to congratulate and talk to the emergency goalie after, so Seabrook's 1,000th game gets totally forgotten. The story of his career!"

Scott gives the game puck to Collin.

"It's his win," Scott says. "I'll take any puck from this game and call it my game puck. I don't care."

The media storms the room and surrounds Scott. They want to know everything about him.

REPORTER: *What are you going to tell your buddies tomorrow?*

SCOTT: *I made about 30 saves in a 1–0 win.*

REPORTER: *What's your day job?*

SCOTT: *I'm an accountant by day. A few hours ago, I was sitting at my computer typing on a 10-key; now I'm standing in front of you guys, just finished playing 14 minutes of NHL hockey.*

REPORTER: *Did you see Joel Quenneville just laughing as you stepped on the ice?*

SCOTT: *I think I would too.*

The Hawks have a spot outside the room where they take photos for special moments—first goals, first wins. Scott goes out and gets one more photo, holding one of the game pucks. When he returns to the room, it's empty. The team has left for the airport. NHL life rolls on. The emergency goalie is alone again.

"I spend five minutes looking for the showers," Scott laughs. "Probably another first for a supposed first star."

Rogowin walks Scott back to the parking lot. He tells him the story is blowing up. There are going to be endless media requests. And then Scott does a strange thing in an age when everyone tries to cash in on their 15—er, 14—minutes of fame. He says, "Nah, I'm good."

"I feel like I've answered all the questions and I'm happy," he says. "I don't want to show up everywhere until everyone is sick of me. It was an incredible moment. But it's time to get back to being a beer leaguer, an accountant, a dad."

Scott comes in through the basement entrance to his house, like always. He wants to run and hug his family. And then he remembers, "Oh yeah, better hang my gear up to dry first." Erin comes downstairs. "Sooo . . . how was your night?" she deadpans, smiling ear to ear.

"There are so many little things that aligned perfectly," Scott says. "Like having my parents up to visit . . . to watch with my wife and daughter. For me to come home to them all after playing in the NHL."

No one is quite sure what to say.

"I just hug him and say, 'You did great,'" Scott's mom, Christine, says.

And then Scott's father, Greg, says the daddest of all dad things in the history of dads: "They said you had seven shots. I only counted six."

Scott shakes his head and laughs.

"They have been the best, most supportive parents my whole life, never yelling and screaming, just telling me to work hard and have fun. And now, in this incredible moment for all of us, he's grinding my shot count."

He tells Dad one of Laine's blasts grazed his head. It's seven. They laugh and sit up for hours, listening to Scott's stories of his night in the big league.

He would say yes to a couple of media requests, including one from the *Ellen* show, because they want his whole family on. He thinks it would be cool for Erin and the girls. Ellen's producers call and do pre-interviews, but make no promises. And then the weekend goes by, and our world-gets-bored-of-everything-in-24-hours news cycle moves on. And so does Ellen.

Scott returns to his normal life overnight. He's back in goal for 200 x 85, one of his beer-league teams, the following Friday. The Blackhawks play their final home game that same night. The rinks are just down the street from each other. And the beer-league schedule is on a public website.

"About halfway through the game, I notice some fans in Blackhawks sweaters come in," he says. "The Hawks game is done before ours, and then suddenly, people are streaming in. They're lined up along the glass, taking photos. It's . . . strange."

Scott's new fans watch their hero, the guy who shut out the Winnipeg Jets eight nights earlier, give up five goals in a 5–4 loss.

"But I *do* get a shutout the next game," he chuckles.

Scott accepts an invitation to the NHL Awards that June in Las Vegas. He and Erin have never been there. He does jokes onstage with Jim Belushi and nails the punchlines. The Hockey Hall of Fame calls. He sends them his cracked game stick and his beer-league jersey.

"It's funny; the sponsor, Wight and Company Construction, gives us a few thousand bucks a year, and they had decided it was the last year they were going to sponsor us. Then their jersey goes to the Hockey Hall of Fame. Let's just say we've gotten a couple more years' sponsorship out of it."

Scott is still an occasional EBUG in Chicago. The rules have changed. Now the EBUG gets a ticket and sits in the stands. Once in a while, he gets tapped on the shoulder by a fan who wants a photo. Or he'll spot a FOSTER sweater. Chicago fans never forget. But mostly, Scott is anonymous again.

Morgan and Wynni still aren't quite sure of the difference between their daddy and the players they see on TV every night, the ones who earn millions of dollars. Their classmates still ask for his autograph, here and there. The accountant smiles, shrugs and signs.

"My girls still think it's the coolest thing that Dad played in the National Hockey League," Scott says. "They'll see the number 90 and say, 'Daddy, that was your number in the NHL!' And it throws you back to when you were a kid, the way you thought of NHL players. It's made me realize how much I love this game. Somehow, through a bunch of randomness, I got a chance to live my dream. How can you ask for anything more than that?"

Short Shifts

Tales Suited to TV Time Outs

"I've got one more quick one for ya."

I loved hearing that while writing this book.

Good stories have no length parameters. Some take a full beer to get through—or three. Some you can tell during a commercial break.

Here is a handful of first-person stories that don't require a full chapter.

Connor McDavid, Edmonton Oilers Captain

The 2015 draft lottery is a huge day for my family. They all come down from our home in Newmarket to Toronto for it. It could go so many different ways. My agent, Jeff, gives me some things to say for each team that might win, just so I'm ready. They start unveiling the draft order, and there are definitely mixed emotions with my family. They want me to be close to home. Toronto is still a possibility. Buffalo is in it. We all think Buffalo is going to win. But they announce the winner, and it's Edmonton. I'm excited . . . but my mom? Not so much at that moment. But she comes around.

I do the interviews and everything that comes after, and about two hours after the lottery, my phone rings. I don't recognize the number, but I pick up. The guy goes, "Is Connor there?"

I say, "Yes, speaking."

He goes, "Hey, it's Taylor Hall! I'm just here with a bunch of the guys. We're in Vegas, and wanted to welcome you to the Oilers."

I'm thinking, "Yeah, right. Sure, you are Taylor Hall." I figure some guy has gotten my number and is messing with me. So I say, "Yeah, I know you aren't Hallsy. Nice try." And I hang up on him.

Well, turns out it was Hallsy, and my future teammates, calling to congratulate me and welcoming me to Edmonton. So . . . great first impression! Of course I end up living with Hallsy. He forgives me . . . eventually. I take all his calls now.

Anze Kopitar, Los Angeles Kings Captain

I get drafted by the Kings in 2005. I come over to training camp. It's the first day. I'm nervous. There are about 60 guys there. They split us into three teams. LA had signed Jeremy Roenick that summer, and I'm put on JR's team.

Andy Murray, the coach, tells all the team leaders to get everyone warmed up. We're in the gym, and JR starts blasting the music. And he starts dancing in the middle of the room. Then he tells us all to start dancing.

I'm 18 years old and I have no idea what to do. I can't dance! I try to find a little corner where no one can see me. I'm so self-conscious. I'm just kind of standing, moving a little bit from side to side. You know in the movie *Hitch*, when Will Smith gives Kevin James the dance lesson? "This is where you live, right here! This is home!" That's me. Just shuffling side to side, hoping no one looks at me.

That's my first NHL moment: dancing with JR in a gym. It's right after that he dances on the ice in Vegas during a pre-season game. It makes perfect sense to me when I see it.

I never get to play with JR. I go back to Slovenia that year, and he's gone when I come back for my rookie year. But we become really good friends. He still dances. I still don't. I've been lucky enough to win two Stanley Cups. Celebrated like crazy. But never danced.

Karl Alzner, Former Washington Capital

Let me start with what Alexander Ovechkin drinks . . . and I don't mean alcohol. A lot of guys drink a Red Bull to get them up for a game. But in his rookie year, Ovie would have three of them in the car on the way to the rink! Then he has another after warm-up and another after the first period. So the guy is crushing five Red Bulls before the start of the second! He's cut it to about three by the time I get to Washington a couple years later. But I've never seen anyone down them like that.

He also has Coca-Cola in his water bottle on the bench for most of my time in Washington. And one of my favourite things about him . . . a lot of guys would do the dip [chewing tobacco] between periods. When they're done, they will spit it out and gargle with Listerine. Ovie would gargle with Dr. Pepper! Everyone would be dying laughing. I don't know how all his teeth are still there.

Ovie has a real funny side. The year we have Dale Hunter as coach, it's pretty clear Ovie and Alexander Semin don't really see eye to eye with him on everything. One game, between periods, Dale rips us, saying, "You guys aren't scorers right now. You need to be plumbers! Get pucks deep and start plumbing!" After Dale leaves the room, Ovie says, "What's a plumber?" We tell him it means Dale wants him to chip pucks in, forecheck, play hard that way. And that a plumber is a guy who unclogs toilets. We do the plunging motion to show him. Ovie chuckles a little. Well, the next day we get on the ice for practice and Ovie has taped a plunger to his stick! It's unbelievable. There is no way anyone would risk pissing off Dale like that. But that's Ovie.

He's generous, too. The year he wins the Hart Trophy, we come in the next fall and he gives everyone on the team a Breitling watch, the ones from Bentley, the car brand. He tells us he couldn't have done it without us. Probably cost him 75 grand. It's one of the coolest things a teammate has ever done. Well, for most of us. One of the guys isn't much of a watch guy, so he sells his to a teammate for half price—cash, and some Lululemon gift cards!

Pierre LeBrun, Writer and TSN Insider

One of my favourite people to cover in 25 years on the NHL beat was the late Bryan Murray. I miss him terribly. He was one of the first GMs to give me the time of the day when I was a rookie reporter back in 1995. Over the years, we would have some very candid, off-the-record chats about the game. I loved his salty language.

One day in December 2015, he calls me and starts asking me questions about Toronto Maple Leafs captain Dion Phaneuf. It wasn't uncommon for Bryan to do that about a player. But he's grilling me pretty good. I tell him I think Phaneuf has been a role model for the younger Leafs players despite their struggles at the time, as far as how he takes care of himself and the work he puts in off the ice. I don't put much thought into the conversation.

Man, was I ever an idiot! You can imagine my reaction when, two months later, February 2016, the Senators trade for Phaneuf as part of a massive blockbuster. I call Bryan and he's already laughing on the other end of the phone before I can even get a word in. "Why did you think I was asking you about him?" he says. "Thanks for the heads-up on the trade," I say, sarcastically. To be fair, Murray had given me plenty of good scoops over the years. On this one, a huge trade between provincial rivals, he had to play it tight to the vest. I understand that. I just can't believe how dumb I was to never follow up after that phone call!

Sidney Crosby, Pittsburgh Penguins Captain

It used to be much more common to have roommates on the road. Today only guys on entry-level contracts have them. In my first two years, my roommate is Colby Armstrong. He'd been called up from Wilkes-Barre, and he's a great guy. He keeps things really loose. For whatever reason, he loves the show *Ellen*. When we get up from our pre-game nap, *Ellen* is usually starting. She always dances with the audience at the beginning. So, Army always dances with her in front of the TV. That becomes my pre-game routine on the road: watching Colby Armstrong dance to *Ellen*.

You spend a lot of time together in hotels. We're in Buffalo, and we always order room-service dessert when we get home from our meal the night before a game. Even if we've had dessert at the restaurant. These were slightly different times when it comes to nutrition! So, we would order this big piece of chocolate cake at the Hyatt in Buffalo. We're waiting for the cake one night, and for some reason, we decide to get in a full-on wrestling match.

We're going back and forth, and now he's on the ground and I come from the other side of the room to jump him. He sticks his knee up and gets me in a . . . well, a really bad spot, if you know what I mean. I just drop. I'm in a heap in the corner in agony. He thinks I'm joking. I'm not. I have some serious swelling. So he starts to panic. "You're gonna be okay—right, Sid? You're gonna play tomorrow, right?" But I'm not sure. I can't move.

We decide we have to tell the trainer. He comes to the room and he's not happy. He doesn't want to tell the coach I'm going to be out because we were wrestling. So, all night, Army is nervous. Every hour, he wakes me up and says, "Sid, are you okay?" He keeps telling me, "You have to play!" He reminds me over and over it was his dream to play in the NHL, and his career depends on me playing. He thinks he's going to get sent down to the minors for knocking me out of the lineup in a wrestling match. So, I grind it out and play, just for Army.

Colby Armstrong, Former Pittsburgh Penguin

I was so scared. Full panic. I'm still waiting for him to have a kid, so I can know I didn't ruin the Crosby genetics forever! But it was kinda Sid's fault. He bull-rushed me. And if you mess with the bull, sometimes you get the horn! We tone down the wrestling after that.

Sid's right about the cake. We love to eat. One night we get into Toronto late, around 11:30 p.m., and we're off the next day. I'm not sure if we are supposed to go out, but a few of us do, just for a couple of beers. Sid is smart. He stays in and goes to sleep.

I'm starving after the bar, so I go to McDonald's and grab a couple of cheeseburgers. I sneak into our room quietly and go straight into the bathroom to eat. Don't want to wake up the Kid.

I'm sitting on the edge of the tub, eating my McDonald's. All of a sudden, the door cracks open a little bit and these tired, squinty eyes peek in. And this little voice says, "Hey, Army, did you get any for me?" So at 1 o'clock in the morning, I sit on the edge of the tub, the best player in the world sits on the toilet, and we eat cheeseburgers. Life doesn't get much better.

The Kid Who Won Everything

Robert Thomas's Parents
Live the Dream

We begin in a backyard.

On a perfect summer evening, on a nice street, in a nice Canadian town, a very nice family is hosting the party of a lifetime. There is endless food and drink, and the best cookie bowl you'll ever eat a cookie out of. It feels like the whole neighbourhood is here.

Debbie Waechter steps out her patio door and looks around, amazed. She grabs her phone and takes a video, scanning the yard.

"Look at all these people! It's all the phases of our life, together. Family, friends, neighbours, billets, coaches and teammates from every level. All here to celebrate with us!"

"Did you get a cookie?" Debbie's husband, Scott, asks a guest who just arrived. "Robert, get him a cookie!"

Scott's son Robert smiles and carries over the cookie bowl. It's big and shiny and silver. And it has Robert's name freshly engraved on it.

He tilts the Stanley Cup just far enough for the guest to grab a chocolate chip cookie. It's delicious. The whole scene is.

There's Brady Tkachuk, chirping his brother Matthew from across the yard. Their dad, Keith, sits at a table near the back, telling stories. Conn Smythe Trophy winner Ryan O'Reilly, Montreal

Canadien Victor Mete, Edmonton Oiler Evan Bouchard—they are all here. The mayor of the town grins as he makes the rounds.

"We're lucky," Scott says, gazing around the yard, not realizing the scope of his understatement.

Robert Thomas has just become the only player to ever win the Memorial Cup, a gold medal at the World Juniors and the Stanley Cup, all as a rookie. Almost every box on the Canadian hockey fantasy checklist ticked off at age 19.

What is that like for a parent? To watch your kid win . . . everything?

I ponder this as I chew on the cookie Robert gave me.

The Thomas family lives just a couple of minutes away from us, in Aurora, Ontario. Just like Robert, my son Jared is a '99 (the way hockey parents identify their children's age). They never played together, and I didn't know the family well, though we have many friends in common. Still, they are kind enough to invite my family to their Cup party, just because Aurora is that kind of town and they are that kind of people.

Back when Jared was playing in pee wee, one of the dads pulled me over to the adjacent rink between periods. The York-Simcoe Express, the local AAA team, was playing. The dad pointed to a kid with hair flowing out the back of his helmet. "That's Robert Thomas," he said. "He might just be the one who makes it."

=====

The same backyard, 15 years earlier.

Scott builds a rink for his two boys, Robert and his little brother, Connor. Robert lives out there. They bring his first hockey team over for practices—a bunch of four-year-olds, whipping around in full gear while their parents sit in the kitchen, drinking coffee.

From the beginning, Robert can skate like the wind. He's forever ahead—playing super 6 at age five, super 7 at six, AAA as soon as he's eligible. But Scott and Debbie are not the kind of hockey parents who believe their boy is destined for greatness.

"All we are really hoping for is to get him into St. Andrew's [a local boys' school with both a great hockey program and academic reputation]," Scott says. "Maybe he'll be able to get a scholarship out of it. Even in his junior draft year, we don't have an agent or anything."

On OHL draft day, they're told Robert has a chance to go in the middle rounds, but they aren't paying much attention.

"We're busy doing other things and just have the computer open on the table," Scott says. "All of a sudden, we hear, 'London Knights, second-round selection, Robert Thomas.' And we're like, 'Oh, that's . . . neat.'"

Robert desperately wants to play for the Knights. "The toughest challenge is my mom and school," Robert says. "I need to show her I'm still going to get a good education. I have a plan to eventually take university classes in London. That's my selling point."

"He comes downstairs and presents the pros and cons to us at the kitchen table, and I'm thinking, 'Wow, that's really well thought out.'" Scott says. "But I still keep pushing, 'School, school, school.' And he looks me straight in the eye and says, 'Dad, I got this one. Trust me.'"

Robert is going to London.

"At first, I'm like, 'Oh my God, I can't let him go,'" Debbie says. "But they get him a wonderful billet family, the McGonigals, and I feel a lot better. We end up being close friends with them."

Debbie isn't the only one who struggles at first.

"My first night away, I'm sitting in my room in London, thinking, 'What did I get myself into?'" Robert says. "I call my mom and dad and tell them I can't do it. I miss them. I miss my brother. I want to come home. But Mom gives me some tough love, and I get through it."

Robert joins a stacked London Knights team, featuring the likes of Mitchell Marner, Matthew Tkachuk and Christian Dvorak. He only plays about half the games his rookie year, but he learns a ton from coach Dale Hunter.

187

In November, Robert plays for Canada (Team White) at the World U-17 Championship. He's the 13th forward, getting three shifts a game.

"That's the first time I see doubts," Scott says. "He comes up to me after a game, and the tears are welling up in his eyes, and he says, 'Dad, I can't find a way through this.'"

He finds a way. Team White wins gold. Robert is a world champion at 16. Scott and Debbie get his Team Canada jersey framed and hang it in his bedroom. "You never know if that's going to be the only championship he wins," Scott says.

Back in London, the Knights go on one of the great rolls in junior playoff history, winning 16 straight to carry them to the 2016 Memorial Cup final in Red Deer, Alberta. Robert plays (not a lot, but plays) in all the tournament games, and leaps from the bench as Matthew Tkachuk scores in overtime to win the Cup.

A second jersey gets framed for his room.

That summer, Tkachuk wants to work with Gary Roberts, who happens to do his training at St. Andrew's College in Aurora, the same school Robert attended. Scott and Debbie take Matthew in for the summer.

"Matthew is one of the most focused young men you'll ever meet," Scott says. "Every single decision is about making the Calgary Flames that fall. Everything he eats, going to bed at the same time every night—Robert sees this and realizes, 'Okay, so this is what it takes to make the NHL.' It's huge for him."

Matthew makes the Flames. And back in London, Robert starts to earn Dale Hunter's trust.

"It's about halfway through that season, his NHL draft year, that we realize this might actually happen," Debbie says. "We better get an agent."

On draft day in Chicago, they are a bundle of nerves.

"We don't eat very much," Scott says. "You are really anxious because you just want it to be a good experience for your kid."

The St. Louis Blues call Robert's name with pick number 20. And an entire arena . . . boos?

"They are tossing cups at him as he walks down the aisle!" Debbie says. The Thomases quickly realize the Blues are the Blackhawks' archrivals. And their son is an instant enemy.

"Robert actually loves it," Scott laughs. "He says after, 'I can't wait to play here now.'"

It's surreal for Scott and Debbie. Robert has won two major titles and is an NHL first-rounder.

The Blues send Robert back to London for another year of junior and a shot at one more dream.

"I had watched the World Juniors my entire life," Robert says. "My brother and I would play all day on the backyard rink and then come in to watch the games with my parents."

This time, his parents will watch *him*. Robert makes Team Canada. On Boxing Day in Buffalo, everyone is there—the Thomases, their friends, his billet family—all cheering Robert as he sets up the opening goal of the tournament against Finland. And when Tyler Steenbergen breaks a 1–1 tie late in the gold medal game against Sweden, Robert is a world champion again.

"I still get goosebumps thinking about that goal," he says.

========

Jersey number three, framed on Robert's wall. There is no room left.

"These things are $400 each," Scott laughs. "Not sure I would have started this if I knew he'd keep winning."

A day after Canada wins gold, London trades Robert to the Hamilton Bulldogs. He's crushed. London is all he knows. But he gets another great billet family (the Sordos) and leads the Bulldogs to an OHL championship, winning the playoff MVP award.

The wall space issues give Scott an excuse not to frame this jersey.

Over the summer, Robert figures he has a good shot at making the Blues, who are thin at centre behind Brayden Schenn. Then, on Canada Day, Debbie is driving him home from the cottage when a St. Louis trade notification pops up on his phone. The only letters he sees are THOM.

"Mom, did I just get traded?"

Turns out the THOM is for Tage Thompson, not Robert Thomas. Thompson is part of the package the Blues are sending to Buffalo for centre Ryan O'Reilly. St. Louis also signs Tyler Bozak that day.

"Now the Blues have three good centres and Robert goes, 'I'm in trouble.'" Scott says. "We tell him, 'It's okay to play another year in Hamilton.'"

But he doesn't go back. He makes the Blues as a winger, finds instant chemistry with Bozak and has a solid rookie season. Oh yeah, and the Blues miraculously come from last place to make the playoffs.

Their second-round series against Dallas goes the distance, and beyond: Game 7, double overtime.

Six minutes in, Robert makes a brilliant move around Stars defenceman John Klingberg, snaps a shot over Ben Bishop's shoulder and hits the post square. The puck bounces behind Bishop, and Patrick Maroon shovels it home. Maroon is the hero, but the play is all Robert's. "That's the moment the team and the city start to believe we can win the Cup," he says.

This is the part where you should probably hear about the flip-flops.

Scott has a red pair he was wearing around the hotel at the U-17s. For some logic-defying reason, he wears them to the gold medal game. Robert wins. So he wears them to the Memorial Cup final. Robert wins. World Junior gold medal game—ditto.

And on a June night in Boston in 2019, he runs onto the ice in the red flip-flops to hug his son, a Stanley Cup champion. The flip-flops are 4–0.

Debbie and Connor join Scott and his exposed toes on the ice. Tears flow.

The flip-flops do not get framed. But Robert's Blues jersey does. Another $400. Scott's not complaining. He hangs it in the bedroom. The U-17 jersey gets demoted to the basement.

===

The backyard, one last time.

It's Christmas 2019. With Robert in the NHL and Connor off at university studying engineering, Scott could have let the rink go. But he's kept it. Kids from the neighbourhood still drop by to play.

Today Robert is back out there. It's the NHL's Christmas break. He's firing shots as Dad makes wisecracks from the side. Robert is 20 now, his whole career ahead of him. Hard to believe, but the kid who won everything is just getting started.

The Salt Lake Room Reno

Ken Hitchcock, Wayne Fleming and the 2002 Olympics

Ken Hitchcock has spent most of his professional coaching career in the five-star life of the NHL. But he knows one-star.

On his very first road trip as coach of the International Hockey League's Kalamazoo Wings in 1993, the team overnights at a motel in Fort Wayne, Indiana.

"I go into my room and it's completely dark," he says. "I try to turn on the lamp . . . nothing. Then I realize there are no light bulbs in the lamp. There are no light bulbs in any of the lights in the room. So I feel around for the phone and call down to the front desk and tell them I have no light bulbs. She says, 'Yes sir, if you want bulbs, you have to put a 10-dollar deposit down.' So, I decide to stick with darkness. Welcome to minor-league hockey!"

Hitchcock is reminded of those dark times when he arrives in Salt Lake City, Utah, in advance of the 2002 Winter Olympics. He has been sent, along with fellow Team Canada assistant coach Wayne Fleming, to do some advance scouting. In 2002, the six world hockey powers (Canada, Russia, the USA, Finland, Sweden and the Czech Republic) are given spots in the Olympic tournament. Other nations have to play in a preliminary tournament to determine the last two qualifiers. So, Hitch and Fleming will scout the likes of Belarus, Latvia and Germany before head coach

Pat Quinn and the Canadian NHL stars arrive for the real show.

Before heading to Provo for the play-in tourney, Hitch and Fleming stop by the rink in Salt Lake City to check out their dressing room. As the host country, Team USA has the large home dressing room. The Czechs have the visitors' room because of their status as defending gold medallists from Nagano in 1998. The other teams are all stuck in temporary rooms built just for the Olympics. There are light bulbs this time, but yeah, they're back to one-star life.

"Basically, it's four walls and a shitter," Hitch says. "And the shitter is right in the middle of the room. There isn't even a separate door to it. All the rooms have the same grey walls and a blue rug. So Wayne looks around and says, 'This is Team Canada. This won't do.'"

A red-and-white room reno won't be easy. It's six months after 9/11, and the security around the building is airtight. But the two coaches have a week before all the teams arrive, so they decide to give it a shot. (Today this would have been an HGTV series where they renovate the room and flip it after the Olympics for a tidy profit.) Salt Lake City happens to be the home of the AHL farm team for the Dallas Stars, the club Hitch has been fired by just weeks earlier. So, he knows some people in the team office. Fleming devises a plan to paint the locker room white and try to find some red carpeting.

"Wayne says, 'I'll take care of it all. You go scout those other games in Provo, and I'll fix the locker room.'"

So, Hitch spends the next few days in Provo, watching Belarus and Germany eventually claim the last two Olympic spots. When he gets back, he asks Fleming, "How did it go?" And Fleming says, "Hitch, I got it all done. It looks great!"

He isn't overselling. Hitch walks in (the reveal—every reno show's money shot), and the room looks completely different. It's red and white, there's a separate door for the bathroom, and the space is suddenly huge.

"I go, 'Wayne, what did you do?'" Hitch says. "'This isn't the same room!' And he says, 'Don't worry, Hitch. It's all taken care of.'"

The Canadians and Americans are the first two teams to arrive in Salt Lake City. The gear has all been moved in, and Hitch and Fleming are hanging Team Canada photos and banners, when they hear yelling and screaming from the room next door. Team Sweden has just arrived.

"I go next door to take a peek, and their room is the width of one lane of a bowling alley!" Hitch says. "They are going ballistic. Wayne has moved the entire wall back, and they have nothing left! The knees of players sitting on opposite sides of the room are basically touching, they are so close! He somehow brought in a construction crew and just moved the walls and took half the Swedish room."

The Swedes never suspect it's Canada that has shrunk their space. They believe the International Olympic Committee is favouring Canada. The IOC eventually figures out something is fishy, but by then, the tournament is well under way. There's little they can do.

The cramped Swedes go 3–0 in group play, including a win over their expansive Canadian neighbours. But they are stunned by 0–3 Belarus in the quarter-finals, one of the greatest upsets in Olympic hockey history. The tiny Swedish room is left empty early. (Fleming decides against using it for another addition.)

Meanwhile, a loss to Sweden, a narrow win over Germany and a tie against the Czechs have caused panic back home in Canada. This is the year they are supposed to end a half century–long gold medal drought.

So, Fleming and Hitch hatch a new plan. Every morning, they get up early and buy every English-language newspaper available at the Athletes' Village, then take them outside and toss them in the garbage. These are the days before social media and iPhones, so papers and TV are the only real connection to back home.

"We'd buy all the copies of *USA Today*, the *Toronto Star* and even the London *Times*," Hitch laughs. "We figure we are doing a service to the country by preventing the players from reading about how heated things are back home. The players probably didn't read anything anyway, but we convince ourselves we're helping. Flem sends Hockey Canada the bill at the end of the tournament for all the papers. They aren't happy."

Even with the Great Newspaper Heist, word gets out. Glen Sather tells Team Canada GM Wayne Gretzky that the negativity in Canada is as bad as it was in 1972 during the Summit Series. Gretzky holds his now-famous news conference after Canada ties the Czechs. He rants against the negativity in the Canadian media, the dirty play of the opposition and the officiating—all to deflect attention away from the team's lacklustre showing. It is often credited as the turning point of the tournament. But Hitch says something else happened in the Team Canada room.

"Four players just take over the team. Steve Yzerman, Mario Lemieux, Rob Blake and Al MacInnis just say, 'Give us the game plan and we'll take care of it.'"

They do. Canada beats Finland, 2–1, in the quarters, destroys Belarus, 7–1, in the semis, and defeats the host Americans, 5–2, for gold. It is a celebration 50 years in the making.

And Hitch and Fleming miss almost all of it.

You may recall a *Gold Rush 2002* DVD that came out after the Olympics.

"It's the three assistant coaches that have to go across the parking lot to shoot interviews for the DVD, right after we get off the ice," Hitch says. "So, while everybody's partying and celebrating this victory of a lifetime, we're doing some television thing for a DVD. We are there for two hours and almost miss the whole thing! We come back into the room and people are already leaving."

I watched *Gold Rush 2002* again. Like everything else, it's on YouTube now. They didn't use any of the post–Golden Game interviews with Hitch and Fleming. Not a single word.

But there is some wonderful celebration footage from the Team Canada dressing room. Ryan Smyth hoots and hollers, points at his gold medal and says, "This is what it's all about, right here!" Eric Lindros hugs Mario Lemieux. Gretzky gives a short speech, telling the players how much they deserved it. Gary Bettman gives Joe Sakic the tournament MVP Award. It's a joyous place.

And remarkably spacious.

Ronan's Ride

A Minor-League Journeyman's
Seven-Year Odyssey

———

The Austin Ice Bats and Corpus Christi IceRays (they like Ice in team nicknames in the Central Hockey League) are brawling in the narrow hallway outside their dressing rooms. A Bat knocked out the Rays' best player with an elbow, the Bats knocked out the Rays, 4–2, on the scoreboard, and now the Rays want vengeance.

The size of the arena doesn't help. The Ice Bats didn't want to pay the rent at their old "real" rink, so they moved to the kind of neighbourhood barn you take your kids to on Saturday mornings, installed a few extra seats and called it home. The two teams use the same gate to exit the ice, and the Rays ambush the Bats outside their dressing room.

As punches, bodies and mouthguards fly, the arena's security guards—"mall cops on steroids," as Ice Bats forward John Ronan describes them—jump in to break it up. They figure their best weapon is pepper spray. Better than using the guns strapped to their hips. It *is* Texas, after all.

So, out come the cans, and the rink cops go Pepper Spray Rambo on every Bat and Ray in the melee. Which is pretty much every Bat and Ray in uniform. Except for one.

"I miss the worst of it, because I happen to score two goals that day and get first star, so I'm doing my victory lap," laughs Ronan.

"As I get off the ice, I see our trainer, Gunner Garrett. He's about 75 years old and is notorious for being one of the most miserable guys in the world. So, of course Gunner is headed right into the fray! I grab him and yank him away. Gunner takes a little pepper spray and I inhale some, but we miss the worst of it. Their goalie, Jason Tapp, gets it really bad. Most of the IceRays do. A bunch of our guys get it bad as well. Complete shitshow."

The pepper spray quickly starts to spread throughout the rink, which might be fine on a typical game night, when most fans would have filed out already. But this is Sunday afternoon, and the team is holding its monthly Skate with the Ice Bats event. Fans and families have come down from the stands, eager to lace up their skates and share the ice with their favourite Bats, who eventually emerge after the Royal Rumble is over.

"The whole rink stinks of pepper spray," Ronan says. "All the boys' faces are beet red, their eyes are watering, they're carrying around Crown and Cokes in coffee cups, and skating around with the fans. A pretty great day all around for the Austin Ice Bats."

===

It's my trainer, Dave Harris, who first tells me about John Ronan. (Yes, I train occasionally; stop giggling.) Dave is a former goalie who has trained a bunch of pro hockey players. I am telling him about this book one day at his gym, and he says, "You have to talk to John Ronan. John lived *Slap Shot*."

Ronan is a Southie. He grows up in South Boston, Massachusetts, then plays three years of junior hockey in nearby Walpole and four years on a half scholarship at the University of Maine, the last as team captain.

In that senior year, closing in on graduation, he gets a call from a former teammate who's playing for the Alaska Aces of the East Coast Hockey League. They need an extra body for their stretch run. It's 2005—the NHL lockout season. The Aces have New

Jersey Devils star Scott Gomez on their roster and look poised for a title run.

"My buddy tells me, 'Our coach wants to sign you. Would you be interested?'" Ronan says. "I go, 'I really can't. I'm a month of school and one summer semester away from graduating.' And then my buddy says, 'We're playing in Vegas this weekend.' Sold."

There's an old *Simpsons* flashback scene in which Homer is about to get accepted into college. His guidance counsellor says, "Homer, sign this application and you're a shoo-in." As Homer grabs the pen, a dog walks by the window with a ham in its mouth. Homer starts laughing and says, "That dog's got somebody's ham! This I gotta see!" and runs out of the office.

That call from Alaska, and the lure of a few nights in Vegas, is Ronan's Homer Simpson moment.

"I sign for the last two games of the regular season, and then we make it to the conference finals in the playoffs, and I play a few games there. I have the best intention of doing my school work along with playing. You'd never guess . . . but the school work goes out the window. And, well, long story short, I end up graduating eight years later. Should have been Dr. Ronan by that time! So, yeah, I pissed away the rest of a free education for $375 a week playing pro hockey. But hey, I'd never been to Vegas before!"

Ronan goes back to Alaska for camp the next fall, but their roster is deep, and he quickly realizes he's in trouble. Aces coach Davis Payne calls him into his office.

"I get along really well with Davis, and he tells me Florida's team in the ECHL is interested, if I'm okay being traded there. No problem! It's already snowing in October in Anchorage, and they're de-icing the plane on my way out. I have a smile on my face the whole flight."

With that, Ronan's seven-year minor-league odyssey is officially under way. His HockeyDB page is a glorious journey through the winding dirt back roads of the game.

» 2004–05 Alaska Aces (ECHL)

» 2005–06 Florida Everblades (ECHL)

» 2006–07 Rocky Mountain Rage (CHL)

» 2006–07 Austin Ice Bats (CHL)

» 2007–08 Austin Ice Bats (CHL)

» 2008–09 Huntsville Havoc (SPHL)

» 2009–10 Flint Generals (UHL)

» 2010–11 Geleen Smoke Eaters (Holland)

» 2011–12 Evansville IceMen (CHL)

Every pro career begins with a rookie party story. I believe it's required under hockey's constitution. In Ronan's case, it's spring break, and the Everblades' tradition is to hold the party on Fort Myers Beach. The rookies all wear Speedos and are sent on a scavenger hunt.

"Just the looks and comments we get and overall stupidity of the situation is really embarrassing," he says. "I don't have a Speedo body. I'm a pale Irish guy with a fat ass. So, it isn't pretty."

Ronan survives Speedo humiliation and spends the entire season in Florida, picking up 26 points in 68 games as a rookie. But at the end of the season, his rights are traded to the Dayton Bombers.

"I'm devastated," he says. "That was a fun year. Hard to leave the combination of hockey, golf and sun. I mean, there are worse places to be playing in the minors. As I would soon find out."

Ronan decides to pass on Dayton and instead jumps to the Central Hockey League, signing with the Rocky Mountain Rage. But they waive him after nine games, and he ends up in Austin, Texas, with the Ice Bats.

"Just a great city, and this collection of misfits on the team who all love playing together," he says. "But the organization is *sooo* cheap. My wife and I have just been married, and when we get down there, they bring us to the apartment and there is a dead rat on the doorstep. So, we just turn around and go right back to the hotel."

Except for the dead rat and a pepper-spray brawl, Ronan loves his year and a half in Austin. Until the Ice Bats fold, and he's hockey homeless.

But school ties never die. An old assistant coach from Maine, Eric Soltys, convinces Ronan to join the team he's now coaching in Alabama: the Huntsville Havoc of the Southern Professional Hockey League.

"It's a pretty legit league today, but back then it's a sideshow," Ronan laughs. "A lot of fighting, a lot of theatrics."

One night Huntsville is hosting the Columbus Cottonmouths when a fan sitting next to the Havoc bench holds up a sign that reads: $100 FOR ANYONE WHO FIGHTS RIGHT HERE.

"Columbus has an older pro named Craig Stahl, and he lines up against one of our vets, Travis Kauffeldt, for a faceoff. Stahl looks at the sign, then looks at Travis and goes, 'You want to make the money?' Kauffeldt says, 'Yeah, screw it,' and they square off. Might have been a salary cap violation, but I believe the fan paid up. And $100 goes a long way in the SPHL!"

He isn't kidding. The league salary cap is under $6,000. For the *entire* team.

"It's actually the most money I make in the minors," Ronan laughs. "About $400 a week on the cap, but I get some money under the table, a couple of hundred-dollar handshakes now and then. Don't know where it's coming from, don't ask."

At Christmas that season, one of the Havoc goaltenders gets called up to the ECHL, and Ronan's brother Mike, a former Division III college goalie, is brought in to replace him.

"We bus overnight to Richmond, Virginia, on Christmas Eve, and wake up on the bus Christmas morning, but at least I have a family member to share Christmas with," Ronan says.

It's a special moment: brothers playing their first pro game together on Christmas Day. Except, midway through the first period, a scuffle breaks out and Ronan gets caught in the middle of it.

"There's a fight, and I get into it with another guy," he says.

"It's barely a scrap, more like a glorified wrestling match with a few punches here and there, but any secondary altercation is an automatic ejection, and I get kicked out. So, yeah, my brother ends up getting his first pro win in his debut, and I get booted in the first. Beautiful family moment."

Ronan's pal Soltys leaves his coaching job in Huntsville after that season, and John is on the move again, this time signing with the Flint Generals of the International (formerly United) Hockey League. It's another organization short on cash, and . . . furniture.

"They are going to put us all in this apartment complex to live, but the apartments aren't ready yet, so we live in this hotel with an Applebee's next door," he says. "We survive on happy hour Bud Lights and mozzarella sticks. Then, when we get in the apartments, there's no furniture. They are completely empty. Finally, this truck pulls up and just dumps a mountain of furniture in the middle of the complex. It's an absolute free-for-all. Some guys get a coffee table, some get a bed frame, nobody gets enough of anything. It's mayhem. I get a lamp and a TV stand."

The entire season rolls that way in Flint. The players have no idea who the owner is, and there are constant rumours of the team folding. In the middle of this mess, Ronan is having his best season of pro hockey, scoring 30 goals.

"I love that team," he says. "We have Jason Muzzatti as our coach. Somehow, Bryan Smolinski gets talked into joining us at the end of his career. And we have Pascal Rhéaume, a Cup winner, playing the Reggie Dunlop player/assistant coach role. Pascal has never been close to that low level of minor hockey. I think his head is ready to explode the whole season."

Ronan is lighting it up, but he's playing on a beat-up old pair of skates that are starting to hurt his feet. And this leads to perhaps the greatest minor-league hockey story ever.

"Something is rubbing my foot the wrong way, and every intermission, I'm in so much pain, I have to take [the skates] off.

So, I go to Muzz and tell him, 'I can't play like this anymore.' But we have no budget for new skates."

So, two days later, the Flint Generals trade a guy to the Port Huron Icehawks. For a pair of skates.

"Technically, they call it 'future considerations,'" Ronan laughs. "But I have a new pair of skates on Monday. Those are the considerations."

The Generals are an average team most of the season. Down the stretch, Ronan believes they need an "act of God" to make the playoffs. Then, suddenly, they start to reel off *W* after *W* and push their way closer to the final spot.

"Part of our motivation is to keep playing for each other, because we enjoy being around each other so much," Ronan says. "But the other part is trying to stick it to whoever the hell owns the team, and make them pay us for a few more weeks."

On the final day of the season, the Generals need a win on the road against the Fort Wayne Komets, or a loss by the Bloomington PrairieThunder, to make the playoffs. It's one of those days when nothing clicks. The Generals are trailing the Komets by two goals late in the third, and have nothing left in the tank, when coach Muzz calls a time out.

"He just starts screaming at us," Ronan says. "He's cursing and yelling, 'Pick it up! What's the matter with you guys?' And then he stops and says, 'Just kidding. Bloomington lost. We're in the play-offs!' Our whole bench goes ballistic, jumping up and down. And 10,000 fans in Fort Wayne are looking at us, going, 'What's wrong with these idiots?'"

Making the playoffs when your team is flat broke leads to some . . . issues. The Generals are out of sticks—a bit of a problem for a professional hockey team.

"I have one Easton left, which I'm only using for games, hoping it will survive until the end," Ronan says. "Pascal is dipping into his NHL retirement money to buy his own sticks. It's ridiculous. But we have some guy who props us up a little and he orders this shipment from an old company called Innovative. The sticks are garbage. Four or five shots, and the blades go flimsy. The righties are this awful royal blue and fluorescent pink. The lefties are black and white, sharper looking. But one day one of our guys is inspecting his and notices something. On the shaft are the four words 'Super High Impact Technology,' and the first letters are bolded. So, yeah, they made no bones about it. These are SHIT sticks!"

The Generals and their SHIT sticks somehow come from 3–1 down to beat the Muskegon Fury in seven games in the opening round, before falling to favoured Fort Wayne in the second.

"We get playoff bonus cheques, a few hundred dollars," Ronan says. "But by the time I cash mine, there is no money left in the account, so it bounces. So I score 30 goals, seven more in the play-offs, and my bonus cheque is minus-nine dollars, for the bank fee."

So ends the story of the Flint Generals. Ronan isn't on many all-time stats lists, but he's elite when it comes to playing for folding teams.

Having experienced pretty much everything in minor pro hockey in North America, he decides to try Europe, signing with the Geleen Smoke Eaters in the Netherlands.

"I take the red-eye into Brussels, and this guy meets me and two other imports, a Canadian guy and an American guy, at the airport. He doesn't speak a word of English. So, we pull into the town the team lives in, and he drops off the other two guys. It looks like a nice town—townhouses, bars and restaurants—but he signals to me that I have to go somewhere else.

"He drives for another half hour and drops me off at this trailer park, with some milk, bread and a couple apples. So, I'm sitting in this trailer in the Netherlands, alone. There's no cell service, no internet, nothing. I start looking around for Bubbles and Ricky. It's nuts! My wife is pregnant back home, and for 36 hours, I am completely cut off from the outside world. Finally, they come and drop off a car, a 1980-something Ford Orion with a choke starter and no power steering. I would get winded parallel parking. My wife moves over after a couple weeks, and she's five months pregnant and can't even fit in the shower.

"Finally, after a couple months, we get moved to the townhouses with the rest of the players. It's a nice town, packed little rink with great fans. But an American coach brought me over, and he gets fired six games in. They replace him with a guy who thinks he's the Dutch Scotty Bowman. So, at the end of the year, my wife is ready to have the baby, and I'm injured. And I just say, 'What the hell am I doing here?' I head home."

That summer, John and his wife, Robin, have a baby girl named Camryn. Fatherhood makes him realize it's probably time to finish that degree he was a few credits short of finishing. He starts chipping away at it, but decides to play one final *Slap Shot* season, in Indiana, with the Evansville IceMen. (I told you they love Ice nicknames in the CHL.)

"We're on the first game on this long road trip, in Tulsa, when I get leg-checked from behind," Ronan says. "We have a bunch of injuries and suspensions and barely have the required bodies, so even though my knee is swollen, I play the whole road trip. I get an MRI when I get back, and then keep playing. It isn't too painful—a bit unstable, but I'm okay. At one point, they drain my knee, and it's red, which I know isn't a good sign. But the guy says, 'No, that's not always bad.' So I just keep playing and never have my MRI follow-up. The season ends, I go in for my medical, and the doctor says, 'Everything looks good. You're good to go,' and he starts to leave the room. And I go, 'Wait, what about the knee?' And he goes, 'Oh right, you had the knee injury!' He starts digging frantically through his paperwork, and then he says, 'Oh, your ACL is totally torn. You need ACL reconstruction!' So, that's my parting gift from minor-league hockey: knee surgery."

And that's the end of Ronan's run. Seven seasons and change, eight teams, 139 goals and a hockey bag full of stories. Ronan is now an assistant coach with Union College in Schenectady, New

York. He lives in nearby Clifton Park, with Robin and Camryn. And has zero regrets.

"Maybe, in hindsight, I could have hung my skates up a couple of years earlier, but hey, I had a lot of fun, and endless laughs," he says. "Plus, I got to make six figures playing a game I love." He pauses. "I mean, if you add up all seven seasons, I think it's almost six figures."

The Scout, the Kid and the Calf

Craig Button and Todd Harvey Team Up on the Farm

There is more to scouting than . . . well . . . scouting. The best hockey scouts will try to get to know players and their families. And, when necessary, help their cows give birth.

Wait. What?

It's the spring of 1993. The Minnesota North Stars have just moved to Texas. The brand-new Dallas Stars are about to take part in their first NHL Entry Draft. And their director of scouting wants to make sure they get the right guy. So, Craig Button spends his May and early June travelling across North America and Europe, meeting with prospects.

"We want to spend time with the players and their families and see the influences the player has had in his life," Craig says. "It's not some 15-minute drop-in. I try to have a lunch or dinner with them, really get to know them, and answer all the questions they might have."

One of Button's 25 or so visits that spring is to a country house in Sheffield, Ontario, a small town northwest of Hamilton. It's the home of top 10 prospect Todd Harvey.

"Craig is the only scout that comes to our house," Todd says.

"And my family and I are really impressed by that. Most of the other interviews I do are the week of the draft. I still remember meeting with the Tampa Bay Lightning. Phil Esposito is asking me questions. I'm really nervous. Phil says, 'The score is 5–3 and you have two goals. What do you do?' And I respond without even hesitating, 'Go for the hat trick!' Phil shakes his head and says, 'You are the only guy who said that!' I guess the other guys all said, 'Play defence, get the puck deep, protect the lead.' I don't think mine was the answer they were looking for. Oh well."

No trick questions from Craig. He's just sitting at the picnic table, chatting with Todd and his dad, Doug, when they hear some strange noises from the family's barn.

"We don't have a real farm. It's more like a hobby farm—we call it a funny farm," Todd says. "We have a little bit of every-thing—cows, sheep, pigs. Just to feed us, really. And we have this very pregnant cow. My mom [Denise] is down in the barn and she screams that she needs help. The cow is giving birth and strug-gling trying to get the calf out."

"The cow is moaning," Craig remembers. "So, they go try to help. And then Todd yells—"

"'Craig, get in here! We could use you!'" Todd recalls. "He's in these nice pants and boat shoes, always perfectly dressed, and he's going, 'What do I do?' And Mom says, 'Get some fucking water!'"

The scout complies, but his chores are far from done. "Denise is holding on with the roe, and two legs of the calf are sticking out, so Todd says . . .

"'Grab a leg, Craig!'

"So, Todd has one leg, I have the other, and he says . . .

"'Pull on three!'

"So, Todd counts, 'One . . . two . . . three!' And we pull on the legs, and out comes the calf! I end up in a pile of mud or shit or something. I know my clothes did not survive the day. But I helped birth a calf!" Craig says.

"Jesus Murphy, what a crazy story! That's actually one of the only times I'd ever been there for the birth of a calf," Todd says, "and the scout of the team I hope to play for in the NHL happens to be there!"

The livestock doesn't hurt Todd's draft stock. Craig drives away thinking, "I really like this kid and his family. Not saying the calf clinched it, but he just seems like a real leader."

A month later, two busloads of Team Harvey—family, friends, the calf (okay, no, but it would have made the story better)—make their way to Quebec City. It's June 26, 1993.

"I'm sitting in the stands, and I just have this feeling it's going to be Dallas," Todd says.

Button is at the Stars' draft table as they await their turn. Alexandre Daigle goes first overall to Ottawa. Chris Pronger is second, to Hartford. Then Chris Gratton, Paul Kariya . . . When the Rangers select Niklas Sundstrom with the eighth pick, Button and the Stars know they have their guy. Coach/GM Bob Gainey steps to the podium.

"We're very proud and happy to make, as our first selection, from the Canadian Hockey League, the Detroit Junior Red Wings, Todd Harvey!"

"I have so many family members and friends from my community there, it feels like the whole arena is standing and cheering," Todd says.

Todd spends the first four seasons of his 11-year NHL career in Dallas. When he retires, he decides he'd like to try scouting.

"I get offered a job with Vancouver, and so I call Craig," Todd says. "He's been doing this for so long, and gives me some really good advice about the tricks of the trade."

Todd still scouts for the Canucks today. Craig now does his scouting for TSN. They run into each other on the road once in a while. They talk about the game, share some stories about the Dallas days, and laugh about their perfectly executed two-on-one—birthing a calf in a barn in rural Ontario.

The Case of the Mistaken McCreary

Referee Bill McCreary
Takes Heat for a Hit on the Great One

The greatest hockey player of all time takes the pass and cuts across the blue line, towards the middle of the ice. We all know where this highlight is headed—to some ridiculously perfect no-look pass and one of his 1,963 career assists. Or maybe to a couple of dekes around desperate, flailing D-men and one of his 894 goals.

Then suddenly, shockingly, out of nowhere, a blue-and-white blur fills the frame and destroys Wayne Gretzky.

It's January 3, 1981. Here's the way the play is described by the TV commentators.

DON WITTMAN: *The puck comes out to centre ice. Here's Gretzky, at the line . . . whoooa, is he hit! Gretzky really belted by McCreary. And he is hurt! Oh, what a check by McCreary!*

GERRY PINDER: *I can't believe it, Witt. He is out on the ice!*

You can watch it on YouTube. For several seconds, Gretzky lies on his back, eyes closed, gloves off. But after the Oilers trainer

210

arrives, he quickly gets to his feet and skates to the bench, shoving away help offered by teammates Lee Fogolin and Garry Lariviere.

The hit is startling because no one could level the Great One.

"It's one of—if not *the*—hardest hits I've taken in my career," Gretzky says. "I remember it like it was yesterday. When we get in the locker room, all the guys are stunned I got hit like that. Dave Semenko asks me, 'What happened?' Well, I get the puck and I see a defenceman, and we have a two-on-one. And a defenceman naturally backs up on a two-on-one. Then, all of a sudden, I just get rolled over. I'm thinking, 'What the hell is *he* doing there?' I realize after it's a forward playing back because the D had pinched. So I get blindsided because I didn't think he'd step up, and I'm vulnerable. It stuns me. I'm mostly mad at myself for having my head down."

The man who delivers the check is rookie Toronto Maple Leafs forward Bill McCreary. When most recount the story of McCreary on Gretzky, they'll tell you it is McCreary's one and only NHL game, and that this would be his final shift. I've heard it told that way multiple times. But hockey lore sometimes alters facts. It is actually McCreary's *second* game. He plays 10 more that month, then never sees NHL ice again.

When Bill McCreary hits 99, his cousin, also named Bill McCreary, is working in a Linamar machine shop in Guelph, Ontario, grinding axles. The other Bill was a hockey player, too, but quickly realized, "The only draft for me is the one in the mug." Bill works part time as a referee, working his way up to the junior ranks.

Guelph just happens to be Refville, Ontario. NHL officials Andy Van Hellemond, Ron Asselstine, Will Norris, George Ashley, Ken Bodendistel and Ray Scapinello are all from the area. So, word gets around quickly that there's another good young official in town. Scotty Morrison, the NHL's vice-president of officiating, invites McCreary out to a referee "prospects" tryout at Maple Leaf Gardens. Three years later, he's reffing in the big league.

JAMES DUTHIE

A month into his NHL career, McCreary works his first
Edmonton Oilers game, against Vancouver.

"Some of the guys are really giving it to me verbally," McCreary
says. "You always get a bit of that as a rookie referee, but this is
different. They are all over me! And soon I realize they think I'm
the Bill McCreary who hit Gretzky! So I keep saying, 'That wasn't
me! I'm the *other* Bill McCreary!' I'm almost begging and pleading. But they won't let up."

"Even the guys who know it isn't him would keep saying it,
just to get under his skin," laughs Gretzky.

The chirping would go on for almost a full season (McCreary
officiates only a handful of Oilers games over that time). Finally,
he tells one of the Edmonton beat writers that the Oilers have the
wrong Bill. And they let up on him.

"I'm 100 percent positive Glen Sather knew the whole time,"
McCreary says with a chuckle. "But he didn't say anything to his
players. I think he enjoyed feeding into it."

McCreary has a history with Sather. The legendary Oilers
coach had played with another McCreary, cousin Keith, on the
Pittsburgh Penguins. When referee Bill is 14 years old, Keith
invites him and his mother down to watch a couple of games in
Pittsburgh. Bill gets to skate with the Penguins one practice and
meets all the players, including Sather. Fifteen years later, Sather
is doing whatever he can to test the young referee.

"Glen would definitely try to intimidate me," McCreary says.

On March 14, 1986, the Oilers are leading the Red Wings, 7–2,
in Edmonton. Detroit coach Harry Neale pulls Greg Stefan and
puts Eddie Mio in goal.

"Back then, we have a rule that a goaltender cannot use col-
oured tape on the knob of his stick," McCreary says. "But Mio's
knob is red, to match the Red Wings' uniforms. So, here comes
Gretzky to talk to me in the corner. Wayne says, 'Glen says it's a
penalty unless he puts white tape on the knob of a stick.' And I say,
'Go back and tell Glen that when it's 7–2, it doesn't matter what

colour the tape is. We're not calling that.' So, Wayne skates back to the bench and must have used my exact words. Glen hollers out, as only he could with his booming voice, 'You are now off my Christmas card list!' People in the stands are laughing, because it's so quiet in there. Middle of a *Hockey Night in Canada* game, and this is the conversation we're having!"

Over the years, McCreary grows to greatly respect Sather . . . and his captain. He would end up officiating some of the most pivotal games of Gretzky's career.

"In the semifinals at the Olympics in Nagano, they are taking forever to decide who is going to shoot in the shootout, and Dominik Hasek comes out of his net and says to me, 'Bill, is Gretzky shooting?' That's the only guy he's concerned about! And of course, Wayne never gets to shoot."

When Gretzky announces that the final game of his career will be at Madison Square Garden, on April 18, 1999, NHL director of officiating Bryan Lewis changes the officials' schedule so that McCreary will referee Gretzky's swan song.

"It's an incredible moment in my career," McCreary says. "I'm standing at centre ice, getting set for the opening faceoff, and Gretzky takes his glove off, shakes my hand and says, 'Thank you.' And I say, 'No, thank *you* for being such a great ambassador for the game.' He comes into the officials' room at the end of the second and takes pictures with us. We delayed starting the third period while he was doing this. Nobody knew. Just pure class."

McCreary joins Gretzky and the game's legends in the Hockey Hall of Fame in 2014. Safe bet he won't have to tell anyone he's the "other" Bill McCreary ever again.

Tucker and the Wrath of the Mighty Quinn

Darcy Tucker Gets a Stern Lecture from His Legendary Coach

"There's a hit on the boards . . . A Leafs player is hurt! Play goes on . . . They score!"

That's Bob Cole, from Game 5 of the 2002 playoff series between the Toronto Maple Leafs and Ottawa Senators. The unnamed Leaf is Darcy Tucker. The player who crushes him into the boards is Daniel Alfredsson—the same guy who scores the game-winning goal seconds later.

It is one of the defining moments of the Battle of Ontario.

SENS FANS: *Clean hit—great goal!*

LEAFS FANS: *Dirty hit! Screw you!*

(I'm paraphrasing here.)

"I break my scapula and dislocate my shoulder," Tucker says. "It's a suspect hit, but in the end, it's a really competitive player hitting another really competitive player. So, I don't have any ill will towards Daniel today. I respect him. But back then, man, I'm

214

angry! I store it in my memory bank and vow to get even down the road."

The Tucker-less Leafs come back to win Games 6 and 7 to take the series. They eventually lose to Carolina in the Eastern Conference final.

During the off-season, Tucker's motivation in training is all about Alfredsson. He's Balboa in *Rocky IV*, climbing the snowy Russian mountains with a log on his shoulders, a photo of Drago taped to the wall of his barn. (Okay, it's summer in Ontario, so not the best metaphor, but just play along.)

"At some point, I'm going to get my pound of flesh from Alfie," Tucker says.

Sometimes, vengeance requires patience. Tucker's anger towards Alfredsson has to simmer for a while. He just can't find the right moment to get even. He does jump into the Senators bench in Ottawa on March 4, 2003, and tries to fight the entire team. But Alfredsson stays out of that melee. Leafs coach Pat Quinn grabs a stick while Tucker is scrapping, and holds the butt-end towards the Senators bench like he's about to go full *Game of Thrones: The Long Night*. They are kindred spirits, Quinn and Tucker.

On October 5, 2005—opening night—two seasons and a lock-out after the Alfredsson hit, Tucker sees his spot and can no longer resist. With Toronto leading, 1–0, midway through the third, he slew-foots the Senators captain. They call him for hooking, which came before the slew-foot. (Tucker gives the ref options.)

The penalty negates a Leafs power play, and Alfredsson scores on the four-on-four. The Senators go on to win—in the NHL's first-ever shootout.

Coming out of the box, Tucker knows he's screwed up. "Pat Quinn has this way of looking at you out of the corner of his eye, like he's not really looking at you, but you can just feel it," says Tucker. "No other coach I've ever had has this ability. You just know how disappointed he is in you, without him even really looking at you or saying anything. And I'm really disappointed in myself, because I've let the team down, and I've let Pat down. And that hurts, because I have so much respect for Pat."

That's a critical part of this tale. Quinn is Tucker's all-time favourite coach. He worships him.

"I wouldn't be the same person I am today—father, husband, human—without Pat Quinn," he says. "He's just a huge mentor in my life."

As Tucker sits in the dressing room stall after the game, head hanging, trainer Scotty McKay comes over with a message: Quinn wants to see Tucker in his office.

"Pat never wanted to see anyone in his office after a game, ever," Tucker says. "He let players do their own thing. So, I know I'm in big trouble."

Tucker doesn't even get dressed. He walks to Quinn's office wearing only his core shorts, a T-shirt thrown over his shoulder. Quinn tells Tucker to take a seat in one of the chairs opposite him.

"Pat always liked to have his stogie, and I'm pretty sure he's already had one by the time I get in there," Tucker says. "He has this gruff voice, and he offers me a Scotch. So he pours me one, and pours himself one, and we sit there quietly for a minute, sipping Scotch. Then Pat sits back, clears his throat with this little cough, and says, 'So, what do you think of that play you made that you got the penalty on?' I can't help myself. I say, 'Pat, I just didn't like his hit back in our playoff series.' And Pat goes, 'Yeah, I didn't like it, either.'"

Tucker instantly feels a little better. His coach is on his side. Plus, he's drinking Scotch with him. So, he keeps going, talking about how much Alfredsson's hit bothered him, how hard he had to work to recover from the injuries . . .

"And Pat goes, 'Let me stop you right there,'" Tucker says. "He clears his throat again and says, 'Tom Lysiak hit me early in my career, one of the dirtiest hits I've ever taken. I never forgot it, but I waited 13 years to get him back. And when I got him, I got him good! You couldn't wait more than a couple of years, and it costs us our home opener. That's not the goddamn right way to do things!'"

Tucker feels himself sliding down in the chair, shrinking.

"And then he gives me this stare I'll never forget," Tucker says. "Just a look of, 'We're never ever having this conversation again.' And Pat says, 'Now get the hell out of here and go get changed!'"

Tucker gently puts down what remains of his Scotch on the desk and slumps out of Quinn's office.

"The way he went from offering me a drink to ripping my soul out is something I'll never forget," Tucker says. "Needless to say, I made it my career goal to never let Pat Quinn down again. I love that man. I wish he would have let me finish my Scotch before destroying me. But I love him."

"Can You Believe It?!"

Jordan Eberle and Canada's
World Junior Miracle

Before Jordan Eberle becomes one of Canada's best World Junior Championship players ever, he is the worst.

"I am terrible, the worst player at the 2008 summer training camp," he says. "They put me on a line with John Tavares, so I figure I'm going to get a good shot at making the team. But I am trying out these brand-new skates and they are awful. So the skates suck, I suck, and the whole camp is a nightmare. Even JT says to me, 'What's going on with you?' And in my exit meeting with the coach, Benoît Groulx, he tells me I was dead last in their evaluations. I leave thinking, 'I may have just blown my chance.'"

He goes back to his home in Calgary, crushed.

"I remember being a kid, watching Jordin Tootoo in Halifax in 2003, watching Sid and all those stars in North Dakota in 2005," he says. "That's when I realized how huge the tournament had become, and how desperately I wanted to be there someday. You really have two dreams growing up playing hockey in Canada: to play in the NHL and win a Stanley Cup, obviously, and to play for Canada at the World Juniors."

Eberle has never been a lock to make Team Canada. Sure, he'd been a first-round selection of the Edmonton Oilers that June, but not a high pick—22nd overall. Ten Canadians are taken before him.

And he's 18, trying to make a team usually dominated by 19-year-olds. As his Western Hockey League season starts with the Regina Pats, his World Junior dream feels like it's slipping away.

Then the hockey gods intervene—specifically, the one in charge of coach recruitment. Groulx gets hired to coach the AHL's Rochester Americans and has to step down as coach of Team Canada. The man who witnessed Eberle's summer camp calamity is gone. And a living legend, Pat Quinn, takes his place.

"That changes everything for me," Eberle remembers. "Quinn had coached me at the World Under-18 Championships that past spring. I had a great tourney, and we absolutely dominated Russia in the final. So, suddenly, I feel a little better about my chances."

The hiring of Quinn helps. And Eberle helps himself, too. His start to the season in Regina is ridiculous, as he scores goals in bunches and launches himself right back onto Team Canada's radar. He earns an invitation to the December tryout camp and makes the team.

Though most of Canada remembers only one moment from that tournament, Eberle has an impact in almost every game, including a key power-play goal in a dramatic come-from-behind win over the Americans on New Year's Eve. Canada looks shaky at times, but goes undefeated and earns a bye to the semifinals against Russia.

There is an early hint it might be Eberle's night. On a five-on-three power play in the second period, Cody Hodgson fires a shot that takes a wild bounce in the air and lands right at Eberle's feet in front of the net.

"Just the luckiest goal," Eberle laughs. "The bounce could not be more perfect. I just throw it at the net, and it goes off someone and squeaks in."

That "someone" is Russian defenceman Dmitry Kulikov. It won't be his last unfortunate encounter with Eberle this night.

It's 4–4 with just over two minutes left, when Dmitry Klopov jams a loose puck past Canadian goalie Dustin Tokarski. The sellout crowd in Ottawa, one of the loudest I've ever heard at a hockey game, falls silent.

My parents have come to the game. They are sitting with me on the TSN set. Jim and Sheila Duthie are almost 80, and I worry about them being caught in the crowd and the heavy traffic leaving the rink in Kanata. Dad hates traffic. So, after Russia scores, I say, "Maybe you guys should go and beat the crowd." They leave. I mean, they probably won't miss anything, right?

Canada has the net empty and is pressing with 45 seconds left when Klopov, the Russian hero minutes earlier, picks up a loose puck near the Russian blue line. He has ample room to skate the puck up ice, but instead seems to panic. He shoots at the vacant Canadian goal. It goes just wide. Icing.

"My heart stops as that puck is going down the ice towards our net," Eberle says. "Best icing ever. And then I notice a couple of the Russian guys are smiling, chuckling. I guess they are thinking, 'Well, that was dumb, but it's over anyway. We've won.'"

The next 35 seconds after John Tavares wins the ensuing face-off are pure mayhem. Or, as Canadians prefer to call it, "poetry." Funny thing is, Eberle is barely involved. He briefly touches the puck right after the faceoff but spends the rest of the time circling near the front of the net. Waiting . . . hoping . . . praying.

Most of the play is on the right side of the Russian zone. Cody Hodgson is down low. Ryan Ellis is on the point, with forward Zach Boychuk out near him. P.K. Subban mans the other point, mostly out of the action. John Tavares is puck-hunting. Eberle only sneaks into the camera frame here and there. A ghost.

So many little plays go into the making of a miracle. With 16 seconds left, Ellis slams his shoulder up against the glass at the blue line to block a Russian clearing attempt. Game over if he misses.

Ellis and Boychuk then battle with two Russian players just inside the line to keep the puck in. Game over if they fail.

With 10 seconds left, Hodgson lifts the stick of a Russian player, preventing another clear. Game over if he doesn't.

And then Tavares finds the puck over by the boards and backhands it blindly towards the net. A soft, harmless muffin.

"The most overused cliché in hockey is 'Just get the puck to the net and hope for a bounce,'" Eberle says. "And that is exactly what happens."

Kulikov, off whom Eberle had ricocheted his shot on his first goal back in the second, drops to his knees to try to stop the puck. He must have it; his entire body is on top of it. But somehow, it sneaks through him. If you're Russian, the moment has a painful Bill Buckner–like feel to it—in slo-mo.

And there is Jordan Eberle.

The puck is on his stick for just a fraction of a second. Quick move from forehand to backhand. Goalie down and desperate. Puck flipped up and over his outstretched stick.

It's 5–5 with 5.4 seconds left. Bedlam.

"CAN YOU BELIEVE IT?!"

Gord Miller, the voice of the World Juniors on TSN, brilliantly calls the goal. Years later, Eberle still can't believe it.

"It's this crazy mix of shock and elation," he says. "People always ask what was going through my head. Nothing. You are just playing. All I remember is peeling off to the corner, going nuts and getting swarmed. You always dream about scoring a last-second goal like that in a huge game, but when it happens, it's . . . surreal."

And at that very moment, listening to their car radio in a parking lot outside the arena, Jim and Sheila Duthie suddenly wish they had stopped at two daughters and not had a third child.

The game is tied, not over. And it still isn't over after 10 minutes of overtime. Quinn taps Eberle to go first in the shootout.

"A week or two earlier, we had done a shootout after practice," Eberle says. "And I went five-for-five. I couldn't miss. So I thought he might go to me if we ever went there."

Eberle slides the puck to his backhand and goes upstairs. Canada leads. Tavares scores on the next Canadian attempt, and

Dustin Tokarski stops the first two Russian shooters. It's over. Canada will play Sweden for the gold medal.

"The one thing I don't realize until later is that in international hockey, they credit the guy who gets the winning goal in the shootout with a goal in the game, so I end up with a hat trick," Eberle says. "Had no idea. I don't think anyone notices. The tying goal is all anyone remembers."

Eberle meets his family after the game. Tears flow.

"Our family planned all of our Christmas vacations around the World Juniors. It was huge to my parents," he says. "I think for me to have been lucky enough to play an instrumental part in a game like that, it was emotional for them. For me, too."

The gold medal game is anticlimactic after the semis.

Eberle scores an empty-net goal in a 5–1 Canada win. It's the country's fifth straight World Junior gold medal.

More than a decade later, Eberle still gets asked about the "Can you believe it" goal by fans everywhere he goes. They all want to tell him where they were, and how much it meant to them. That magical night in Ottawa was 14 months before Sidney Crosby scored the Olympic winner in overtime in Vancouver. So, for an entire generation of Canadians, Eberle's goal is their first Paul Henderson moment.

"Noah Dobson [his New York Islanders teammate] just brought it up the other day," Eberle says. "He says it's his most memorable World Junior memory growing up. It's nice to hear, but man, it made me feel old."

It's remarkable how a moment like that can stick in one's memory. Apparently, even the memory of hockey executives trying to improve their team. In 2017, Eberle is traded from the Edmonton Oilers to the New York Islanders.

"One of the reasons the Islanders tell me they traded for me is to play with John Tavares, because of our World Junior chemistry," Eberle laughs. "We barely played together! That one play—a blind backhand by him and a lucky bounce to me—it's remembered as 'chemistry.' It's pretty hilarious."

During their time with the Islanders, Tavares and Eberle have a running joke about the goal. You see, after Gord Miller yelled, "Can you believe it?!" his analyst, Pierre McGuire, followed instantly with, "I can! . . . Tavares had to step up and make a magical play! The crowd loves it! Tavares's magical play!"

"JT would rib me that it was his 'magical play' that should have gotten all the credit," Eberle laughs. "I mean, it was a smart play by him to get the puck towards the net, but it wasn't really a special play. And the goal wasn't any genius play by me. The whole thing was mostly luck, really. So, we just bust each other's balls about who the real hero was."

Eberle's goal remains one of the most dramatic and replayed moments in our nation's hockey history. It's never fading. But what will surely be forgotten as the decades slide by is that the very next year, he did it again.

Canada trails the Americans, 5–3, with under three minutes left in the 2010 World Junior gold medal game in Saskatoon, Saskatchewan. Eberle, now 19 and a household name in Canada, does the unthinkable: he scores twice in 1:20 to tie it, 5–5.

"I cannot believe it," he says, unintentionally paraphrasing Gord Miller. "In my head, I'm saying, 'Oh my God, I did it again! This is insane!' To me, it's more shocking than the Russia game the year before. And if you look at those two goals, they are pure crap. The first is a one-timer on the power play that I completely fan on, and it fools Jack Campbell and goes five-hole. The second one bounces off about three guys. Just unreal luck. It's a rare feeling in sports, like you can do no wrong."

But this time, the Eberle storybook ends with a painful twist. US defenceman John Carlson beats Martin Jones on a three-on-one 3:20 into overtime, and Canada's five-year gold medal streak is over.

"That one really stings," Eberle says. "Being in my home province with all my family and friends there, my last World Juniors, and the gold medal streak on the line. I tear up in the dressing room after. I just don't want it to be over."

Ponder for a moment Canada winning that game. Let your imagination stretch a little further, to see Eberle scoring the overtime goal. He might have gotten a statue before he'd played a single NHL game. Instead, the silver in Saskatoon becomes just a footnote in Canada's collective hockey memory. It's the Russia goal that is eternal.

"My brother got married in Jamaica last year, and one night my dad and I sat around and had a few drinks and started talking about that game," Eberle says. "My wife was pregnant, I was about to become a father for the first time, and I just really wanted to know what it was like for him as a father to watch a moment like that. He said he just couldn't believe it was happening. How we'd always watched that tournament together, and now his boy was playing a part in such an unforgettable game. You're a kid when it happens. You really don't think about it much. But as you get a little older, you really cherish it."

It's a good thing he has those memories, because there are almost no souvenirs from that game. The puck Eberle scored the tying goal with remained in play and was never saved. And he took the stick he scored with back to Regina, broke it and threw it in a garbage bin, not even thinking of its place in history.

Fortunately, the Pats' trainer was well aware of what it meant. He retrieved it from the trash and taped it back together. Eberle gave it to his mom. The stick that saved Canada remains in her house in Calgary.

The Draft Email Disaster

Insider Tales from Darren Dreger

═══════════

TSN's Darren Dreger is staring at his phone in disbelief.

"Oh my God, what have I done," he says to himself. A million thoughts are sprinting through his head, but one is loud and clear: "Brian Burke is going to kill me."

One hour earlier, the team tables that line the arena floor at the 2011 NHL Draft in St. Paul, Minnesota, are mostly empty, with one notable exception: Brian Burke, the GM of the Toronto Maple Leafs, likes to be early to every draft. He is the first and only GM on the floor. So, Dregs seizes an opportunity to hunt for a scoop.

"I saunter up to Burkie and say, 'Do you have anything in the works?' And surprisingly, he says, 'Yes.' So, I keep pushing him and pushing him, and finally he tells me he's made a trade but can't tell me the details because the player doesn't know yet. There is some legal work to be done before it gets completed."

To an Insider, that's like having a cake placed right in front of you and being told you can't take a bite. (Free cake, I should qualify, from a comped media meal. Helps the simile.) So, Dregs strikes a deal.

"I tell him, 'Burkie, I'm going to be scrambling around once the draft starts, so just tell me the deal right now so I can have it all ready to report, and I promise I won't send anything out until you give me the green light.'"

JAMES DUTHIE

Untied tie hanging around his neck (obviously), Burke ponders the request, and finally agrees.

"We're getting John-Michael Liles from Colorado for a second-round pick," he says. "And you better keep it quiet."

Dregs repeats his vow of silence until he's given the okay. Knowing how busy his day is about to get, he types a draft email to TSN Hockey announcing the trade. (TSN Hockey is the group email chain used to send out hockey information at The Sports Network. There are hundreds of TSN staffers from all across the country on it. This will become problematic shortly.) When Burke gives Dregs the go-ahead in a couple of hours, all he'll have to do is call up the email and hit send. He's done it many times before.

"My only concern is that I can't get a hold of Bob McKenzie," Dregs says. "I am trying to give him a heads-up so he can work it from his angle, so he isn't blindsided when I report it. But Bob isn't answering his phone. I figure I'll just run up to our panel set, just to let him know."

As Dregs bounces up the stairs towards the TSN set, he stumbles and fumbles his phone. It takes a couple of hard bounces off the concrete.

"My first thought is, 'Oh no, I've killed it! It's probably the biggest day of the year for hockey news flying around, and I've destroyed my phone.'"

But somehow, the screen is intact and all the buttons still work. (There is probably room here for a mid-book ad for OtterBox cases.) Dregs exhales and resumes the climb towards Bob. When he gets there, he checks the phone to see if he has missed anything on his five-minute hike. He's puzzled to see a chain of emails with the subject heading "Liles traded to Toronto."

"My first thought is, 'Who scooped me on this in my own company?'" Dregs says. "Then my eyes quickly scan the chain and I realize the first email had come from . . . me! I must have had the draft email open, and somehow, when I dropped my phone, one of the bounces hit send."

Cue panic.

"I'm dead," Dregs says. "I had pestered Burkie relentlessly and he finally confided in me. Now I've sent it out before he's given me the go-ahead. There is no pulling back from this. There are so many radio stations and Twitter feeds on that TSN Hockey group email that the trade is already out there . . . everywhere!"

Dregs is great at his job because he's earned the trust of executives like Burke. There is nothing worse to him than breaking a promise, no matter how cartoonish the circumstances. He has no choice.

An hour has gone by since Burke gave him the scoop, and the draft floor is now full, buzzing with word of the trade. So, Dregs heads straight to the Maple Leafs table and falls on his sword . . . for falling on his phone.

"I have to own this. So, I'm waving at Burkie, asking him to come over to me so I can tell him quietly. I tell him what happened, as dumb as it sounds. It's painfully awkward. Burkie says something like, 'You're such a dickhead.' Thankfully, he decides he won't murder me. Probably too many people around. Though I know I won't be breaking any more Leafs news that day."

"I believe him," Burkie says. "He's never screwed me before and he hasn't since. I'm angry, but he dropped his phone—it's an accident. I'm just pissed off because players shouldn't find out they are traded in the media."

"That part bothers me, too," Dregs says. "Players find out that way often around *TradeCentre* [TSN's trade-deadline show], but never quite like this."

Been there, Dregs. During *TradeCentre 2015*, our producer tells me in my ear that Chris Stewart has been traded to Minnesota from Buffalo, and Stewart is on the phone now. So, I bring him on live television and say, "Chris, what's your reaction to the trade?" And Chris responds, "Where have I been traded to?"

Awkward silence.

"You mean . . . you . . . don't . . . know?"

"No."

"Well, it's Minnesota."

That's how Chris Stewart finds out he's going to the Wild. So, yes, players do sometimes find out they've been traded through the media. Just not usually from a Hockey Insider dropping his phone and hitting send on an email.

Draft-day disasters like this have been rare for Dregs. He has broken countless deals on that floor. Usually, the source prefers to remain anonymous. *Usually*.

"At the 2009 draft, I get a tip that Philadelphia is about to acquire Chris Pronger from Anaheim. I'm thinking, 'Holy smokes!' Pronger is still a huge name. This is a major deal. I get the details and post it. Usually, we get our tips from player development guys or scouts, not the top executives at the table. No one wants to get caught tipping a reporter off. So, the source will never make eye contact with you from the table. They act like they don't know you. But in this case, it's one of the senior executives, a huge name in hockey. So, as everyone hears about the trade and you can feel the buzz around the room, I glance over to the team's table, and the source is smiling at me and gives me this huge thumbs-up, right in front of everyone. He just doesn't care. Definitely one of my most entertaining scoops."

Dregs's biggest scoop is also one of his first. In 2005, he is still a host, not an Insider, when he gets the tip of his career.

"The late, great John Ferguson was one of my favourite guys and one of my first sources," Dregs says. "I love that man. He's with the San Jose Sharks when I get to know him, and one day I'm doing my regular cold calls, just fishing around, and I ask Fergie if anything is going on. He says, 'Yeah, we're just about to acquire Joe Thornton from Boston.'"

Sorry . . . what?

"'Oh my God, this is a blockbuster!' I'm thinking. So, I write it up. This is before Twitter, so I put the trade out on our website and write, 'Joe Thornton has just been traded to the San Jose Sharks. More details to come.'"

Then Dregs sits and waits for the teams to confirm it. And waits. And waits.

"There is nothing . . . crickets!" Dregs says. "Hours go by. *Hockey Night in Canada* is doing its 'Hot Stove' segment and they say nothing, except that there is some phantom report out there about a Joe Thornton trade. I am in a full-sweat panic, thinking the deal has somehow fallen apart. I age about five years in a few hours."

Finally, the teams officially announce the trade. Joe Thornton is officially a Shark. And Darren Dreger is officially an Insider.

Butch's Battles

Garth Butcher Gets Black Eyes and Big Mini-Bar Bills

Both teammates and opponents are frightened of Garth Butcher during his career, for two very different reasons.

Let's start with the obvious: his fists. Butch is one of the most feared fighters in the league during his 16-year NHL career. But he is too humble to talk about that toughness. Tough guys, in general, are (or *were*—there aren't many left) usually the nicest, most humble guys in hockey. In fact, Butch never talks about the fights he won. He much prefers tales of battles lost.

"One night I go at it with Bob Probert in Detroit," Butch says. "We're 45 seconds or so into it, and I'm doing really well. I'm landing a few and thinking to myself, 'Hey, I'm fighting Probert and I'm holding my own! Look at me!' I'm getting really tired by this point, and figure it should be just about over. 'Let's go, linesmen—break this thing up.' And then Bob pulls his shirt off and I realize, 'Oh crap, that was just the warm-up for him! He's just getting started!' I'm completely done, my arms are about to fall off, and Bob's like, 'Let's do this!' So, yeah, it didn't go so well after that."

From the first time he drops his gloves, Butch doesn't like fighting. But his lip tends to gets him in trouble. And occasionally, his teammates' lips do as well.

One game, a couple of Canucks rookies, who haven't learned the rules of engagement yet, decide it would be a good idea to chirp Edmonton Oilers tough guy Dave Semenko from the bench before a faceoff.

"Semenko finally turns to face our bench, and I'm sitting there and I look to my right and left, and the guys who were chirping are suddenly tying their skates," Butch says. "So, now Semenko's looking right at me, saying, 'You are dead.' Thanks, guys! It's amazing how those laces came loose all at once!"

The Oilers are never much fun for Butch.

"I really hate playing them in my early years in Vancouver, because you can't win no matter who you go out against," he says. "You could end up out there against Gretz and just look stupid. You could face Mess [Mark Messier] and Glenny [Glenn Anderson], and they are just flying around you. Or you get to play against Semenko. I would sit there before the game and go, 'Do I want to go minus-5 tonight or get beat up?'

One time, Butch fights two other Oilers tough guys—Jeff Beukeboom and Marty McSorley—in the same game. A couple of days later, his wife gives birth to their first child, a son named Matt.

"He's a New Year's baby, and so the local paper runs a photo of me holding him, smiling, with the purplest, blackest eye you'll ever see. I'd like to tell you I did well in those two fights, but baby photos don't lie!"

Truth is, Butch more than holds his own in almost every scrap over his 16 seasons in the NHL. Most opponents don't want any part of Garth Butcher. And neither do teammates. You see, Butch is an elite snorer. A taboo trait for an NHL roomie.

"Every roommate I have in hockey ends up leaving in the middle of the night because he can't take it," Butch says. "But it works out, because I get my own room!"

Perhaps because Butch is alone, his hotel room becomes a gathering place on nights off or after games. The boys come to Butch to have a few. And sometimes a few more.

"One road trip when I'm playing with the Blues, we have a night off in Winnipeg before flying out the next morning," Butch says. "Most teams seem to get extra days off in LA, but the Blues always seem to get them in Winnipeg. Oh well. So, we decide to have a little gathering in my room. Hully [Brett Hull] and Chaser [Kelly Chase] are there, and we have a couple of new Russians on the team. We want to give them a friendly Blues welcome. So, we invite them up for a few beverages.

"Before long, they are into the mini-bar, and specifically the vodka. I have to call down a couple of times to replenish the stock. And then, after a while, we move on to other spirits. This goes all night. Everything is going . . . fast. I guess at some point, we go to bed. It's blurry. But when I wake up the next morning, I check the mini-bar and the entire thing is empty. I mean, everything is gone. I have to go check out. Back then, there was a sheet in your room you had to fill out to say what you took from the mini-bar. So, I grab a pen and just start putting checkmarks beside everything on the sheet. Drank that—check! Drank that—check! Yup, that too. With refills!"

When Butch gets down to the lobby to check out, all of the Blues coaches and execs are standing together near the front desk.

"GM Ron Caron is there, head coach Brian Sutter, assistant coach Bob Berry—you name it," he says. "They are giving me the eye because it probably looks like we've had a night. So, I'm carrying this mini-bar sheet, trying to be very discreet and quiet as I explain things to the guy at the front desk."

Which leads to the following exchange between Butch and the Winnipeg Westin check-out guy:

BUTCH [*softly*]: *Hey, here are my incidentals . . . Could you please just put the whole charge on my credit card?*

CHECK-OUT GUY [*the opposite of softly*]: *THE WHOLE THING?*

232

BUTCH: *Hey, keep it down, pal . . . Yes, please just charge the whole thing to me. Thank you.*

CHECK-OUT GUY: *YOU EMPTIED THE ENTIRE MINI-BAR?*

BUTCH: *Please, just take my Visa!*

The Blues brass watches all of this, collectively shaking their heads. But Loud-Voiced Desk Clerk isn't quite done. He's now going through the list, item by item.

CHECK-OUT GUY: *EVEN THE ALKA-SELTZER?*

BUTCH: *[Sigh.]*

Cuatro por Papi

Auston Matthews's NHL Debut

He unwraps the first present and squeals in delight. It's a Coyotes jersey.

That's how he found hockey, bouncing on the knee of his dad at the games in Glendale when he was a toddler. Not old enough to really understand what was going on. But old enough to know he loved it.

He pulls the jersey on and smiles proudly.

"There's one more gift for you in the garage, Papi," says his mom, Ema. He bounces off to find it. Moments later, he charges back into the living room, stickhandling the whole way.

A 'Yotes jersey and a new hockey stick! Best birthday ever! Granted, it's only his fifth.

"If you work hard and keep playing hockey, someday you might get a scholarship to college," Ema tells her little boy.

He stops stickhandling and stares at her.

"But I don't want to go to college, Mom," little Auston Matthews says. "I'm gonna play in the NHL!"

⸻

Thirteen years later—the day before his five-year-old prophet self is proven right (with four exclamation points)—Auston sits

234

with Ema and his dad, Brian, in an Italian restaurant in Ottawa. It's October 11, 2016. The Toronto Maple Leafs will open their season against the Senators the following night. Auston's NHL debut.

They avoid talking hockey. "We're all nervous, but Auston's trying to act like he isn't nervous, and we're trying to not say anything to make him nervous," Brian says. "But the unspoken thing for Ema and I: we want him to score a goal. Just one. So it's not hanging over his head."

A goal in your kid's first NHL game is a lot to ask. Or, apparently with this kid, not nearly enough.

Game day feels normal to Auston. He's working on his sticks at the rink when Maple Leafs coach Mike Babcock comes over and asks if he's nervous. When Auston answers no, Babcock says, "You will be. Just be careful not to spend all your energy in the pre-game warm-up."

Game day does not feel normal to Brian and Ema. "We're so unprepared," Brian says. "We think we have lots of time to get to the rink, but there's a huge line of fans waiting for a shuttle bus. We try to get an Uber, and finally end up jamming in this 10-person bus with 20 people. There's tons of traffic, and I look at Ema and say, 'I don't think we're going to make it.'"

==

Papi's passion for the game is so intense, it delays his youngest sister's birth.

All of the Matthews babies are huge—nine pounds plus. The youngest, Breyana, is going to be 10 pounds if she goes full term. So, Ema and Brian schedule an inducement.

Oops. It's the same day as Papi's first-ever hockey practice. They know it will crush him to miss it. So, Brian rushes Papi to the rink and back home before taking Ema in. Breyana waits a few extra hours to join the world.

==

Brian and Ema make it to the Senators' rink in Kanata. Barely. They scramble to their seats just in time for puck drop. One goal, son. Just get one.

He doesn't make them wait long. On Auston's third shift, he heads to the net as William Nylander breaks in down the right wing.

"Willy makes this unbelievable move at the blue line, and suddenly I'm alone in front," Auston says. "He makes a great pass, and I have a wide-open net. I'm thinking, 'Oh my God, I'm going to score right here!' But I wait too long and Derick Brassard strips me from behind. My elbow pad gets stuck, and I kinda shake my arm to get it loose. And then I'm open again. I scream at Zach Hyman for the puck. He gives it to me, and . . . it's in the net! I just go insane. I lose complete control of my mind and body."

Brian and Ema leap from their seats and hug. Brian fist-pumps the sky. "It happens right in front of us," he says. "I say to Em, 'Now we can relax!' We can see it in Auston's face, too, because he looks up towards us after he scores and . . . the stress is gone."

Six minutes later, Auston strips Mark Stone at the Senators blue line. He tucks the puck between Stone's legs, and then Mike Hoffman's, pushing it back towards centre ice. He beats Kyle Turris at the red line and circles to the left wall. Hoffman gives him a half shove/half cross-check from behind, and the puck slides towards Erik Karlsson along the boards in the Senators' end. Karlsson has it briefly, but Auston lifts his stick and dances past him, cutting towards the net. Goalie Craig Anderson looks like he's expecting a pass, but Auston shoots and fools him five-hole.

He has just beaten five of the six Senators on the ice for his second goal. In his first NHL period.

"I think I black out after that one," Auston says. "I have no idea what's going on at this point."

The disbelief is genetic.

"Oh my God, did that really happen?" Brian says to himself.

It's still happening, Dad. Your boy is just getting started.

==

"Where's Auston?" Brian asks, over and over. But the kids in the dressing room just stare back blankly.

He's seven now, and hockey is all he wants to do. They have to drag him out of the rink. But no time for that today. His older sister Alex has a soccer game right after his hockey game. Brian and Ema have told him to hurry out so Alex can make it on time.

But now the game is long over, and Auston is nowhere to be found. Alex is losing it. Ema is fuming.

"GUYS, WHERE IS AUSTON?" Brian repeats, getting frustrated that the kids won't snitch on their friend. Finally, one little boy at the back of the room puts his hand up.

"Who is Auston?"

It hits Brian. No one calls his son Auston. It's always been Papi. Ema is originally from Mexico, and "Papi" is a common nickname for the first-born boy in a family. Even Brian and Ema only use "Auston" when they're mad at him. Like . . . now.

"Where is . . . Papi?"

His teammates, now realizing Papi and Auston are the same kid, give him up in a heartbeat. They show Brian to another room, where he finds Papi, still with half his gear on, playing mini-sticks with some other friends.

Alex makes her game, but demands supplemental discipline for her little brother.

==

Morgan Rielly is Auston's first close friend on the Leafs. They hang out all through the World Cup of Hockey the month before Auston's NHL debut. A minute and change into the second period in Ottawa, Rielly carries the puck the entire length of the ice along the left boards. He spots 34 in front and threads a perfect pass.

Auston one-times it through Ottawa defenceman Dion Phaneuf's legs and past Anderson.

"I just look at Mo and start screaming, 'What a pass! I love you, man!'" Auston laughs.

It happens so fast, Ema doesn't see who scores. The man sitting next to her says, "It's a hat trick!" It's Nazem Kadri's dad, Sam.

"We're so incompetent, we don't even realize the Kadris are sitting right next to us until that moment," Brian says. "We're just two deer in the headlights the whole night."

Hats litter the ice. There are always thousands of Leafs fans at games in Ottawa. But Brian and Ema don't know that. Until now.

"It's like a home game!" Brian says. "It feels like the whole building is going crazy."

Ema sees the hats, sees Auston's teammates mauling him, and starts crying. Brian hugs her and gently kisses the top of her head.

"We're just so happy for him," Ema says. "He's come so far."

==

Mom and Dad sit in front of their TV, in stunned silence, watching their 15-year-old boy in agony on the ice. They're home in Arizona, live-streaming Auston's second game with the United States National Development Program. An opponent has stuck out a knee, sending Auston somersaulting. He's stretchered off and taken to hospital.

"I'm calling and calling and can't get anyone to answer the phone," Brian says. "Finally, I reach his billet family and ask them to bust down some doors and find out how my son is. She gets back to me and says, 'It's not his knee; it's a broken leg. But, Brian, it's not just a normal broken leg . . . He needs surgery.'"

Brian rushes to the airport and catches a red-eye to Detroit.

"When I get to the hospital, the entire team is there—Matthew Tkachuk, Charlie McAvoy, Noah Hanifin, the coach, the trainer, all of them," Brian says. "The camaraderie on that team is unreal. They're trying to cheer him up. But it's not working. The coach, Donnie Granato, pulls me aside and says, 'Listen, Brian, surgery went really well. But Auston's a mess. He thinks he's never going to play again.'"

The team leaves, and it's just father and son. For six hours, Brian tries to boost Auston's spirits. Tries to get him to forget the three screws and four pins sticking out of his leg. Tries to reassure him it will be okay. Finally, he leaves to get a coffee. To give his boy some time alone.

"I call Ema, dejected, and tell her, 'I don't think I'm getting through,'" Brian says. "I come back after 25 minutes or so, and his hospital room is empty. I walk around the corner, and he's hopping down the hall with the nurse, dragging the IV behind him. And the look in his eye is so determined . . . I call Ema and say, 'We're good. He's back.'"

＝＝

By the second period, the entire hockey world is watching Ottawa. No other games have started yet. NHL superstars are texting each other: *Are you seeing this???? Matthews WTF!!!!*

Brian's and Ema's phones have spontaneously combusted. Keith Tkachuk, Shane Doan, Auston's old coach Granato—everyone they've ever met in hockey is texting. Christine Simpson from Sportsnet comes down to interview them. Suddenly, everyone in the stands realizes they are Auston's parents. There are endless high-fives, and fans yelling, "Thank you for birthing him, Ema!"

"Leafs fans are the best," she laughs.

In the dying moments of the second, Jake Gardiner flips the puck up ice to Auston. He spots William Nylander, feeds him and races to the net. Nylander saucers a perfect pass over Chris Wideman's stick, and Auston chips it over Anderson's pad.

Cuatro por Papi. Auston Matthews is the first player in hockey's modern era to score four goals in his NHL debut. There is no primal scream this time. No leap into the glass. His face is . . . blank.

"I'm just paralyzed," Auston says. "I don't know if it's real anymore. I'm trying to look calm, don't want to piss off any of the veterans, trying to act like I've been there before. But my head is spinning."

"My mouth is just wide open, like, 'Wow! What did I just see?!'" Ema says. "I brought my camera to take pictures of his first game, but it's so crazy, and I'm so excited, I forget to take any."

The Leafs would lose, 5–4, in overtime, the only downer in a wildest-of-dreams night. Steve Keogh, Toronto's director of media relations, comes to get Brian and Ema in the stands.

"I think the Leafs realized we were clueless," Brian says. "We're sitting there, with no idea what to do or where to go, when Steve comes up and says, 'I'll take you to him.'"

When parents and son reunite in the bowels of the rink, there are no words. None needed.

"I'm crying again," Ema says. "And we're all speechless."

"I give them both a really big hug and then we just stand there and look at each other for a minute in utter shock that this happened," Auston says.

They only have that minute. NHL life moves fast. Auston is off to catch the team charter.

"Mitchy [Marner] and I get on the plane first and sit near the front," Auston says. "As the veteran guys get on, they all stop and shake my hand to congratulate me. That's one of the coolest moments."

He spends the whole flight on his phone.

"As selfish as this sounds, I couldn't not see myself," Auston laughs. "Everywhere on social media, even on accounts that I follow for basketball, football, baseball—that would never tweet about hockey—suddenly, I'm all over their accounts. Hilarious memes about being on pace to score 300 goals . . . It's just bonkers."

He specifically remembers a tweet from Dallas star Tyler Seguin:

I don't even know what to say. Just a treat to watch tonight @AM34

"Just awesome to have a guy like that tweeting about your first game," Auston says.

That's when you remember he's 18. Up until tonight, he was an NHL fan, like everybody else. Now he's blown up the internet, with the greatest debut in hockey history.

As their boy flies back to Toronto, Brian and Ema quietly head back to their Ottawa hotel.

"We don't sleep a minute that night," Brian says. "We just lie there, trying to let it all sink in. Eighteen years of your son dreaming of this moment . . . all the early-morning skates, the workouts, the broken leg . . . and this happens in his first game? We're just so proud."

Carlo's Commute

Carlo Colaiacovo Races between Paternity and Playoffs

Unspoken fact: professional hockey coaches and GMs would prefer that their players do their baby-making in the late fall. Ideally October to December, if you want specifics. Summer births never interfere with playoff runs (until 2020). But that's a tough clause to get into a contract. Sometimes you can't fight the miracle of love . . . and life.

Which lands us in Mannheim, Germany, in March 2017. After 14 seasons in the NHL, Carlo Colaiacovo is winding down his career, playing with Adler Mannheim in the top German league, the Deutsche Eishockey Liga.

His wife, Gina, is back in Toronto, their hometown, pregnant with their second child. We're talking "last minute of play in the third period" pregnant. She is due any day. And the playoffs are about to begin.

Mannheim's first-round schedule goes like this:

- » Game 1: Tuesday (Home)
- » Game 2: Friday (Road)
- » Game 3: Sunday (Home)

"I have a plan, as best as you can plan these things," Carlo says with a laugh. "My wife Gina's due date is the Friday. So, I'll fly home Wednesday morning after the Tuesday game, hopefully get lucky and have the baby over the next day or two, and make it back for the Friday game."

The plan starts smoothly enough. Mannheim wins Game 1 at home in overtime.

"This makes me feel less guilty for leaving the next day," Carlo says. "I fly home with my fingers, toes and testicles crossed that my son Leo would come before Friday's game."

Carlo learns quickly that he can control a power play, but not a womb. Wednesday and most of Thursday go by with no action. Sometime late Thursday night, Leo decides he's just about ready to make his debut in the league we call Life.

"Gina starts having contractions that night, so I know I'm not going to be there for the Friday game," Carlo says. "So, Friday comes and I'm praying for a few things: First and foremost, a healthy baby boy and Gina getting through it. Second, please let us win the second game, so we'll be up 2–0 in the series. Then maybe the team won't rush me back for Game 3. I can spend more time with my family and newborn son. And third, maybe Gina can hold off delivery until the game is over, so I can watch it on my phone in the hospital room!"

Can't fault a guy for aiming high.

He gets two out of three. Gina holds Leo off until after the game is over. Terrific defence. And most importantly, he arrives healthy and beautiful.

"Gina is the MVP," Carlo says. "She lets me watch the whole game before Leo is born! We lead three different times in the game, but lose, 5–3. I'm elated over Leo. But I'm furious because we should have won, and after seeing how we lost, I know my phone is gonna blow up from coaches and management telling me to get back for Game 3 Sunday afternoon."

Sure enough, just as Leo is making his grand entrance, Carlo can feel his phone vibrating constantly in his pocket. When he checks later, there are endless texts from teammates and coaches asking if Leo has arrived . . . and when Carlo plans on rejoining the team.

"I'm so grateful to my teammates, coaches and GM for allowing me to come home," he says. "Some teams in Europe don't give their blessings like they did. But I know they are anxious. I return a missed call from my GM, who starts by being excited about Leo, but I know the whole time the question is coming. 'Congratulations! That's amazing! There is nothing like witnessing the birth of a child! And oh . . . by the way . . . when are you coming back?!'"

Carlo doesn't have an answer. Despite his earlier plan to return as soon as possible, seeing his son being born changes things.

"I don't want to leave, and definitely not without the blessing of my wife," he says. "But we have a heart-to-heart and she is really supportive of me going back to a team where I'm wanted . . . and needed. That was a feeling I didn't have in my last few years in the NHL. That's special. We are both incredibly thankful that I was there for Leo's birth, so we decide I'm going back to play."

Carlo books a 5 p.m. flight back to Germany. It will get him into Mannheim around 7 a.m. for a 1 p.m. game.

"As long as I get a comfortable seat on the plane, and a decent sleep, I know I can do it."

But just as the plane is set to take off from Toronto, the pilot announces mechanical problems.

"As much as I want to play, I'm secretly fist-pumping because now there's no way I can make the game, and I'll be able to stay home with my family for a couple more days."

Carlo gets off the plane, but just as he's about to leave the airport and go home to Gina, Leo and their daughter, Mia, there's an announcement for all passengers to stay close to the gate. They have another plane.

"I'm like, 'What the hell ?' How is there just a random empty plane waiting around the airport that has nowhere to go?"

The new flight time is 7:45 p.m. By Carlo's updated calculations, his flight will arrive in Frankfurt around 9:45 a.m. local time. By the time he gets his luggage, goes through customs and drives to Mannheim, it will be around 11 a.m.—two hours before the puck drops.

"How the hell am I gonna do this?" he thinks. "I haven't skated since Tuesday's game."

To summarize: no hockey in four days, barely any sleep, and an eight-hour overnight flight with a six-hour time change, to play a critical playoff game. Oh, and there's one more little complication.

"I eat dinner on the plane. I'm sitting in that premium economy section and they serve chicken and rice," he says. "It's actually pretty good, and I fall asleep right after. But four hours in, I wake up with this incredible pain in my stomach. Now the sweats are activated! I'm a mess. My go-to every time this happens when I fly is a ginger ale. Usually, I'm good after. Not this time! I rush to the bathroom and plant myself there for at least an hour. Finally, I come out and I don't even make it back to my seat before I have to go again. After two and a half hours of this, I finally seem to get rid of it all. I need sleep so badly, but now it's too late, and I'm too anxious."

The wheels touch down in Frankfurt just before 10 a.m. Herman, Mannheim's team services guy, picks Carlo up at the airport. It's less than three hours to game time.

"Herman is the human version of the Jiffy app," Carlo says. "He does everything. There are no speed limits in Germany, and Herman just flies on the autobahn. A normal 45-minute drive to Mannheim takes us 23 minutes."

They head straight to the rink. Carlo is dehydrated, jet-lagged, physically and mentally exhausted, and about to be on the top pairing in Game 3 of a playoff series.

"The guys in the room are excited because they can't believe I'm there after hearing everything I went through," he says. "That helps get me going. So, I say to myself, 'No excuses. I'm here. Find a way. Make it happen.' I know adrenaline exists because that's all I played on. I want to show my teammates, coaches and GM that I am willing to give it my all for them in return for the experience they allowed me to share with my family."

Apparently, self-pep talks can turn into self-fulfilling prophecies.

On a Mannheim power play, Carlo fakes a shot and fires a pass to a teammate for a back-door tap-in. Then, in the dying seconds, clinging to a one-goal lead, he knocks down a dump-in and flips a high shot towards the empty net. He hears his bench collectively scream, "Nooooo!" fearing the puck will go wide for an icing. They clearly don't understand destiny. The puck bounces a couple of times . . . and finds nothing but net.

"They didn't remember I was four-for-four on empty-netters that season," he laughs. "It was an automatic."

Carlo has the game-winning assist and the clinching goal. He is named the first star. Afterwards, he sits in his dressing room stall, delirious.

"I'm looking around, and all I see is happiness," Carlo says. "I literally can't move. I just hit a wall of complete exhaustion. I can't believe that at age 34, I'm able to do what I just did. No sleep, hardly any food (that stayed in me), jet lag, the emotions of watching Leo being born. But I did it. I like to think that story represents what my career was about. Family and perseverance."

Leo's still way too young to understand the complexities of his birth story. Someday, Carlo will tell him the whole tale. How Dad was the first star. How Mom was the MVP. And how Leo is the only part that ever really mattered.

The Apprenticeship of Jim McKenzie

A Tough Guy Learns the Ropes

I didn't know anything about being a hockey player. Luckily, I had a lot of guys who taught me along the way.
—JIM McKENZIE (14 NHL SEASONS, 9 TEAMS, 1,739 PENALTY MINUTES)

―――――――――

Lesson 1: Don't Let the Coach Intimidate You

Jim McKenzie's hockey education begins in Moose Jaw, Saskatchewan, in 1986. He's a wide-eyed rookie with the Western Hockey League's Warriors.

"We have a horrible coach. I don't even want to name him. He's just a complete idiot," McKenzie says. "So, Mike Keane is on the team, and Keaner is just one of those guys who is 30 years old in a 17-year-old body. And he sees right through this coach from the beginning. The coach thinks he's really tough, but Keaner knows he's a phony. So, he calls him 'Cupcake' right to his face—'Hey Cupcake, what time is practice?' Every. Single. Time. Well, one night we are playing the Saskatoon Blades, and they aren't a hockey team—they are a work-release program. They have Chaser [Kelly Chase], Twister [Tony Twist], Kerry Clark, Kevin Kaminski . . . just a bunch of donkeys. Anyway, somehow, we blow a 3–1 lead and lose.

"So, we get home from Saskatoon at two in the morning and Cupcake says, 'Anyone who wants to be on the team tomorrow, put your gear on. We're going to skate.' We're at the Crushed Can [the Moose Jaw Civic Centre], and Cupcake can't figure out how to get the lights on. It's dark, except for the score clocks at either end of the rink. And Cupcake is just screaming about how terrible we are. Then he suddenly pauses and says, 'Where the fuck is Keane?' And from the back you hear, 'Right here, Cupcake!' Keaner has gone into the room and come back out with the trainer's penlight taped to his helmet, like a miner's hat. We all crack up. Cupcake is so mad. He bag-skates us for an hour. But he could have skated us all night and it wouldn't have mattered after that.

"Another time, we are on a bus trip to Medicine Hat and Keaner buys all these little plastic BB guns. The vets at the back of the bus are shooting at the rookies. But soon enough, we see this hail of BBs over our heads right at Cupcake, who is trying to take a nap. Well, Cupcake is furious and comes back and takes some of the guns, but Keaner had hidden one under his leg. As soon as Cupcake walks back towards the front, Keaner nails him right in the head. Now he's furious and comes back, waving this sawed-off broom he has for cleaning up the bus. He says, 'Do you know what this is, Keaner?' And Keaner says, 'Your job next year, Cupcake.' We all just lose it."

Lesson 2: Don't Chirp a Chirper

During McKenzie's last year in Moose Jaw, he is coached by a Canadian sports legend, Gerry James. James was a two-sport athlete—a four-time Grey Cup champion football player with the Winnipeg Blue Bombers, and a Stanley Cup finalist with the Toronto Maple Leafs. He is also a dark comic genius.

"We show up at practice one time, and they tell us our cheques aren't going to be there," McKenzie says. "So Gerry tells us, 'You guys should go on strike. If they aren't going to pay you, just stay home, don't practise. That's what I would do.'

"Well, we think this is a great idea! So, we all go home. The next day, we come in and our envelopes are there, and there is only 10 bucks inside instead of 20. We say to Gerry, 'What the hell is this?' And he says, 'I had to fine you because you took the day off yesterday.' He's an absolute beauty!

"Gerry was a brilliant chirper. I could never chirp. I always take it personally when guys say things to me, so I never wanted to say anything to anyone else. But one day I walk in on game day and Gerry is wearing this ugly yellow jacket. It looks like a Century 21 blazer. So, I work up the courage to rip him. I'm like, 'Hey coach, hear you sold your hundredth house and they gave you a jacket!' He turns around and it's a Canadian Football Hall of Fame jacket. Without missing a beat, he says, 'Nope, got it when I got inducted.'

"I thought my line was hilarious, practised it a hundred times in my head, finally worked up the courage, and *boom*! He shoots it down, just like that. I was like, 'Okay, just gonna go hide here in the corner and put my skates on and never say anything, ever again.'"

Lesson 3: Prank When They Least Expect It

In McKenzie's rookie season in the NHL, his Hartford Whalers trade for Mark Hunter. McKenzie is the first guy at the rink the morning after the deal is made. He's sitting alone in the dressing room, sipping a coffee, when Hunter walks in.

"I've never met him before. I'm just a rookie, and he's this vet who has been around," McKenzie says. "So, he gives me a little nod and then he goes to the bathroom. He comes out with shaving cream and scissors. He goes around the room and cuts the laces on every pair of skates and puts shaving cream in all of their gloves! Then he looks at me and says, 'I was never here,' and walks out of the room. We just traded for the guy the night before!

"The room starts to fill up, and Hunter walks back in like he's just arrived. He goes around, introducing himself to everyone. So, guys start putting on their stuff, and realize their laces are cut and their gloves are a mess. They're all swearing and looking at me, because they know I'm always the first guy in the room. I'm going, 'Wasn't me, guys. I was in the trainer's room!' Hunter knows this is the one time no one is ever going to accuse you of a prank, on your first day with the team. No one would have the balls to do that on their first day! Mark never admits to it. He would do stuff like that all the time, and no one ever knew."

Hunter becomes McKenzie's Mr. Miyagi of pranking. And the student uses everything he's learned from the master before his final NHL season, in Nashville in 2003.

"We do this bonding thing where we go down to Orlando for a few days. We use the practice facility for the NBA team, but the hotel is 20 minutes away, so they rent us vans—two for the players and one for the coaches—Barry Trotz, Pete Horachek and Brent Petersen.

"They are out on the ice one day, and I'm bored because I tore my ACL in training camp. I'm walking around and see the keys for the coaches' van. So, I grab the keys, sneak outside and take the seats out of the back of the van and hide them inside, under the stairs. We get back to the hotel, and I tell all the guys to wait in the lobby. The coaches arrive, and pour out of the dirty little van with no seats, and they are just miserable. Was not a fun ride.

"That night, after curfew, I get our equipment guy, Frosty Scoppetto, to drive me back over there because he has the security pass for the facility. Frosty and I move all the couches and chairs out of the coaches' room and replace them with the van seats. The next day, the coaches are desperate to know who did it, so they make the poor video guy, Robert Bouchard, pore over all the security camera footage at the complex. All he can find is this grainy black-and-white footage of this big guy with a giant head limping into the building with a van seat. It looks like those old Bigfoot movies we watched in the '80s. That's me . . . Sasquatch!"

Lesson 4: Know Who You Are Fighting

McKenzie is an NHL rookie in 1990–91 with the Hartford Whalers. He's up and down between the NHL and the minors, trying to find a way to stick with the big club.

"I don't consider myself a fighter," he says. "I didn't have that many penalty minutes in junior and never looked for fights. I don't really even understand the role of the tough guy at that point. I'm just trying to stay in the league as a player."

The Whalers are in Calgary on December 29, 1990, and getting destroyed. It's 8–1 in the third when McKenzie goes upstairs on Rick Wamsley for his first NHL goal.

"Even though we get smoked, I feel pretty good about myself because I scored. Rick Ley is our coach. I love playing for him. He would end up playing the heck out of me. But on this night, he's mad and he just starts carving everyone. Then he gets to me and says, 'You didn't hit anyone. You didn't fight anyone. You did nothing!' I'm thinking, 'Hey, I scored a goal!' So I'm rattled, thinking I'm going to get sent down. As we bus to Edmonton, I'm playing mind games with myself. 'You scored a goal, but the coach said you sucked. Maybe you *do* suck.' I'm a mess."

During warm-ups for the Oilers game, McKenzie bumps into an Oilers player near centre ice. He thinks nothing of it. But the Oilers do.

"One of their little yappy guys, Keith Acton or Ken Linseman, looks at me, looks at the big guy I bumped into and says, 'Holy fuck, Brownie, this kid is trying to show you up in your own building. What are you going to do about it?' And the big guy looks at me and says, 'You're dead.' I'm like, 'Whatever, buddy.' I have no clue who he is. My mind is still obsessed with getting yelled at by the coach 24 hours earlier. For the rest of the warm-up, we bump a few times and make eyes, stupid *Slap Shot* stuff. Kelly Buchberger, my old junior teammate who plays for Edmonton, skates up and says, 'Buddy, what are you doing? Do you have a death wish?' But I'm not paying any attention to him. I'm clueless."

251

In the dressing room after the warm-up, McKenzie can't understand why no one will look at him, like he's a dead man walking (er, skating). The extra players scratched from the lineup seem relieved not to be playing.

The game starts, and a couple of shifts in, the big guy on the Oilers challenges McKenzie to a fight. They go. It's a great tilt, and the rookie holds his own. But as he sits in the box, his head is still spinning.

"The few fights I had in junior and the minors, I usually won. I did okay in this one, but I didn't win. I scored a goal and the coach yelled at me. I'm probably getting sent back down. Maybe I should just quit and go back to Saskatchewan and be a cop like my dad. These are the things I'm thinking, sitting in that box! I'm just miserable."

When the five-minute major ends, McKenzie senses something strange. There is an energy on the bench. His teammates had never seen him fight before. He can tell they're pumped. He's felt this after a fight, but never quite like this. Coach Ley sends him right back out on the ice.

"In this age, if you don't feel you do well enough in your fight, you get back out and go again. I see the big guy, give him a whack and say, 'Let's go!' And he goes, 'Settle the fuck down, kid.'"

The rematch doesn't happen. Now it's the third period, and the Whalers trail by a goal. McKenzie is glued to the bench. He's moping. He sits at the very end next to his good buddy, Whalers backup goalie Daryl Reaugh.

REAUGH: *What's wrong with you?*

McKENZIE: *I'm getting sent down. I score and the coach yells at me . . . Now I can't even win a fight against this guy.*

REAUGH: *Wait. You don't know who you fought?*

McKENZIE: *Yeah . . . Some guy named Brown.*

REAUGH: *That's Dave Brown.*

McKENZIE: *Oooh, big deal. Dave Brown . . . Charlie Brown . . . Downtown Brown . . . who cares?*

REAUGH: *No. DAVE. BROWN.*

(PAUSE.)

McKENZIE: *What do you mean? The Dave Brown . . . of the Flyers?*

REAUGH: *Dave Brown who got traded from the Flyers to Edmonton, you idiot! Dave Brown, the toughest guy in the league!*

McKENZIE: *Oh crap.*

McKenzie feels the blood leave his face. He had no idea he had poked the biggest, baddest bear in the NHL.

"Now coach Ley is signalling to pull the goalie to try to tie it," McKenzie says. "I'm like, 'Maybe just leave him in there and be happy with the one-goal loss!'

"If they score an empty-netter, I'm going to have to go back out and fight him again. That's how it worked back then. Luckily, no one scores. I'm the happiest guy in the world. I jump over the bench like we've won a playoff game! It's crazy that I didn't know who it was. He had been in Edmonton awhile, but I wasn't in the league yet. I wasn't really sharp when it came to following who was where. All the guys on our team thought I was this courageous, heroic tough guy. And really, I was just dumb."

Lesson 5: Mario Can Do Whatever He Wants

In 1994, McKenzie gets traded from Dallas to Pittsburgh at the deadline. The Penguins have won two Cups in the last three years.

"We have a neutral-site game in Cleveland, and I've just gotten there, so I don't really know anyone," McKenzie says. "It's an afternoon game and I get on the bus and see 15 guys or so. I don't see Mario. I don't see Ron Francis. I don't see Ulf Samuelsson. I look over at Rick Tocchet and say, 'Where are they all?' And he says, 'They are driving down with their families. We'll meet them there.' I'm thinking, 'What? That's not how it's done.'"

When the Penguins arrive in Cleveland, McKenzie finds Ron Francis in the dressing room, working on his stick. All the players who have come down separately are there. But still no Mario. Finally, he walks in, just as the players are about to head out for the warm-up.

"It's strange, but I figure he'll just throw on his gear and get out there," McKenzie says. "So we go out for warm-up, and when we get off the ice, Mario is still sitting in his street clothes, sipping on a coffee, reading the paper. I'm like, 'What the hell is going on?' Finally, he gets dressed, goes out and gets two goals and two assists! One of the goals is amazing, and the assists are ridiculous. We beat Boston, 6–2. And he's the first star. I have never seen anything like it."

Walking to the bus, McKenzie is still shaking his head when he feels a little tap. It's Mario, whom he still hasn't had a real conversation with.

"Mario says a quick hello to welcome me, gives me a wry little smile and says, 'See ya Tuesday.' We have practice Monday. So yeah, I figure out pretty fast that Mario is on a different schedule. (Turns out he was just pulling my leg; he did show up Monday.)"

The next thing McKenzie notices, besides Mario's flexible schedule, is the shoeshine box 66 has in his stall.

"My dad had been in the RCMP and always had this big shoeshine box, and I notice right away Mario has the same thing because he can't bend over to tie his skates. His back is just so messed up. On the plane, they have this board with straps on it that they would put on his back after takeoff and tighten to keep it straight. He would sit in the aisle in something that looked like one of those director's chairs and play cards with the guys. He would never talk about it, never complain. It just amazes me what he goes through physically to play."

McKenzie also learns quickly that Mario has a dry sense of humour.

"Anytime we go into overtime, he gives me a little elbow on the bench and says, 'Watch this.' He throws one leg over the boards, looks back at E.J. [Penguins coach Eddie Johnston] and says, 'E.J., who's up?' And he just starts laughing. Because he knows E.J. is never not saying him."

Penguins play-by-play voice Mike Lange would always say, "Elvis has left the building" after a late Penguins goal wrapped the game up. Soon, Penguins fans are dressing up as Elvis for games.

"We're in the playoffs in a tense game in the third period," McKenzie says. "During the TV time out, they put on an Elvis song, and the spotlight keeps hitting all these different fans in Elvis costumes. I'm not paying attention because I'm nervous, just thinking about the game. Then I feel a little bump, and Mario says, 'It's great your dad made it down.' And he nods towards the other side of the rink, where the spotlight is on this huge Elvis with his giant gut hanging out. Then Mario jumps over the boards and scores the game winner. What a talent. He could do whatever he wanted."

Cammi's Flame

The voice over the loudspeaker stops practice at the rink in Downers Grove, Illinois. The boys and one girl on the ice freeze, in mid-drill, to listen. It's February 24, 1980.

"We have an important announcement! Team USA has won the gold medal in Lake Placid!"

Cammi Granato and her teammates start jumping up and down, hugging, like it's *their* gold.

And isn't it? They are eight years old and have just been told that you can grow up playing hockey in America and become the best in the world. Inside little Cammi, a flame is ignited.

ABC makes a movie called *Miracle on Ice* a year later. Not to be confused with the 2004 Kurt Russell film *Miracle*, which our generation knows and quotes endlessly ("I'm sick and tired of hearing about what a great team the Soviets have. Screw 'em! This is your time!"), the 1981 version is a hastily put together made-for-TV movie with Karl Malden as Herb Brooks and Steve Guttenberg (!) as US goalie Jim Craig.

"My brothers and I play that tape in our VCR until it's wrecked," Cammi says. "We know every line and re-enact every scene in our basement, over and over. 'If you can't stand the heat, get out of the kitchen!' 'Fool me once, shame on you! Fool me twice, shame on me!' Every Brooks-ism Karl Malden uses! And we'd play the Russia game again and again, everyone wanting to be Mike Eruzione, scoring that last goal."

Two decades later, Granato is no longer reliving Lake Placid; she's living *in* Lake Placid. It's where Team USA trains for the first Winter Olympics to be held in their country since those 1980 Games.

The little girl who used to pretend she was Mike Eruzione is now an American hockey legend herself—a trailblazer, an Olympic hero—though, as it will become clear shortly, she doesn't really grasp that yet. Four years earlier, in the first-ever Olympic women's hockey tournament in Nagano, Japan, Granato captains the US team to an upset 3–1 win over Canada in the gold medal game.

Now she'll get that rare chance to compete in an Olympics at home. The wait is agonizing.

"Our team lives in Lake Placid, on and off, for two years," she says. "There is nothing to do there except train and practice. So, we have to create ways to kill time. Barb Gordon and Alana Blahoski come up with this scheme of putting birdseed in people's beds. Most bizarre prank ever! You'd get in your bed, and there would be this giant pile of birdseed under the sheets. Anything to keep ourselves laughing so we don't go stir-crazy."

Finally, it's February 2002. The team arrives in Salt Lake City.

"Those first couple of days are the most exciting time ever as an amateur athlete, because this is your moment," she says. "You're going to be on the world stage for the next two weeks. You know every ounce of work that you have put in has been worth it. You've made it."

The American team practises the day before the Opening Ceremonies. As Cammi is leaving the locker room to get back on the bus, Chris Plyman, the team's PR rep, grabs her by the arm.

"The look on her face is like she has won the lottery," Cammi says. "She pulls me aside and says, 'You aren't going to believe this. They've asked you to be part of the torch relay at the Opening Ceremonies!' It doesn't compute. I never, ever, thought it was possible that I would even be considered for something like that."

That's Cammi. It makes perfect sense to the rest of us that the captain of the first team to win gold in women's hockey might be a good choice to carry the torch. But it has never crossed her mind.

Hours later, Cammi arrives at the stadium for rehearsal. She has no idea what she'll be doing. And for a while, no one tells her. She just stands and watches as they practise handing off the torch.

Figure-skating legends Dorothy Hamill and Dick Button run the torch into the stadium. They hand it to fellow skaters Scott Hamilton and Peggy Fleming, who skate it across to skiers Phil Mahre and Bill Johnson. Then it's back on ice to speed skaters Bonnie Blair and Dan Jansen, followed by father–son Olympic sledders Jim and Jimmy Shea.

"I'm watching all this happen, and I start to realize, 'This is getting really close to the stairs up to the cauldron,'" Cammi says. "And that's a spot reserved for someone really special . . . not someone like me. And then they tell me, 'Cammi, you and skier Picabo Street are carrying the flame up the stairs.' I can't believe it! The Olympics had meant everything to me my entire life. And now I'm doing this? I can't breathe."

It gets better. They tell Cammi that, at the top of the stairs, they will hand the torch to Mike Eruzione, the guy she pretended to be all those years ago, playing in the basement with her brothers. Eruzione and the entire 1980 team will light the cauldron.

"The whole thing is just surreal," Cammi says. "I still get choked up thinking about it."

The next night, the Olympic Stadium is packed with Granatos. Cammi's parents are there, her brothers and sister, her aunts, nephews and nieces—everyone who matters in her life.

"I tell them I'm going to be carrying the torch in the stadium, but I don't tell them where," she says. "They all turn their phone lights on at the same time and wave them in unison, to show me exactly where they are in the stadium."

When the moment comes, Cammi wears a wide smile all the way up the stairs, one hand on the torch, the other high-fiving the crowd that lines the route.

"One of the things they tell me in rehearsal is that when we get to the top of the stairs, we should turn around and face the stadium, to show the torch off to everyone. That's our moment. So, that's what we do. But Mike jumps his cue. He starts walking over to us to get the torch as soon as we get to the top of the stairs. So, we have to turn our back on him to face the crowd. He's left standing there, alone, for a few seconds. I feel bad about that. But I am so grateful for that moment. It's different from winning a gold medal, because your teammates aren't there. But it's right up there."

Cammi calls her mom as soon as she's back in her seat.

"They were doing the same thing I did in rehearsal—watching all the torchbearers, saying, 'Where's Cammi? That's not Cammi. That's not her, either . . . Oh my God! She's carrying it up the stairs!' And my mom tells me she looked over at my dad, and tears were just streaming down his face."

Cammi doesn't get the *Miracle* ending at this Olympics. Canada edges the US, 3–2, in the gold medal game. The loss still stings almost two decades later. But she would retire with gold and silver Olympic medals. The Hockey Hall of Fame comes calling a few years later.

And to this day, that view, from high atop the stadium in Salt Lake, torch held above her head, is burned into her memory.

Hully

Kelly Chase Rides Shotgun to Brett Hull

One day during his superstar prime, Brett Hull pulls up to the arena in St. Louis. There is a new security guard at the ramp into the garage where the players park. Hull has no pass with him. The guard says, "Can I help you, sir?"

"I don't think so," Hull responds, indignantly.

"Are you with the Blues?" the guard presses.

Hull doesn't hesitate.

"I *am* the fucking Blues!" And off he drives, down the ramp.

Kelly Chase rides shotgun for six years of those legendary Hull-isms. He's Brett's best friend and roommate on the road during their time in St. Louis. Whoever first paired the two gave us all a gift. Chase is a brilliant storyteller. And in their time together, Hull hands him a *Harry Potter*–length collection of tales.

On January 9, 1990, the Blues are playing in Los Angeles, one of the NHL players' favourite towns for going out after games. The Kings score to tie it, 3–3, six minutes into the third period. St. Louis coach Brian Sutter doesn't trust the Golden Brett in his own end at this particular moment, so Hull is glued to the bench. With a minute left, Sutter sends out his checking unit: Bob Bassen, Dave Lowry and Rich Sutter (Brian's brother)—the Green Beret Line.

Hull has had enough.

"He jumps over the boards and heads to the faceoff circle," Chase says. "And Richie yells, 'Hully, get off!' Hully just goes, 'Fuck off, Richie.' He doesn't move. He won't even turn to the bench! Sutter and everyone else are yelling, 'Hully, get off!' He won't even acknowledge them. He's so sour that he hasn't been playing that he's staying on the ice, no matter what.

"Finally, the ref says, 'Someone has to get off or you're going to get a too-many-men penalty.' And so Richie kind of shrugs and leaves the ice. The puck drops, we lose the draw, and LA is swarming us. Hully is just doing loops, like he's not even trying. Cujo [Blues goalie Curtis Joseph] makes a couple of saves and the puck goes off the left-wing wall to Hully. He cuts through the middle of the ice, fires an absolute bullet and beats Kelly Hrudey. We're up, 4–3, with 25 seconds left in the game! Hully doesn't even let anyone congratulate him. He just skates over to the bench, hops over the boards and says, in his perfect sarcastic Hully voice, 'Like we're playing overtime in LA.'"

On the Blues bench, Chase is sitting next to Dave Thomlinson, who has just been called up from the minors. Thomlinson turns to him and says, "Did that just happen?"

"Yeah. It happens a lot," Chase replies with a chuckle.

The moment is peak Hully, in both personality and performance. He scores 72 goals that season, 86 the next.

"Brian Sutter is such an intense guy, and you can tell he's so mad at Hully for not obeying orders," Chase says. "He wants to strangle him, but Hully has just won us the game, so there is nothing he can do about it. Hully is just so damn good, you just shrug and take the *W*."

Hull is half hilarious, half ruthless. One game, Nathan Lafayette is up on the boards, ready to replace him at the end of a five-minute power play.

"Hully has been on forever, and Bob Berry is the coach," Chase says. "Nathan has been waiting for about two minutes, and Bob finally gets Hully to consider coming to the bench. Then Hully sees Nathan up on the boards and says, 'Bob, not him!' And he turns around and rejoins the play."

That legendary lip would occasionally get Hull in trouble. Not just on the ice.

"One time, this guy in a car cuts us off when we are walking across the street in St. Louis and he pulls a gun on us," Chase says. "Under my breath, I'm saying, 'Hully, don't you say a word!' Because knowing him, I figured he might say, 'Go ahead, pal. Try me!' But Hully has street smarts. He says, 'Don't worry, Chaser. Just keep walking.' And then the light changes and the guy pulls away. One of the few times I've seen a guy shut Hully up!"

Chaser and Hully usually go out together on the road, but when the Blues are in Alberta, Hull is on his own. Chase's family comes to the games and he hangs out with them afterwards.

"One night I've just gotten in bed when I hear the key in the door," Chase says. "I pretend I'm asleep because if he knows I'm awake, Hully is going to talk my ear off about the game we just played. He will open the mini-bar and we'll be up all night. So, he stumbles in and he's clearly had a few. I'm chuckling to myself quietly in the dark. I can see because my eyes have adjusted. He's trying to be quiet, but he's struggling to get undressed. Then he catches his thumb in his sock and he starts bouncing across the floor. He just drills his head into the TV! Now he's down in front of the TV, moaning. I'm trying so hard to be quiet, but I can't stop laughing. I'm dying."

Hull pulls himself up and stumbles to the bathroom to assess the damage.

"He turns on the light in the bathroom, and because of the mirror, I can see him looking at himself. He has this massive growth on his forehead! He finally shuts the light off, and now he's trying to find his way back to the bed. He's going to do one of these big falls into bed. But as he falls, he catches the edge of the bed, leg-whips the wall, and he's down again, holding his ankle and moaning and groaning. I'm in my bed, just howling."

The next morning, the Blues have practice before flying out of town. Chase tries to revive his sleepy, wounded roommate.

"I'm saying, 'Let's go, Hoss. We have practice!' But Hully isn't budging. I yank on the covers, and finally he sits up and tries to get out of bed. He takes one step and moans because his ankle is swollen. Then he runs his hand through his hair, and he has this knot sticking out of his head like he's a unicorn! So he says, 'I can't practise today! I blocked a shot last night and I got high-sticked in the head!'

"I say, 'Are you fucking kidding me? You hit your head on the TV and leg-whipped the wall when you got in, you drunkass!' And then he does that Hully laugh— 'Heh heh heh'—and limps into the shower."

After another game on the road, Chase gets a double dose of Hully when Brett's dad, Bobby, goes out with them. The trio get back to their hotel (the Drake in Chicago) about 2 a.m. There are no rooms left for Bobby, so he's going to bunk with Brett and Kelly.

"The Drake has this elderly gentleman working the elevators, all dressed up with white gloves on," Chase says. "He recognizes Bobby right away and says, 'Mr. Hull, pleasure to meet you.' Bobby says, 'Good evening, young man. Could you press floor one for me?' And Brett goes, 'No, Dad, we're on three.' Bobby says, 'Goddammit, I said press one!' And out he goes on the first floor.

"We go up to our room, and a few minutes later, in walks Bobby with this food tray. He's got a quarter of a clubhouse sandwich, a piece of pizza and a couple of chicken wings. I'm like, 'What the . . . ?' And Bobby says, 'Wasteful bastards! This is how Stan Mikita and I ate in the old days. He took the even floors, I took the odd!'

"This is my idol! Then they bring the cot up, and Bobby is insisting on sleeping on the cot. Well, there is no way I am letting Bobby Hull sleep on a cot, so I take it. Bobby goes into the bathroom, comes out, whips his rug off his head, hangs it on the bedpost and gets in bed. The first time I meet my idol, and he's eating off food trays left outside people's doors and his hair is hanging on the bed!"

Chaser and Hully could be its own six-season Netflix show. But Chase is careful not to let the comedy overshadow the career.

"He's the greatest player I ever played with," Chase says. "You never went to a big game and worried about whether Brett Hull was going to show up. Never, ever, ever. And he was so tough. The beating he took with aluminum sticks so he could stay in front of the net and score was unreal. And he would never go in the training room. He hated it. He would just put a heat pack on his back and sit on the floor, stretching and doing crosswords.

"He could have scored so many more goals. He wouldn't score empty-netters for the longest time—he felt like they were tainted. And he never wanted to score more than three in a game. He'd say, 'If I score four or five and embarrass the other team, then I'll have some little asshole trailing me all over the ice, hacking me.' I think if Adam Oates had stayed in St. Louis, and if Hully had scored empty-netters and not let up when he had three in a game, he would have scored 150 more goals in his career."

Hull finished with 741. He would have to leave St. Louis to win his two Stanley Cups—with Dallas, in 1999, and Detroit, in 2002. But he eventually returns to the Blues organization, and is front and centre during their remarkable run from last place to Cup champs in 2019, gifting Chase with another volume of Hully stories.

"We get backstage for the rally after the parade, and I realize he's been into the tequila early, and he says, 'I'm going onstage!' I'm going, 'Hold on, Hoss, you probably shouldn't go up there right now.' But he walks past the cops, and they aren't going to stop him because they all love him, and he grabs the microphone and . . . you know the rest."

Hull's parade speech—er, is speech the right word? Let's go with performance—is one for the ages. He strolls onstage holding a beer and wearing a T-shirt that reads "Ric Flair Drip," with a photo of Hull giving someone the finger in the stands during the Cup final (Chase says it was one of Hull's buddies a section over). The crowd is chanting, "Let's go, Blues!" and Hull says, "You can say, 'Let's go, Blues' all you want. But you know what? We went! We don't have to go anymore, because we already did it . . . So instead of saying, 'Let's go, Blues,' we're going to say, 'We went Blues! We went Blues!'"

Tequila-driven gibberish or pure poetry? It's a fine line.

Backstage, a nervous Blues executive is urging Chase to give Hull the hook.

"I say, 'There is no chance I'm going up there and pulling Brett Hull off the stage during the Stanley Cup rally! This city loves him!'"

It's about then that Hull breaks into the most epic off-key version of "Gloria," the Blues' theme song, that human ears have ever heard. It would get mixed reviews, but only a good one from Hully's old roomie.

"No one gives a shit in St. Louis. They all thought it was hilarious. Hully always said if the Blues ever won the Cup, it would be the biggest party ever, and that's exactly what he made it. He doesn't care what people think. He never has. That's what makes him Hully. That's what makes him a legend. And I fucking love him."

Bobby Mac vs. Tretiak

The Original Hockey Insider
Takes His Shot

Vladislav Tretiak stares down the shooter from his net. He settles into his familiar crouch, the one we saw lead the Soviet Union to 10 world championships, three Olympic gold medals and brilliant performances in the 1972 Summit Series, the 1981 Canada Cup and "the greatest game ever played," against the Montreal Canadiens on New Year's Eve 1975.

Tretiak taps both posts with his stick. *Come at me.*

The shooter takes the puck from the faceoff dot and heads up ice. The move is already carefully planned out in his head. It's his go-to. He's been waiting for a chance like this his whole life. After all, the penalty shot is the purest mano-a-mano showdown in hockey. And he's facing one of the greatest goalies in the history of the game.

Bob McKenzie crosses the blue line and winds up for a slapshot.

"Bob, you never played the game."

I cringe when I hear it. I've sat across the panel from Bob McKenzie, the most respected media voice in hockey, for years. I know that's the one thing a player can say to get his back up. And now Jeremy Roenick has gone there.

It's the spring of 2007. Roenick is a guest on the TSN panel during our playoff coverage. We're talking about a headshot the night before, and debating whether it's worthy of a suspension.

"In those early years of the headshot debate, I'm like the safety inspector for the National Hockey League," Bob says. "To me, any hit to the head is a penalty. If it's a bad hit to the head, it's a suspension. Obvious today, but back then it's a contentious argument. And on this particular hit, JR and I are going back and forth, arguing. He says, 'It's a man's game, and that's a good hit.' I say, 'No, it's a headshot and a suspension.'"

And then JR plays the "you never played the game" card.

"I'm like, 'Oh man, here we go,'" Bob says. "I love JR. He's a great guy. But I can't let this one slide. I say, 'Well, JR, I have no comeback for you. You're right. I never played the game at any high level like you did. But if every time you and I are on this panel and we have a disagreement, and your response to our disagreement is 'You never played the game,' I have nowhere to go with that.'"

The argument slides into the commercial break.

"Okay, JR, so your opinion is more valid than mine because you played the game," Bob says. "Then it should also stand to reason that if a player who is better than you has an opinion that's different than yours, then his opinion will be more valid."

"What do you mean?" JR asks.

"Okay, for example: What if Bobby Orr has a different opinion than you?" Bob says. "And you are having an argument with him, and he says, 'Well, Jeremy, I'm sorry, but your opinion doesn't matter because I'm Bobby Orr and you're Jeremy Roenick.' Would that be okay with you?"

"Absolutely!" JR says.

Bob comes back with: "Good. I talked to Bobby this morning and he said that hit is a suspension. So, we're right, and you're wrong."

First rule of Panel Fight Club: don't mess with Bobby Mac.

Besides, Bob *did* play the game. No, nowhere near NHL level. But long before he's the Insider, Bob's a right winger for the Scarborough Lions of the Metropolitan Toronto Hockey League. Bob Park, father of future Hall of Famer Brad, is his coach. Bobby Mac and the Lions go to the prestigious Quebec International Pee Wee Tournament. And play in front of a Leafs legend every week.

"Monday night at Scarborough Arena is our home night, and we love it because Dave Keon Jr. plays for the younger team that plays right before us. So his dad, Dave Keon, is always in the stands for our games. For a Toronto kid growing up in the '60s, having Dave Keon at your games is pretty much the coolest thing ever."

Young Bobby Mac is a self-described "soft" player, until one night in minor midget.

"There's a really big, tough guy on the other team, and I accidentally high-stick him," Bob says. "He turns around, looks at me, and says, 'I'm going to kill you.' I go back to the bench and my stomach is in my mouth. I'm thinking, 'What am I going to do?' And then I realize I have a decision to make. I'm either going to walk out of the rink tonight and quit playing competitive hockey, because going through life scared is no way to live, or I'm going to go back out there and mix it up.

"I decide I'm going for it. I go back on the ice and just tear after him, running into him, yelling at him, 'Come on, you want to go? Now I'm gonna kill *you!*' I notice this hesitation, a little bit of fear in his eyes, like, 'What is wrong with this guy?' I realize, 'Hey, this works!'

"From then on, I lose my fear. I have a lot more jam. In juvenile, I get in some fights and get beat up a bunch of times. But I'm not afraid anymore. I think it's a good life lesson that it's okay to be afraid. The definition of fearless to me isn't not being afraid. It's overcoming your fears."

Courage isn't enough to take Bob much farther in hockey. "I just wasn't very good," he laughs. But it helps him relentlessly chase an alternative dream: to cover the game at the highest level.

He writes for the *Sault Star* and becomes editor-in-chief of *The Hockey News*, a columnist for the *Toronto Star*, and finally, the original Hockey Insider at TSN. It's in that TV role that Bob gets one last shot at on-ice glory.

He is assigned to work on a TV show taping at Maple Leaf Gardens. Canadian Tire has sponsored a contest where winning teams get to play in a three-on-three tournament and skills competition against stars of the 1972 Summit Series. Paul Romanuk is the host. Bob is the analyst/skills demonstrator.

"There are about 2,500 people in Maple Leaf Gardens, and Paul and I are both on skates," Bob says. "I'm demonstrating all the skills—accuracy shooting, puck relay, blue-line-to-blue-line sprint. And the last one is a shootout. Vladislav Tretiak is the goalie.

"Vlad, who is a great guy, comes up and gives me a little wink and says, 'Don't worry. I let you score.' I want no part of that! I say, 'Vlad, if I want to score on you, I'll score on you.' And I laugh and wink back. His eyes twinkle a little and he says, 'Okay, you try to score, I stop you.' Now my juices are flowing. I say, 'No, Vlad, I'm gonna score.'"

One other thing I've learned about Bob over our two decades together—don't ever underestimate his competitiveness.

"So, I come in, and I have this really good go-to move," Bob says. "But it's very complicated for a penalty shot. When I get to the top of the circle, I wind up for the biggest clapper you could possibly imagine, which is to try to get the goalie out of the net. Then I'm going to do a big, deep fake. I'm a right shot, so I'll fake to my backhand. Then I'm going to pull it back real fast to my forehand, extend my arms right out, go around the goalie, who's coming at me, and I should be able to tap it in the empty net.

"And it works like a charm! At least, at the start. As soon as I wind up for the clapper on Vlad, who is into this thing now, he comes racing out at me. But what I don't anticipate is that he's going to go two-pad stack! I'm in the middle of my backhand move when I realize, 'Holy shit, he's laid right out and coming at me really fast! How am I possibly going to get around him?' Somehow, I manage to pull the puck back really fast to my forehand and I'm able to jump out of the way of a sliding Vladislav Tretiak. He slides by me, but the puck is getting too far in front of me. I reach over and lean forward and just flip the puck into the empty net, top shelf. It's beautiful! But the problem is, I am going so fast and leaning over so far . . . that I fall and go crashing into the end boards.

"I have no equipment on, except a tracksuit, gloves and a stick. And I instantly know exactly what has happened. I separated my shoulder. You remember the 2020 World Junior Championships, when Barrett Hayton separated his shoulder? That's me. So, now there's 2,500 people at Maple Leaf Gardens and all these legends watching. Plus, it's on camera. I get up and I'm in absolute agony. It's like there's a knife going through my AC joint.

"I turn around, and Vlad gets up and he looks at me. He laughs, and I'm grimacing. People probably think I'm grinning like an idiot—'Mr. Big Shot juvenile hockey player just scored a goal on Vladislav Tretiak.' Now I'm skating back to talk to Paul Romanuk, who's got the microphone, and we're supposed to continue with the show. And as I'm skating up to him, I can see Paul Henderson and the other legends staring at me. I can just see the looks on their faces like, 'What a dick! What an absolute dick, making Vladislav Tretiak look bad!'"

What the legends don't know is that Bob *has* to score, or risk eternal ribbing from a friend. A few years earlier, when Bob is at *The Hockey News*, he assigns one of his writers, Steve Dryden (the man who would later become TSN's Quizmaster), to attend a Philadelphia Flyers fantasy camp in Montreal. Tretiak is the guest goalie for the camp.

"They have this 'pros-versus-Joes' scrimmage at the end, and the Quizmaster fancies himself a bit of a hockey player," Bob says. "He scores a beautiful goal on Tretiak. It ends up being the main part of the story he writes for *The Hockey News*."

Finally, it was just me and Tretiak . . . Tretiak was out of the crease, challenging. I wound up, pulling back my Murray Craven–model Sher-Wood . . . and fired the best shot of my life. Low. Far corner. Goal!
(STEVE DRYDEN, *INSIDE HOCKEY*, JANUARY 1989)

"So, when I get my shot at Maple Leaf Gardens in front of a few thousand fans, I can't let the moment pass," Bob says. "I have to score, or Steve will never let me hear the end of it."

Bob is in agony through the rest of the TV show, desperately trying to not let anyone see that he's hurt. Twenty-five years later, he still has the bump on his right shoulder. It hangs lower than his left.

"It was worth it," he laughs.

So there. Next time you try to tell Bob McKenzie he never played the game, remember that he scored on a brilliant diving deke against one of the greatest goalies ever. And then stayed on the ice and finished the "game" with a busted shoulder.

(Maybe just leave out the part about the TV show, the fact that Bob was supposed to be doing a demonstration, and that Tretiak wasn't exactly in Summit Series shape. Irrelevant details.)

Jonny Hockey

A Courageous Fan Becomes a Hockey Hero

Does it drive you crazy that you can't play hockey?
It keeps me awake at nights. I dream of it. I'm playing the game, flying down the ice. Scoring. And then I wake up. And just wish I could go back to sleep.

The boy's face appears on the giant screen above the ice and the crowd begins to applaud. Usually, that would be it. It's just a TV time out. The game will start again shortly. But the cheers keep building. And building. Soon, all 18,000 are on their feet, roaring.

He is wearing a perfectly tailored suit, a gift from a friend. He smiles, and waves from his wheelchair. Most kids his age would be uncomfortable or overwhelmed by the adulation. He is neither. He never sought attention. Never wanted any of this. But he humbly accepts it, only because it means he's having an impact. Maybe some of those standing and cheering will take the time to learn about his disease. Hopefully, it will help other kids who have it. His world is full of *maybes* and *hopefullys*.

The ovation is the kind the crowd usually saves for its hockey heroes. And then it hits you. To them, he *is* one.

It's April 22, 2015—one of the last Ottawa Senators games Jonathan Pitre will ever attend.

People with your condition, they call them "butterfly children." Why do they say that?
They call us "butterfly children" because our skin is as fragile as a butterfly's wings. As much as a butterfly is pretty and gentle, we have the hearts of warriors. We are very much stronger than we appear.

You may already know Jonny. Our TSN documentary and another from Barcroft TV have more than 45 million combined views on YouTube. ESPN profiled him on its magazine show *E:60*. His hometown newspaper, the *Ottawa Citizen*, covered every agonizing step in his battle with the rare skin disease epidermolysis bullosa (EB). I'm not going to tell those stories over again.

This is about a boy and his love for hockey. And how hockey came to love him back.

When is the last time you had one pain-free moment?
Never. I've never had one.

Maybe this is why he bonds so easily with hockey players. Hockey loves toughness. And Jonny is the toughest kid you will ever meet.

He was born with EB. It tears and blisters his skin from head to toe, including his throat. Even eating is agonizing. When his story first becomes public, he is 14, and he hardly looks like a tough guy at 4-foot-7 and 60 pounds. But as soon as hockey players hear his story . . . as soon as they understand the pain he lives with every second of every day of his life . . . as soon as they see how hard he fights, and how little he complains . . . they embrace him. He is one of them.

"It's hard to explain, but the players just understood him," Tina Boileau, Jonny's mother, says. "A lot of adults would talk to him like he was two years old, or always look at him like a kid in a wheelchair. The players were never like that. They would crouch down to his eye level and have normal conversations with him. They treated him like one of the boys. They'd just say, 'Hey, bud, how's it goin'?' And talk to him about hockey. He never felt different around them."

When you dream, what do you dream about?
I would play sports all day. And I would not stop. And I would be the most fit person in the world.

Jonny does play hockey. Once. In Grade 3. Ball hockey in the school gym. EB is degenerative, so at eight, he can still run.

"Are you going to come to watch the final, Mom?" he asks. Tina isn't sure she can. She's terrified. The other kids are aware of Jonny's condition, but they are still . . . kids.

"My heart stops because the ones he is playing with are not being careful. They don't really understand," Tina says. "If he gets hit or falls hard, he could be really hurt. He's that fragile. But he wants to play so badly. So I sit anxiously on the bench and watch. And his face is just beaming the whole time. He scores a goal and the other boys are all cheering for him. He is so proud."

Blisters cover every inch of Jonny's feet after. He can't walk for three days.

"It was worth it," he tells Mom.

What kind of toll did playing take on your body?
A big one. Soon, I just knew I couldn't do it anymore. It was tough. I had a lot of trouble swallowing that one. The one thing I just loved to do . . . was gone.

But hope is in Jonny's DNA. Maybe he can still be involved in hockey—as a coach, a scout or a commentator. He mentions these dreams in the first article written about him, by Andrew Duffy in the *Citizen*. The paper lands on the desk of Ottawa Senators GM Bryan Murray. The Sens invite Jonny to a game and sign him to a one-day contract as a scout.

When the day arrives, Murray approaches and introduces himself. Jonny knows Murray is battling cancer and says, "I'm very sorry to hear what you are going through."

Murray has to turn away, fighting tears. He tells a friend later, "This kid is going through this horrible disease, and he apologizes for what I'm going through?"

"That is Jonathan," Tina says. "It's pretty impressive at 14 years old to think of others, when you have every reason to think about yourself."

Jonny spends the game doing scouting reports with Pierre Dorion, then the Senators' director of player personnel. Afterwards, he goes in the dressing room to meet the team.

"You guys played good," he tells them. "A few turnovers, but you got the *W*. That's what counts."

He then grills captain Erik Karlsson about whether he wants to stay in Ottawa long term. The two become fast friends.

"I've never really met anyone like him," Karlsson says. "It's hard being around sick kids who may not have a future. But not Jonathan. It was always so easy to be around him. He has this terrible skin disease, but that's not what you see. He makes you look past that. All you see is pure joy."

What position did you see yourself playing?
Centre. I've always been . . . not the scoring type like Ovechkin . . . I'm more of a Crosby type. I see the ice well.

Though the Senators are his team, Sidney Crosby has always been Jonny's favourite player. After the TSN documentary airs, Tina gets a call from the Penguins. Sid needs Jonny's measurements. He wants to have a suit made for him by his personal tailor, Domenico Vacca.

"It the kindest, sweetest gesture," Tina says. "Sid heard that Jonny went to a lot of games, so he wants him to look like he's one of the guys."

"I want him to feel like a pro," Crosby says. "Here's a guy who is going through something so painful, and his first thought is always, 'How can I help others?' When I was young, I'd watch on TV the players coming to the rink in their suits. That was a cool part of being an NHL player. I want him to feel that, to make it as real as possible for him."

Tina tries to discreetly measure Jonny while she's changing his dressings. But he's way too smart for that.

"Um, Mom, why are you measuring me? Am I going for surgery again?" he asks.

"No, no!" Tina replies, trying to reassure him and come up with a good lie, all in the same breath. "The doctor needs them just to make sure they have proper dressings next time you are in."

A few weeks later, the sharp navy blue suit shows up at their front door, along with a couple of ties, an autographed stick and a handwritten letter from Sid.

"His eyes just light up," Tina says. "Jonny always liked to be well-dressed, and he just loves having his own suit. It fits perfectly. He looks so good in it."

And he will soon have the perfect place to wear it. In June 2015, Jonny is invited to attend the NHL Awards in Las Vegas. Mom likes surprises, so she decides not to tell him he's going onstage until the last minute. But the pain and meds make Jonny tired constantly. At one point during the show, he falls asleep.

"Jonny, wake up. You have to go up onstage in a minute!" Tina says.

"What?! What am I doing?" he says in a half daze.

The NHL has a special presentation for Jonny. They have arranged for someone to push his wheelchair onstage, but he calls a last-second audible.

"He had a really rough day, but he is determined to walk on that stage and show off that suit," Tina says.

A crowd full of NHL superstars and executives gives him a long standing ovation. Actress and Paralympian Amy Purdy interviews him and compliments his suit. Jonny does a full runway-model 360 for the crowd.

"Here it is!" he says, smiling ear to ear.

Karlsson, Murray and several other Senators surprise Jonathan onstage and announce that the NHL will make a large donation to DEBRA, the EB awareness organization.

Keep fighting. Keep making an impact.

There is no hockey player Jonny makes more of an impact on than Kyle Turris. Kyle and his wife, Julie, are deeply affected when they read Jonathan's story. On that first night when the Senators make him a scout, Julie brings Jonny a special Senators jersey for his dog, a Boston terrier named Gibson (the true love of Jonny's life). The Turrises form a close friendship with Jonny and Tina.

"He's this old soul and his spirit just draws you in," Julie says. "And he's so smart when it comes to hockey. He'd say to me, 'They're playing well, but Kyle really needs to do more of this or that.' He really knew the game."

Jonny and Kyle start emailing regularly.

"I am just amazed at his positivity," Kyle says. "In all our conversations, he never mentions his condition or the pain he is in. The amount he teaches Julie and I about how to approach life is indescribable."

When Jonny and Tina move to Minnesota for a stem cell transplant they hope will extend and better his life, Kyle brings the whole Senators team to see him during a road trip.

"They come straight from their flight," Tina says. "Two big buses show up at our apartment building. I know about it, but I want to surprise Jonny, so I tell him we are just going for a walk. We get off the elevator, and there is the entire team! Jonny is about to go in for his second transplant (the first failed), and we delayed his hospital admission so he could see the guys. It means everything to him."

Canadian diplomat Khawar Nasim invites Jonny to help lead the Wild crowd in its traditional pre-game cheer. Just like in Ottawa, the crowd goes crazy for Jonny.

After the visit, Jonny's Senators go on a playoff roll, coming within a Game 7 overtime goal of the Stanley Cup final. It's Sid and the Penguins who beat them—and go on to win the Cup. Jonny can live with that.

"When he's healthy enough, he's constantly on his phone, getting updates," Tina says. "But he's on a lot of meds at that point. A lot of days, he's just too sick."

Jonny suffers endless setbacks in Minnesota, many of them life-threatening. But he fights on, hoping the second transplant takes and he can grow new cells, new skin.

Hockey is never far away. Minnesota native Matt Cullen and his wife, Bridget, also befriend Jonny and Tina. Jonny begs doctors to let him out of the hospital for a Wild–Penguins game, where he meets Cullen and Crosby—for the first time in person.

He's still in Minnesota in November 2017, in and out of the hospital, when Kyle Turris is traded to Nashville.

"Jonny's heartbroken," Tina says. "His first worry is that he's never going to see him again."

Kyle quickly emails to reassure him that their friendship has a no-trade clause. It isn't going anywhere.

"Hockey people are just different," Tina says. "We got the chance to go to a lot of different sporting events when Jonny became well known. All of the athletes were very kind, but they would hand him the jersey, take the picture and move on. Which I completely understand. But the hockey players, and people around the game, they wouldn't leave. They would email and call. In his heart, Jonny always thought of himself as a hockey player. They treated him like one. They related to how hard he battled. He was always my hero, but he became everybody's hero."

What is the life expectancy of someone with EB?
Twenty-five years, approximately. It's not a lot. If you think of it, I'm over half my life. One fear I do have is that I'll get to the point that I can't live life to the fullest. But I'm not going to let it happen. That's a promise, not a statement.

I *will* win. I *will* beat you. It's the belief of every great hockey player. Even when reality says otherwise. It was Jonny's attitude for all of his 17 years.

The last time I see him is February 2, 2018. I'm in Minnesota for the Super Bowl, and I spend the afternoon with him and Tina at their apartment. His face and body are badly swollen from all the steroids he's being treated with. We talk about hockey, of course. And the sci-fi novel he is going to write. The words he uses are upbeat as always. "I'm gonna get better. The transplant's gonna work. It has to." But he looks tired. Even the heart of a warrior can only take so much.

I'm at the Masters in Georgia two months later when Tina calls. Jonny's gone.

He finally succumbed to complications from septic shock—when a rampant infection destroys your organs.

"Kyle cried when he heard," Julie says. "Jonathan changed him. He always says that if Jonathan could get through everything he was dealing with, then the things Kyle is going through in hockey that seem like a big deal, really aren't. He gave Kyle and I so much more than we gave him."

"It's a sick feeling to hear those words, that he's gone," Kyle says. "He fought so hard. He was the toughest hockey player I've ever met."

Jonny dies on a Wednesday, but most of the world doesn't find out until Friday. Just hours after Canada learns of his passing, a truck hits the Humboldt Broncos' team bus on a quiet road in Saskatchewan.

As a country mourns, Ottawa artist and author Kerry MacGregor draws a sketch of a bunch of Broncos players, standing with their sticks, ready for a game. They're facing a boy with a hockey jersey that says PITRE on the back. The caption reads, "Hey, you play?"

They used to call EB the "worst disease you've never heard of." But millions know of it now because of Jonny. From the time he decided to tell his story, until his death four short years later, he raised more than $600,000 for EB research.

A butterfly starts as a caterpillar. Then it starts growing. Then when it gets to the part of the butterfly, it's free. When we find a cure for EB, we will have no more pain and no more wounds. Our limitations are gone. We are free now. We can do whatever we want to do. That dream is very bright and I think it's coming soon.

—

(The quotes in this chapter are the words of Jonathan Pitre, taken from my interviews with him for the TSN documentary *The Butterfly Child*, and from the ESPN documentary of the same name.)

The GQ Style Guide

Lessons in Fashion from Teddy Purcell and Connor McDavid

Teddy Purcell struts into the rink in Boston with swagger. It's December 2, 2010. Purcell is 25, finally a regular in the NHL, and having a strong first season with the Tampa Bay Lightning. And on this night, he's wearing a brand-new custom suit. It's grey, with a subtle black-and-purple windowpane pattern. His dress shirt is light purple, and his tie has a black, grey and purple pattern.

His tailor talked him into the combo, telling him it's "edgy and cool." Perfect. Teddy likes the idea of being both of those. It's all coming together for the native Newfoundlander.

Until the game happens.

Purcell and the Lightning lose, 8–1, the team's worst defeat in a decade. He lingers in the rink afterwards, chatting with his Boston-based agent. He ends up being the last Lightning player to board the team bus. As he steps on, he passes GM Steve Yzerman, who's in his usual seat at the front. Yzerman gives Purcell a nudge and a side nod, signalling that he wants a quick chat with his forward.

"I'm like, 'Fuck, here we go,'" Teddy says. "The bus is like a morgue after a loss like that, and now I'm getting pulled aside by the GM. But I'm thinking, 'Wait, I didn't play that bad. I had my man!' So Steve gestures for me to lean over close to him, and he says, 'Besides the fact we just lost, 8–1, that is the worst shirt-and-tie combo I've ever seen. Wear that again, and I'm going to trade you.'"

Purcell starts giggling, the only sound on a dead-quiet, defeated bus. Apparently, in hockey, you can have a terrible loss and a terrible tie on the same night.

"It's the coolest thing ever, this legendary guy who always appears so serious, who keeps everything close to the vest, ripping me about my tie right after we lose, 8–1," Teddy says. "That's the thing people don't know about Steve. He's pretty witty. Anyway, I get home and take off the tie and never wear it again. When Stevie Y rips your fashion, you listen."

It's the second harsh style lesson Teddy has learned in the NHL. He had shown up for the Lightning's first road trip with the team-logoed travel bag they'd given him in training camp.

"Vinnie Lecavalier and Ryan Malone are all over me," Teddy says. "They say, 'Look like a professional and go get a Louis Vuitton bag.' I'm like, 'How much is that, guys?' And they say, 'Only 1,200 bucks.' In my head I'm going, 'That sucks. That's a lot of money.' But I go to Louis Vuitton. And the girl there is pretty cute. She gives me a beer. Then another beer. She sucks me in. She says, 'Try the one with the roller.' Perfect!

"So, I'm strutting around the store with this roller bag, thinking I am the man! I'm in the store, flirting with this girl for an hour, and then I get to the cash and she says, 'That's $3,500.' I'm like, 'What?!' So the guys basically pranked me, knowing I'd end up spending a fortune. But, hey, I still have that bag to this day!"

Six years later, Teddy is an Edmonton Oiler, and a seasoned vet when it comes to NHL style sense. He's learned his lessons. Now it's his turn to teach. His pupil is an 18-year-old Oilers rookie named Connor McDavid.

"From the beginning, Teddy is just all over me about my fashion choices," Connor says. "He's relentless."

"He's the nicest kid," Teddy says, "but he has no clue on style.

He shows up his rookie season and he's got this giant Erie Otters travel bag. So I say, 'Connor, you aren't in junior anymore. You don't wear a track suit. You're the man now! Go out and buy yourself a proper duffel bag.' So he does. But he still doesn't have a tailor. His pants are awful. We work with him, and by Christmas, he's starting to look better."

"Now he tells me I need a nice watch," Connor laughs. "So he sets me up with this guy, and we find the perfect watch for me, and the guy goes, 'Just send me a cheque.' I say, "I'm 18 years old. I don't even have a chequebook yet!"

"I'm like, 'You're going to make $300 million! You don't have a chequebook?' Teddy says. "So I pay for the watch. It's a few grand. And Connor pays me back when he gets his next paycheque."

Purcell takes pride in the fact that he helped the best player on the planet look the part. And he feels incredibly lucky he got to witness the true style of McDavid—on the ice.

"I remember when he broke his collarbone," Purcell says. "I had broken mine before and remember how painful it was. He was lying on the table in the dressing room, not moaning or crying. He just had tears in his eyes, saying he felt like he'd let the guys down. Can you believe that? I went up to him and said, 'You didn't let anyone down. You are going to come back and probably win MVP five years in a row.' He's a special kid."

Teddy's style student has come a long way. McDavid is featured in *GQ* magazine in September 2018. In the article, he tells the story about Purcell chirping him over the travel bag. Here is the exact quote:

> *I showed up for my first road trip and all the guys have these Gucci bags and these Louis Vuitton bags—you know, these sweet bags. And I showed up with my Erie Otters team bag, and [Oilers vet] Eddie Purcell was like, "Dude, what are you doing with that?" Well, what do you mean, it's my bag, what am I supposed to do? "Go out and buy yourself a nice bag."*

Sure enough, had to go out and buy myself a nice Tumi bag. Next thing you know, they're chirping my hair. "You gotta go get a nicer haircut than that—that's awful." I think it's a little bit better now, but I still have some work to do.

That's right. After getting ripped by Stevie Y over his outfit, and all his other style faux pas, Teddy Purcell finally makes the pages of *GQ*.

And they call him Eddie.

The Golden Goalie

Roberto Luongo and the 2010 Olympics

The bus is quiet when the goalie feels his phone vibrate.

It's February 21, 2010. Canada has just lost, 5–3, to the Americans in the preliminary round of the Vancouver Olympics—the most important hockey tournament in the nation's history.

Roberto Luongo watches the game from the bench. He's gotten used to that. Four years earlier in Turin, Luongo backed up Martin Brodeur. He played one game, a rout over Germany, but that was it. Brodeur started the rest, and was in goal when Canada was eliminated, 2–0, by Russia in the quarter-finals.

The starter and backup roles are less clear when the 2010 Games begin. Luongo shuts out Norway to open the tournament. Brodeur wins a tougher game against Switzerland, 3–2, in a shootout. When head coach Mike Babcock goes back to Brodeur against the archrival Americans, it feels like the New Jersey Devils legend might be The Guy again. But Brodeur allows four goals on 22 shots against Team USA.

Forty-five minutes later, Team Canada's bus is rolling through the streets of downtown Vancouver towards Canada House, where they'll meet up with their families. Luongo's phone starts buzzing.

"I look down and it's a text from Babcock," Luongo says. "It reads, 'Lui, come see me at the front of the bus when we get there.'

Right at that moment, I'm like, 'Oh shit. Here we go.' I have a pretty good idea what it's about. So, I stop and see him at the front of the bus, and Babcock says, 'It's your tournament now.'

"I've never been so nervous in all of my life as that moment. I feel like the blood just drains right out of me. And then I go see my family a minute later, and they are looking at me, going, 'What's wrong with you? You're white as a ghost.' And I tell them, 'I guess I'm The Guy now.'"

Luongo has waited for a chance like this his entire life. And now that it's here, he wants to throw up.

"You're now the starting goalie for Team Canada . . . in the Olympics . . . in your home country . . . in Vancouver—your city. The pressure is more than anything I have ever felt."

With the loss to the US, Canada finishes sixth in the preliminary round and has to play an extra elimination game just to get into the quarter-finals. While this causes a minor national panic, it's not the worst thing for the anxious goalie and his team. They rout Germany, 8–2, and Luongo gets to find his sea legs before the madness that lies ahead.

The quarter-final game is now just a footnote in the 2010 Olympic story, but in the moment, Canada's showdown with Russia is one of the most hyped hockey games of our generation. It's the sport's original great rivalry—featuring Alex Ovechkin and Sidney Crosby in their primes. Not to mention, Russia eliminated Canada in the very same round four years earlier.

Luongo is tense, almost uncomfortable, when the puck drops. But Ryan Getzlaf scores 2:21 in. Then Danny Boyle. Then Rick Nash.

"That start really helps me settle down," Luongo says. "The guys are just flying, and the nerves go away."

Canada wins, 7–3, but the goalie isn't happy. He lets in two he feels he should have stopped. And across the country, there are still murmurs about whether Luongo really is The Guy.

What else is new? Doubt has followed Luongo around his entire career. It's his permanent backup. He has been one of the best, most consistent goalies in the NHL for almost a decade. But from the moment he is picked fourth overall by the Islanders in 1997, people have always expected . . . more. The occasional bad goal at a bad time, the lack of a defining win—it all feeds the doubt. Maybe that's part of the reason he feels sick when Babcock tells him it's his tournament: if he fails, maybe they'll be right.

The semifinal against Slovakia is a microcosm of Luongo's career. Canada is cruising, up 3–0 midway through the third. The goalie has been perfect. The adoring Vancouver crowd worships him with every save: "Looouuu!" Canucks fans have always done this. But now it echoes across the country. In between, they chant, "We want USA!" This game is over; bring on the Americans for gold.

And then, with 8:35 left, Lubomir Visnovsky sends a harmless backhand towards the net from below the goal line. It goes off Luongo's leg and in. Three and a half minutes later, Michal Handzus bangs home a rebound: 3–2. Stunned silence replaces the chants. The cameras show endless close-ups of Luongo. *Are you The Guy?*

"I feel like the first one is bit unlucky, but I know it looks bad," he says. "Anytime you allow a goal from there, it's a bad goal. But it's weird. Even after the second one, I'm not rattled. There is no time to be nervous. No time to think about the pressure. About what this means."

Now the Slovaks are swarming, desperately pushing to tie it. With 11 seconds left, Marian Hossa takes a shot from the high slot that Luongo gets a pad on. The rebound comes right to Pavol Demitra, the goalie's friend and Canucks teammate, alone at the side of the net. Luongo has no chance. Demitra lifts the puck up over his pad. In slo-mo, it looks like he's already starting to raise his arms in celebration. But Luongo contorts, reaches back with his glove in desperation and somehow gets a little piece of the puck.

The save of a lifetime. 3–2 Canada, final. *Looouuu!* He's mobbed by his teammates. In the handshake line, Demitra smiles, shakes his head and says, "That was incredible, Lui. That was robbery."

(Tragically, Demitra dies just 19 months later in a plane crash in Russia. It claims the lives of the entire Lokomotiv Yaroslavl team from the Kontinental Hockey League.)

Suddenly, the panic that overcame the goalie when Babcock handed him the job has vanished. He will start in what is arguably (it's a fun argument) the biggest game in Canadian hockey history. And now he knows he belongs there.

There is a day off before the gold medal game. Luongo and the team spend most of it in the Athletes' Village. It's his favourite part of all of his Olympic experiences—mingling with the competitors from different countries, from different sports. That night, he and Danny Boyle do the same thing they have done before every game in the tournament: they go to McDonald's in the village and have six McNuggets. (Somewhere, Gary Roberts cringes.)

Luongo has had his own hotel room on the road for his entire NHL career. But in the Olympics, he shares a small apartment with five other players, and a room with forward Brenden Morrow.

"Brenden is a great guy, but I don't like that part. We goalies are different; we like to do our own thing. Like if I want to lie naked on my bed," he laughs. "One time, at the World Championship, I'm rooming with Anson Carter. He snores so bad, I can't sleep at all. But Brenden is nice and quiet. I sleep well that night."

The men's gold medal hockey game is the final event of the Olympics. It starts early, 12:15 p.m. local time in Vancouver. That helps Luongo.

"There is no time to sit around and think about how big the moment is," he says. "We get up, eat, go to the rink and get ready to play."

And Canada is ready to play. Jonathan Toews scores midway through the first period. Corey Perry adds another, seven minutes into the second. The entire country can taste gold.

But with seven minutes left in the period, Ryan Kesler deflects an innocent shot over Luongo's pad and under his blocker. He gets a piece, but it trickles through. It's a one-goal game. During the second intermission, Kesler—another of Luongo's Canucks teammates—is interviewed by Ryan Rishaug on the CTV telecast. He says, "Lui looks like he's fighting the puck a little bit, so we're just gonna keep throwing pucks on net."

It's an odd chirp at a guy Kesler will share a dressing room with again two days later. You could see him perhaps doing it before the game, trying to rattle Luongo—that's Kesler's style, and all is fair when it's USA–Canada for gold. But in the second intermission, when there's no chance the goalie will hear about it until after the game? Just . . . strange. The two never talk about it after. And Luongo still doesn't understand it to this day.

Kesler and the Americans do fire everything they can at Luongo in the third. For the 20 million Canadian fans watching, the period feels about three hours long. The Olympics have been a massive success for the country. But, right or wrong, this is now the only part that really matters. It's Canada. It's hockey. It's everything.

The last two minutes are chaos in the Canadian end. With 25 seconds left, Patrick Kane picks up a loose puck to the left of the Team Canada goal, whips around and throws it towards the net. It hits the skate of American forward Jamie Langenbrunner. Luongo sees that and reacts, moving slightly to his left. But then the puck also hits Zach Parise's skate at the top of the crease and changes direction again. It hits Luongo, but he's lost sight of it. He quickly glances to his left, searching for the puck. But the rebound is already on Parise's stick. Luongo kicks out his right leg in desperation, but Parise is a millisecond faster. It's 2–2.

There are 24.4 seconds left.

"We're stunned," Luongo says. "You can feel it through our entire team, through the entire rink. I'm just so glad that there is a break before overtime. We get to go to the dressing room and regroup. If OT started right away, I think we would have been in big trouble. But in the room, Scott Niedermayer says, 'We're in overtime in the gold medal game of the Olympics in our country.

What other place would you rather be? Someone is going to be a hero in this room, so let's just go out there and get it done.' That settles everyone down."

Seven and a half minutes into OT, Niedermayer circles his own net and tries to pass the puck across the ice to Shea Weber deep in the Canadian end. Joe Pavelski, chasing Niedermayer, intercepts the pass, spins and fires towards the top corner.

"I don't have much time to react. I just lift my elbow and am lucky enough to make the save."

Looouuu!

"Funny thing is, I cover the puck and want to freeze it, just to calm things down, but Scott calls for it behind the net, so I slide it back to him. If he doesn't do that, we have a faceoff in our end. But instead . . . well . . ."

Niedermayer takes the puck from Luongo, circles the net and heads up ice. He finds Sidney Crosby streaking down the right wing. Crosby tries to bust through the two American defencemen but gets held up, and the puck rolls harmlessly to US goalie Ryan Miller, who steers it into the left corner. Crosby gets there first and turns back up the boards towards the blue line. But the puck gets caught briefly in the skate of referee Bill McCreary, and Crosby changes plans. He pokes a pass to Jarome Iginla in the corner and spins towards the goal.

"It looks like an innocent play off the wall from my vantage point," Luongo says. "It's not one of those plays where you antici- pate something happening."

I'm sitting exactly opposite Luongo, a few rows up, behind the American net. The crowd is so tense, so quiet, that everyone in the building can hear the one word Crosby yells.

"Iggy!"

As Iginla is being knocked to the ice by Ryan Suter, he slides the puck to Crosby, who has a step on Brian Rafalski. Crosby touches the puck twice—once for control, once for history. His shot beats Miller five-hole.

Goal. Gold.

"It happens so fast," Luongo says. "I see Sid raise his arms, and it hits me all at once. It's over. We won. I don't even sprint to the pile. I just put my arms in the air and look to the sky. I just feel all the pressure of those whole two weeks lift off my shoulders."

It's bedlam on the ice. In the stands. In the streets. In every bar, and most every home in the country. Most of it is a blissful blur to Luongo.

After the ceremony, he can't wait to get to the dressing room, to celebrate with his teammates. But as he steps off the ice, gold medal around his neck, he gets pulled aside.

"I get drug-tested!" he says with a laugh. "For the fourth time in the tournament! I'm so mad. And I can't pee that night. My body has nothing left in it. So, you try to go, and it's not enough, and you have to start over again. It takes forever. Biggest win of our lives, and I'm stuck in a washroom with some stranger for 45 minutes, trying to fill the container."

(Washrooms always seem to find their way into Luongo stories.)

Later, at Canada House, his whole world is waiting for him. His wife, Gina, his parents, his brothers, his in-laws, his nephew, friends. There are tears, although Luongo says none are his, only because the last drops of liquid in his body went out in the urine sample.

"The great part is, they all want to tell me what it was like for them when Sid scored—where they were standing, who they were hugging. We relive it over and over."

A decade later, he still does. Every once in a while, someone will post a clip on Twitter, or a fan (or book writer) will ask him about it. Feel free to keep asking. It never gets old to him.

Luongo retires in 2019. The gold medal tops his personal podium of career highlights. The other two are the trip to the Cup final in 2011 ("Some of it, not all of it," he says), and the Game 7 OT win over Chicago in the first round that same year (one of the greatest playoff series of all time).

He would win one more gold medal, in Sochi in 2014, this time backing up Carey Price. No dramatic texts from Babcock needed. Price is brilliant. And Luongo is more than happy to let him be The Guy. He had his time. The time of his life.

"Sometimes, I still can't believe how it worked out," he says. "The perfect storm . . . the perfect story . . . the perfect ending."

The Boy Who Came from Away

A Syrian Refugee Finds His Hockey Community in Newfoundland

Yamen scored a goal.

He can't wait to tell me about it. The boy is still learning English, and though a translator sits beside him, he eagerly answers most of my questions in his new language.

"How are you, Yamen?"

"I am good! Nice to meet you!"

But when I ask about the goal, he starts in English, then switches quickly to Arabic, because there is so much he wants to say. The words come racing out, his voice full of excitement and pride.

Mohammad Al-Maksour, our translator, listens intently and smiles. "He says he was right in front of the goal, and his friend shot it," Mohammad says, Yamen's play-by-play still filling the background. "The puck came to him, he focused and he put it in."

Just another rebound. On another rink. In another Saturday house league game.

Or much more.

Michael Doyle gets the email on a Friday afternoon in January, a week before the storm of the century hits his home—St. John's, Newfoundland. Michael is a former teacher turned stay-at-home dad and kids' hockey coach. A friend is wondering if he knows of any apartments available for a refugee family. Fatima and her four children fled war-ravaged Syria and came to Canada almost a year ago. But they are still looking for a permanent home.

Oh, and one more thing. Could Michael get one of the kids, eight-year-old Yamen, into hockey? The boy has fallen for the game. Hard. He's been playing non-stop in a neighbour's basement.

Michael writes back that he isn't sure about the apartments, but will look into hockey right away. He calls Mark Sexton, president of the Avalon Minor Hockey Association. Asks if there is any way to get Yamen into the league this late in the season. Sexton is away in Halifax at a tournament, but promises to do whatever he can.

In the meantime, Michael digs through his basement. Finds a pair of old skates and a brand-new helmet that he drops off for Yamen. The boy spends Saturday taking his first Canadian skate on the Loop, an outdoor rink in the neighbourhood.

Sexton calls back early the next week. They would love to have Yamen play in the league. He'll start on Michael's team.

"I call my friend back and tell her Yamen is good to go," Michael says. "And she says, 'Great. Now, how do we get him equipment?'"

Michael decides to send out a tweet.

> A neighbour has asked me for hockey equipment for a young Syrian boy who lives around the corner. All our stuff is sort of small. I got him a new helmet but looking for everything else. DM please and I'll gladly pick up in the metro area. Also looking for skates for sis and older bro.

A couple of St. John's media friends retweet it. People message Michael instantly, offering sticks, pads, pants. Soon, bags full of equipment start showing up at his front door.

"I didn't know so many people knew where I lived," he laughs.

Only hours after he sends the tweet, as Michael stands freezing in a park, watching his kids play, he gets a message from a journalist named Muhammad Lila. He mistakenly thinks it's the guy CBC Radio just hired for its local morning show.

"He asks me about the boy who needs the hockey equipment, and I message him back, saying, 'He lives in Churchill Square, down by the CBC where you'll be working!'" Michael laughs. "Muhammad writes back, 'I don't work at the CBC.' And I say, 'You aren't working with Krissy on the new morning show?' We have this hilarious back and forth until I realize he isn't from Newfoundland—or coming to Newfoundland. He used to be a war correspondent for CNN and ABC. He saw the tweet and has taken an interest in Yamen's story."

Muhammad asks Michael why he won't accept money. Some had offered it. But Michael is leery. He doesn't like the idea of people thinking he's asking for cash on Twitter.

He gets a long string of messages back from Muhammad about refugees. How welcoming Canadians are to them. How we generously offer clothing and items they need to start their lives here. But how those things are never brand-new.

"He says, 'Imagine how Yamen would feel if he got shiny new skates, new equipment—clean gear, not used by anyone else.' And I think about a few days earlier, when my son Charlie had been complaining that the palms were ripping out of the hand-me-down hockey gloves he got from his brother," Michael says. "We had bought him a new pair but hadn't given them to him yet. So I run in and get them and give them to him in the car. Charlie's eyes just light up. 'Thank you, Daddy! I love them!' It tugs at my heart."

He messages Muhammad back.

"You got me. How should I do this?"

Muhammad suggests that Michael accept e-transfers. So he sends out a new tweet.

A lot of people have offered money and at first I resisted but if you want to help get new equipment for them you can dm me. @ NISportscraft have offered equipment at cost and getting them fitted properly. Thank you everyone.

Michael figures he needs $700 to outfit Yamen head to toe. Within a few hours, he gets a message from a local woman, saying, "We don't have much money. But I want to give you $20. And my boyfriend does, too." Soon, another Twitter stranger, Suleman Ahmed from Toronto, messages and asks what he can do to help. He puts Michael in touch with the Syrian Outreach Program. They offer translators and any other support Michael needs. Ahmed also finds Michael a donor who sends him $500.

"Then the money starts flying in," Michael says. "Fifty dollars here, 25 there, 40 here. By that night, I have too much!"

On January 16, 2020, just six days after Michael received that first email, Yamen is at Sportscraft, getting fitted for equipment. With each new piece he puts on, he stares in the mirror, smiling endlessly. He walks around the store, shaking each staff member's hand, saying thank you, over and over.

"I am so excited," Yamen says. "But I do have a question in my head: how will I move with all this on?"

We hear ya, Yamen. We all thought the same thing the first time.

The only thing that can keep Yamen from hockey, apparently, is Mother Nature. He is supposed to make his debut that Saturday. But Newfoundland gets buried. The biggest storm in its history. St. John's shuts down for a whole week. It only comes back to life the following Saturday. Just in time for Yamen to finally hit the ice. Despite his fears at the store, he moves around in all that new equipment just fine.

"I love it!" Yamen says. "Hockey is very exciting. And I have made many friends. I skate as fast as the Canadian kids now!"

I ask Yamen what games he used to play in Syria, and Iraq, where the family fled before making it to Canada.

"None," he responds. And then he's quiet for the first time.

His mom, Fatima, fills the silence, telling me the kids had to stay inside. They couldn't even go to school. Playing a sport was not possible. Until Canada.

Now Yamen is a hockey player. And soon he has company.

Michael gets a call from a friend who teaches English as a second language. She has seen the photos he posted of all the equipment Newfoundlanders donated. There is another Syrian boy in her class, Anas, who would love to play hockey. Maybe he could have some of the gear, if there is enough?

"I tell her, 'Sorry, I don't have used stuff for you—I have enough money left over to buy him all new gear!'"

Turns out Anas has a sister, Areej, who also wants to play. Michael calls a few friends and comes up with enough money to buy equipment for her, too. The next week they both get fitted at Sportscraft. Areej dances in her skates in the middle of the store.

They join the same team as Yamen. The following Saturday, all three are on the ice together.

"Hey! These are my friends!" Yamen yells. He knows them from Association for New Canadians events.

Michael helps the trio with drills, works them in with the rest of the kids.

"I can't get them off the ice at the end," he says. "They are overjoyed. The Zamboni driver is coming on the ice, saying, 'C'mon, let's go!' But he's smiling, too. People in this province, and from all over Canada, made this happen with their generosity. It's just a small thing . . . but it's not. It's big."

Hockey isn't perfect. It has warts, and scars, like the rest of life. But it overflows with good people. Some of them play in the NHL. Or the minors. Some coach. Some referee. Some are our neighbours.

And some are strangers. Who chose to help a kid who came from away feel like he was home.

Acknowledgements

My dad loved telling stories. Even in his final days, as we sat next to his hospital bed in Ottawa, he would spin tales of his time in the RCMP or of his boxing matches. I recorded some of them on my phone's voice memo folder, just so I can still hear his voice now and then.

"I was fighting this one huge guy and he came out and started yelling at me like a crazy man, trying to put me off," Dad says. "Uncle Fred, my trainer, warned me he was going to line me up and take one giant swing. Sure enough, he does! I duck, he misses. And I knock him out with one punch."

I think Dad would like this book. He loved hearing a good story as much as telling one.

If my love of storytelling came from him, my passion for writing came from my mom. She was a teacher, and she proofread all of my essays. Probably bumped my average 15 percent a year. I'm an honour-roll fraud. She proofread this book, too, just like the first three. Love you, Mom.

It takes a small army to finish one of my books—there are that many typos. Besides Mom, my sisters Merydee and Kristy, friend Puffy (Sean Cameron), and Brad Fritsch—the only copy editor/professional golfer around—all generously took a turn reading it over. Special thanks to Steve Dryden, TSN's managing editor of hockey. His corrections and suggestions, all made by his trademark pencil, were invaluable.

The team at HarperCollins was terrific. Jim Gifford made *Beauties* happen. Editor Brad Wilson guided me through every step from start to finish and could not have been more helpful. Erin Parker did the hardcore editorial edit, while taking care of her two-year-old son, Max. (Shocking amount of similarity between raising a toddler and dealing with me.) Erin made this book better. As did Lloyd Davis, our excellent copy editor.

Brian Wood has been my supportive agent for all four books. Seems like he does about 90 percent of sports literature in Canada, but he says mine are his favourites.

(That is not a direct quote; rather, it's a liberal paraphrasing of "James is one of my clients.")

I am fortunate to have a team at TSN/CTV that supports my writing books between hosting sporting events on their networks. Stewart Johnston, Shawn Redmond, Nathalie Cook, Ken Volden, Paul Graham, Mike Lane, Dave Krikst . . . they all lent a hand with *Beauties* along the way. My entire TSN family is endlessly encouraging.

Thank you to Jen Entin from Creative Artists Agency, who arranged time with several players who are swamped with requests in the middle of a hockey season. And to Jessica Johnson of the NHL, who helped with several of the photos.

I have the most tolerant family. When I write, I'm lost in space. My wife and three children have long since gotten used to asking me questions 17 times before I glance up from my keyboard. My wonderful wife, Cheryl, and amazing kids, Jared, Darian and Gracie, are everything to me. I'm back, guys! I will now respond to your questions after no more than three to five attempts! (Also, thanks to canine supporters Buddha and Willow, who sat on my lap on the couch for the entirety of the writing. Buddha, a Boston terrier, would drop his rubber toy on my keyboard over and over. We played fetch and wrote a book together for six straight months. He was also my scapegoat for the typos.)

Finally, thank you to all the hockey people who shared their stories. They gave me hours of their precious time and tolerated countless follow-up calls and texts. I hope I did their tales justice.

I went into this project knowing that hockey stories can be like fish stories. In my early days of sportscasting, I kept hearing this one great tale about Gordie Howe. Gordie was attending an event where everyone wore name tags. They simply wrote "Mr. Hockey" on Gordie's. Well, one of the attendees, who clearly wasn't a hockey fan, saw Gordie's name tag.

"'Mr. Hockey' . . . well, that's an interesting name!" she said. "What's your first name, sir?"

"Gordie," Howe answered politely.

"Gordie Hockey! What a neat name!"

Years later, I hosted a luncheon where Gordie was the guest of honour. I told that story. The crowd laughed, and Gordie smiled and nodded knowingly throughout. When I sat back down, I leaned over and whispered to him, "I've always wondered, is that story 100 percent true?"

"Not a word," Gordie replied with a wry smile. "Never happened. But I enjoyed it."

So, we made sure the stories in *Beauties* are all true. More or less. We have fact-checked to confirm that the games, dates, scores and details match reality. (Many thanks to Hockey-Reference.com and HockeyDB.com . . . you are invaluable.) But if there is a minor embellishment by the storytellers in places, so be it. I'd be disappointed if there weren't.

I know my dad won that boxing match. But I have no idea if he really knocked the big guy out with one punch. But that's the way I'm telling it to my grandkids.